PORTRAITS OF GREAT AMERICAN SCIENTISTS

PORTRAITS OF **GREAT AMERICAN SCIENTISTS**

EDITED BY

LEON M. LEDERMAN, NOBEL LAUREATE

AND **JUDITH SCHEPPLER,** PH.D.

ILLINOIS MATHEMATICS AND SCIENCE ACADEMY

Prometheus Books

59 John Glenn Drive
Amherst, New York 14228-2197

Photo credits

Clifford Geertz: Randall Hagadorn; Mary-Claire King: courtesy of M. King; Marvin Minsky: courtesy of M. Minsky; Story Musgrave: NASA; Steven Pinker: Donna Coveney; Sally Ride: NASA; F. Sherwood Rowland: courtesy of F. S. Rowland; Vera Rubin: courtesy of V. Rubin; Paul Sereno: courtesy of P. Sereno; George Smoot: Lawrence Berkeley National Laboratory; Charles Townes: courtesy of C. Townes; Geerat Vermeij: courtesy of G. Vermeij; Edward O. Wilson: courtesy of E. O. Wilson; Edward Witten: Robert P. Matthews; Dawn Wright: CMC Photo Services. Student photos: Lifetouch Prestige Portraits.

Published 2001 by Prometheus Books

Inquiries should be addressed to
Prometheus Books
59 John Glenn Drive, Amherst, New York 14228–2197
VOICE: 716–691–0133, ext. 207; FAX: 716–564–2711
WWW.PROMETHEUSBOOKS.COM

05 04 03 02 01   5 4 3 2 1

Library of Congress Cataloging-in-Publication Data

Portraits of great American scientists / edited by Leon M. Lederman and Judith
    Scheppler.
        p. cm.
    Includes bibliographical references.
    ISBN 1–57392–932–8 (pbk. : alk. paper)
    1. Scientists—United States—Biography. I. Lederman, Leon M.
II. Scheppler, Judith A.

Q141.P668 2001
509.2'273—dc21
[B]   2001041932

Every attempt has been made to trace accurate ownership of copyrighted material in this book. Errors and omissions will be corrected in subsequent editions, provided that notification is sent to the publisher.

Printed in Canada on acid-free paper

CONTENTS

PREFACE

The new millennium brings with it new hope for many things—a cure for cancer, the desire for world peace, and the dire need that we preserve our environment for generations to come. However, many of these hopes depend upon the type of education our students receive . . . they need a deep education in mathematics, science, and technology with a strong background in the arts and humanities and an ethical leadership commitment to solve important problems. The state of Illinois recognized a need to encourage talented students to explore careers in mathematics and science, to develop expertise in mathematics and science, and to catalyze the improvement of teaching and learning throughout Illinois. From this context, the Illinois Mathematics and Science Academy (IMSA) was born.

Now in its fifteenth year, the Academy has graduated over 2,400 students, with over 60 percent of them pursuing majors or careers in mathematics and the science. IMSA students and staff have served thousands of other Illinois students and teachers through our unique Center@IMSA, designed to provide professional development and outreach.

As a learning enterprise that builds the capacity of students, teachers, and policymakers, IMSA strives to advance and transform teaching and learning. Our residential program serves Illinois students in grades 10 through 12 through an academically rich and rigorous program of studies, providing learning experiences that are competency-driven, inquiry-based, problem-centered, and integrative. Simply put, our students are being prepared to be thoughtful ethical leaders who will have the skills to carefully and boldly face their futures and to help decide societies' fates.

One of IMSA's unique opportunities is our Student Inquiry and Research program, designed to provide learning experiences both in and out of class for students to pursue compelling questions of interest. Students conduct authentic research in many fields of science, craft original creative works, and invent products and services. These are shared through presentation, publication, and collaboration with other students, mentors, scholars, researchers, and inventors throughout the world. It is within the context of this program that this project, a book of biographies, *Portraits of Great American Scientists*, emerged.

In 1998, I came to IMSA as inaugural Resident Scholar in the Great Minds Program. Our goal is to bring some of the best minds of the world to IMSA to share with students, teachers, and the community through a variety of formal and informal venues. The "biographies" project is one such venue, where students question and probe the lives of some of America's leading scientists.

With the strong encouragement of founding IMSA President Dr. Stephanie Pace Marshall, I sent out an invitation to IMSA students to write this book, through research and interview; the project would be a compilation of biographies of their favorite scientists. The word spread and soon we had fifteen enthusiastic writers, including a student from neighboring Batavia High School, eager to engage in this project. Working with me on this endeavor were IMSA staff member Dr. Judith Scheppler, coordinator of IMSA's Inquiry Program, and Dr. Neill Clark, a member of the English faculty. A list of over one hundred potential candidates from scientific areas, broadly defined, was assembled.

Students divided the list, focusing on an area of intense interest, each taking five to ten names. Over a four-month period, each narrowed their selection to one. This involved numerous questions, conversations, discussions, and preliminary research. The learning process was rich. Together we discussed the appropriate audience for the book and decided it should be written for their contemporaries—middle school and high school students. However, we decided we wouldn't mind too much if parents and grandparents also read it.

Content and interviewing techniques were discussed. Before the interview, each writer had read books and articles by and about their scientist; hence, they really understood their scientist's principle contribution. We also encouraged them to explore the societal implications of the work where it was relevant.

Through all of this I remembered my own experience as a high school student, reading such books as *Microbe Hunters*[1] and *Hunger Fighters*[2] by Paul DeKruif, both biographies of biologists; chemists and how were treated by Bernard Jaffe in *Crucibles*.[3] These were important books in shaping my own interest and science.

Between fall 1999 and spring 2001, each of our students interviewed their scientist by telephone for an hour, recorded the interview, and frequently followed up with e-mail questions. Fortunately, I personally knew most of the scientists selected and was able to warn them that a telephone call was coming. And then came the writing drafts, editing, and rewriting. (Fortunately, no one's computer crashed!)

This has been an interesting journey, but now we have fifteen chapters in a most remarkable book, covering fields of science as diverse as cultural anthropology with Clifford Geertz and string theory with Edward Witten. We believe this book is unique. There is no better audience to attract young minds and to encourage them to imagine the scientist's life than the budding young scientists who are the authors of this book.

America is indeed at a crossroads. It is imperative that we rekindle the sense of awe, wonder, and imagination of possibility in our young. It is our mission to encourage them to explore the mysteries of the natural world, to embrace questions that they are passionate about, to seek answers to puzzling dilemmas, and to continue to just keep trying to figure things out.

We are in an amazing era in terms of our emerging knowledge of science. This is a time when the imaginations of our young people must be rekindled, because it is our hope that children who read this book will be the scientists of the future. The inspiring stories of the lives and works of these great American scientists will surely open their eyes to the wonders and the possibilities of being a scientist in the twenty-first century.

Our sincere thanks goes to our fifteen scientists, Drs. Clifford Geertz, Mary-Claire King, Marvin Minsky, Story Musgrave, Steven Pinker, Sally Ride, F. Sherwood Rowland, Vera Rubin, Paul Sereno, George Smoot, Charles Townes, Geerat Vermeij, Edward Wilson, Edward Witten, and Dawn Wright, who participated in this project with their generous gift of time. Generously providing photographs and diagrams, they also found time for interviews and follow-up questions amidst their own very hectic and busy research and travel schedules.

A number of people have read and commented on our writing drafts. They are IMSA staff members Neill Clark, Donald Dosch, John Eggebrecht, Gene Skonicki, and Susan Styer plus Rena Lederman (Princeton University) and Margaret Geller (Harvard University). Editorial assistance was provided by Linda Regan, Christine Kramer, Art Merchant, Mike Petryshyn, and Jacqueline Cooke of Prometheus Books and Lauren Kafka of The Write Stuff. Expert secretarial skills were provided by Denise Koehnke, Jeannie Mowrer, and Cindy McGrail.

The Illinois Mathematics and Science Academy and our Great Minds Program is supported by both public and private funds. We thank the State of Illinois, the IMSA Fund for Advancement of Education, and the fund's donors and supporters for providing the environment that nurtures projects like these.

INTRODUCTION

LEON M. LEDERMAN

WHAT IS SCIENCE?

R ichard Feynman, one of the greatest American physicists of the twentieth century, was asked to define science and it made him think of a poem:

> A centipede was happy quite, until a toad in fun said:
> "Pray, which leg comes after which?"
> This raised his doubts to such a pitch,
> He fell distracted in the ditch,
> Not knowing how to run.[1]

The point Feynman was making was that all his life he had been doing science (He even won a Nobel Prize!), but when he was asked to define science, he was terrified that not only was he unable to define it, but that he would go home and no longer be able to do his research, just like the poor centipede, who, when forced to think about walking, could not put foot after foot.

Science is first a human activity. The search for explanations began back in the dim mists of prehistory and rested for eons on myths, on gods and demons who would mischievously place the stone on which you would stub your toe, or who would shake the earth or belch flames out of mountains or flash lightning and thunder to terrorize the sailor at sea.

THE ORIGINS OF SCIENCE

A wonderful compilation of explanations were embedded in the Greek mythology of 600 B.C.E. and earlier. Then there arose, in the Greek colony of Miletus, a new outlook which offered to replace mythology with a new spirit of reason. This was so successful that the haze of myth was rather quickly dissipated and replaced by efforts at logical explanation of natural phenomena. This was science. The Miletians were not small thinkers. Not only did they try to understand such processes as the condensation of moisture, but also the formation and workings of the world. These became purely natural events from which the Miletians deleted all supernatural powers.

These earliest scientists adopted the premise that has guided science for the past 2,600 years: a single order underlies the chaos of our perceptions and furthermore, we humans are able to comprehend that order. Considering the limitations of the ability of these Greek citizens, this idea was extraordinarily bold. So, historians generally agree that the replacement of mythology (mythos) with logic (logos) took place in this Greek city in about 650 B.C.E. and constitutes the beginnings of science.

To illustrate the change, consider that the ancient Egyptians listed all the wonderful uses of fire—for warmth, for rendering foods edible and tasty, for hardening bricks, and for cooking metals out of certain kinds of earth, but they never asked why—why does fire do these things? The Greeks asked "why?" and the "why" is the essential difference between invention or technology and science.

To illustrate the nature of science, the ancient Greeks believed that everything in the world can be understood. But the world and everything in it is complicated. We know about stars, galaxies, and planets; the sky, air, clouds, mountains, and oceans that cover the surface of the Earth; and living things, like plants, bugs, lions, and monkeys—we know not only all these things but also how they change: night and day, the seasons, clouds move, apples fall, there is thunder, and the earth quakes—all these things are included in the world in which humans are born, grow, and somehow manage to survive. And in their activities of searching for food, shelter, and safety, humankind somehow, when things were not too difficult, found the time to wonder how and why all these things of the world work. Small wonder that the easiest explanations lay in myth and superstition, gods and demons. But it was in ancient Greece, so the scholars tell us, that humankind began the effort to account for it all by "natural causes." Later Greek scholars give the credit to Thales of Miletus, hailing him as the founder of a new kind of philosophy—that which we now call science.

Thales (650 B.C.E.) was a mathematician and an astronomer. It is said that he was able to predict eclipses of the sun—a remarkable achievement one thousand years before the invention of the telescope. But his most famous contribution was typical of the scientific idea that underneath all the complexity of the world is some very simple mechanism. To illustrate this idea, consider a large city, say New York or Chicago.

One sees a skyline of buildings, tall ones, short ones, square and round ones, narrow buildings, and buildings of great width. The variety of buildings is enormous. Now let's pretend that the only building materials that exist are bricks and cement. No steel beams, no concrete pillars, just bricks and cement. Then we can make all the buildings in the city out of bricks and cement. (Perhaps skyscrapers would be unsafe, but that is a minor detail in my example.) So, the huge variety of buildings is all made of different arrangements of just bricks and cement.

Now we return to Thales' effort to explain the complex world in terms of something very simple. Thales said, "Everything is made of water." The earth floats on water. Now why did Thales pick water? Well, it is the only thing known that exists naturally as solid (ice), liquid, and gas (water vapor). Also, almost anything when heated gives off water. Rivers, emptying into the sea, deposit mud (earth) seen as deltas; that is, it looks like water converting to earth. Often cracks in rocks contain water. Water is also essential to life of both plants and animals. The warmth of life is a damp warmth. Though we know that this simplification doesn't work, it was soundly rooted in observations and it wasn't a bad guess. Hydrogen is a basic constituent of water and we now know that well over 90 percent of the universe is made of hydrogen; it was, in fact, an inspired guess. Today, the search for "what the world is made of" is a basic scientific goal.

NOW, WHAT IS SCIENCE?

Contemporary definitions of science call it a unified, rational view of nature; a search for laws with universal validity—valid in New York, Chicago, Calcutta, on the moons of Jupiter and, we have good reasons to believe, in solar systems that belong to galaxies ten billion light years away.

Apples don't fall from trees willingly or frivolously. They fall because of the law of gravity. Generalizing, the laws of nature supervise all the activity in the universe.

Concluding this long definition, we should clearly distinguish science, the search for pure knowledge about nature, from technology and invention. Technology is the application of science to useful things. Our modern world is dominated by technology that is based on scientific knowledge. For example, the television tube, an arguably useful gadget found around the house, works because science discovered a subatomic particle, the electron, learned how to control its motion, and how to devise a coating on glass which would give off light when struck by a stream of electrons. Cell phones, computers, fax machines, jet planes, X-ray machines, and artificial limbs are all examples of technology that came out of scientific understanding. Inventions, like the cotton gin or the sewing machine, are inventions more beholden to clever tinkerers than to any scientific principles. Some science is close to technology—like the study of the properties of materials, and some is very remote—like extragalactic astrophysics. The history of science is a history of very abstract science, remote from human experience, eventually giving rise to vast technologies that have changed human life and behavior. A good example is the history of the atom. In 1900, the atom was like a new world governed by seemingly bizarre laws of nature. It was so abstract that some prominent scientists didn't believe that atoms existed. In the year 2000, the understanding and control of atoms accounts for a major fraction of the Gross National Product of all the industrial nations.

ABOUT OUR BOOK

Perhaps the best way to define science is by what scientists do, and so these biographies of living, breathing, working scientists should give the reader the best possible description of what science is.

The breadth of the scientific work covered in this book is impressive: abstract mathematical physics, cosmology, astronautics, atmospheric chemistry, paleontology, genetics, oceanography, linguistics, artificial intelligence, cultural anthropology, . . . Whew! Still, we do not cover all of science by any means, but by telling the stories of these fifteen scientists, we hope to give you a sense of science.

We should learn from these stories that science can be very abstract and very far from being useful. Useful science can be useful in two senses. One is as technology. The invention of the laser is a good example. The study of the structure of molecules gave rise to one of the most useful technologies of the twentieth century. The other useful sense of science is that knowledge in one field is often essential to progress in a different field. An example is that the discovery of quantum theory is essential to understand how atoms work, how they are constructed, and what properties they have. This was a contribution of the physicists we discuss in this book. But the knowledge gained was absolutely crucial to progress in chemistry and molecular biology.

One of the lessons of our book is the importance of scientific knowledge in the preservation of the environment and in the economic prosperity of the nation. However, often there are conflicts between these goals, as illustrated in the Sherwood Rowland biography.

THE "NEW" RELEVANCE OF SCIENCE

Science in the twenty-first century has extended its influence far beyond economics and environment. Just think of all the devices in homes, automobiles, jet airplanes, factories, and hospitals. Inventions stemming from an understanding of quantum science enables the cell phone, the home computer, e-mail, the Internet, the global reach of communications, and businesses, plus the increase in longevity and the conquest of some diseases.

Human behavior is changed by the relative ease of travel, of communications, and of the availability of information, such as the Internet, TV, and radio. Progress in molecular biology has lead to mapping the human genome and a much clearer understanding of human genetics with the awesome possibilities of biotechnology. Then there is the exploration of the dark depth of our oceans, the geology of our planet, and the outer space of our solar system. The pace of these researches is increasing as tens of thousands of scientists and engineers work in laboratories all over the world. The easy communications between scientists worldwide, adds to the pace of "progress." Incidentally, because U.S. scientific activity tends to be extremely robust, English has become, de facto, the international language of science.

All of this means that it becomes very important to discern, as best we can, what the future may hold for science and for the new world that science is creating. And we have not begun to understand the full implications of progress in the more abstract fields; the beginnings of a complete history of the universe from its birth in the big bang, a summary of the most fundamental particles and forces out of which matter and energy are made, and the growing progress in the neurosciences, that is concerned with how we learn, how our brains control body functions, and what it means to be conscious of ourselves as reasoning, feeling human beings.

THE SCIENTISTS

Science, the doing of science, requires a variety of human qualities. But before giving examples, we should be clear in recognizing the distinction between scientists and the subject: science. Scientists are members of the class: human being. As such, they share the strengths and weaknesses of people, wise and foolish, ego driven and serene, saints and sinners. The science is somehow protected. Over the millennia, since the ancients discovered processes, science evolved through the contributions of the Great Ones, and has developed a set of criteria for what is accepted as valid scientific behavior: a tradition of openness, a necessity for skepticism, a profit from democratic governance, a patience with tentativeness, and a tradition of rebelliousness. The body of scientific knowledge and the culture that controls access is truly universal. Science is the most communal of human endeavors. It is the same in the West as it is in the East, North, and South. There is a strong consensus that if intelligent life evolved on other planets, it would discover the same science, the same laws of nature.

These comments then train us to look for such qualities in prospective scientists. We know that curiosity is often a driving force for scientists, so we expect scientists to be curious about nature. But this curiosity may be highly focussed so as to be invisible to outsiders as part of the daily life of the scientist or it may be widely exhibited so that the scientist develops a broad sense of the outside culture in the process of following up on his curiosity. Scientists should be eager to listen to ideas, however bizarre, from whatever source. However, as science has become a large effort with huge budgets, there are scientist-administrators who seem to be paid not to listen to young people or to people with "strange" ideas. They develop a class name: the Establishment. It is the traditional and honorable quality of a good scientist to rebel against the Establishment because scientific revolutions are, by definition, lead by rebels.

MOTIVATIONS

Finally, it is interesting to look at the deeper motivations of scientists who may very well be too shy or reserved to expose them—but who, occasionally, will write about them. The sensitivity to the transcendent beauty of nature is most dramatically expressed by Einstein's contemporary, the French mathematician Henri Poincaré:

> The scientist does not study nature because it is useful to do so. He studies it because he takes pleasure in it; and he takes pleasure in it because it is beautiful. If nature were not beautiful, it would not be worth knowing and life would not be worth living. . . . I mean the intimate beauty which comes from the harmonious order of its parts and which a pure intelligence can grasp.[2]

Much is made, fairly often of the similarity in the driving force of scientists and of artists and musicians. Here is an example from Ludwig Boltzmann, a creator of thermodynamics:

> Even as a musician can recognize his Mozart, Beethoven or Schubert, after hearing the first few bars, so can a mathematician recognize his Gauss, Jacobi, Helmholtz or Kirchhoff after the first few pages.[3]

However, whereas styles in describing a new theory may vary, ultimately the constraints in science forces one to provide the experimental justifications. Thus, whereas the artist, musician, and poet can create beauty out of his imagination, the physicist is stuck with merely describing nature and wondering. Here is Einstein, describing his theory of relativity:

> Scarcely anyone who fully understands this theory can escape from its magic.[4]

The lesson of all this is that science is an activity of humans and the best way to understand it is to understand the individuals who practice it. As we see from these biographies, science flourishes best when it is free to use all the tools, without any preconceived notions of what science ought to be. There is also the ubiquitous presence of passion, the love of research, of exploration; the challenge, as Einstein wrote, of contesting to know the mind of "the Old One." We have learned from the past four hundred years of science that nature's imagination is far richer than ours.

A BRIEF HISTORY OF THE WORLD

In the very beginning there was not much: no plants, no animals, no planets or suns, no space, and no time—only some kind of unstable false vacuum and, presumably, the laws of physics. The nascent universe exploded with the release of enormous energy, instantly creating mass, radiation, space, and time. I know "explosion" isn't the right word—here it is used poetically. The enormous density and temperature insured that matter could exist only in its primordial form (quarks and leptons, we think). Quarks and antiquarks annihilated each other to give rise to photons. After an initial surge of exponential growth, the universe entered a phase of expansion and cooling. Soon, all of the antiquarks were consumed in the annihilation, leaving only one quark out of 100 million photons, still enough to create the hundreds of billions of galaxies. The cooling proceeded to the point where quarks could safely combine to form the nuclei of hydrogen, deuterium, and other light elements.

Eventually, at about 500,000 years after genesis, the dense and opaque plasma of charged particles thinned out to permit the flooding of the universe with radiation that cooled to become the cosmic microwave background. The universe cooled enough to form atoms. Condensation begins to form galaxies and stars. Our astrophysicists have plenty of difficulties these days, so if you meet one, take her to lunch. Recently, they seem to have discovered that the dark matter and the chemical elements combined, only account for less than half the content of the universe. But let's follow the planet story.

About five billion years ago, a sun turned on in the Milky Way galaxy. Small globs of matter maintained a separate existence and formed orbits around the sun. The inner planets had a rough time;

gases trapped in their interiors were boiled out to form atmospheres. Surfaces were convulsed; volcanoes abounded; water smoothed the surfaces of the globe. Wind and water eroded the land, but mountains also grew. Large masses of the Earth were mobile so that continents moved and changed shape.

The mix of atmosphere and sunlight, created a rich chemical brew of molecules, forming, dissolving, and reforming over time in ever more complex organizations. The oceans collected these and protected them. Molecules connected and twisted other molecules so that they could catalyze still others. Loops of molecules were formed by reactions and became interconnected with other loops. The whole was fueled by energy from the Sun. Nucleic acids were formed and soon (approximately one billion years or so) made proteins. Then, in a process which is still mysterious, a new breed of molecules (prokaryotes) was formed, one which could use the rich brew of complex molecules in the nutritious ocean, to make an accurate copy of itself. Somehow, it contained a set of instructions for its own replication. When, by all kinds of chance, the set of instructions was altered, new versions of the thing were produced. Mutations were preserved and replicated. Conditions changed, the composition of the atmospheres changed, the complexity of molecules was initially limited to plants, which could work with air, water, minerals, and sunlight. Animals became parasites on plants. In time, a rich array of plants and animals began to cover the Earth. Competition and greater specializations took place. Evolution, involving lots of time—billions of years—happened. However, the resiliency of life was impressive. Living things thrived on the top of Mount Everest and in the deepest darkness of the oceans, where one could find life thriving in hot, concentrated sulfuric acids.

After 4.5 billion years, intelligence evolved, passed on genetically—but also extra-genetically by learning, by memory, and by books. The future of evolution, nature's way of trying everything and selecting the best, will almost certainly be affected by modern human ability to engineer and alter its own genes.

From the time we first think about these things we are confounded by the incredible unlikelihood of our own existence. Wasn't it astronomer Fred Hoyle who found the idea of life arising from randomness so incredible that he compared it to a tornado sweeping through a junkyard and assembling a 747? So even Hoyle underestimated the power of geological time.

This story embeds much, if not all, of the scientific disciplines: physics, chemistry, biology, astrophysics and cosmology, planetary science, paleontology, geology and oceanography, anthropology, and ultimately genetics. The exciting frontiers today include brain research and human consciousness, the basic laws of particle physics, the study of complex systems, and so much more.

The greater tragedy is that so little of this is known by our average citizen. So we have this worldview of transcendental beauty and wonder, expressed from time to time by scientists who carry the gift of articulation. I know, in their books, they speak for all of us: Victor Weiskopf, Sylvia Earle, Brian Green, Rachel Carson, Carl Sagan, Jane Goodall, Margaret Mead, Steven Weinberg, Dian Fossey, Steven Hawking, Richard Feynman, and many others.

The importance of public understanding of science may be in that scientists also need to be selected, loved, and appreciated. Unappreciated science may be as futile as unappreciated music or art or poetry . . . or a Chicago Bull's team when and if they ever resume playing basketball!

But there is a deadly serious aspect to scientific illiteracy which is characteristic of our times when the technology that is streaming out of our science lays out issues of awesome significance for the well-being—even the survival—of our children and grandchildren.

MOTIVATION FOR SCIENCE LITERACY

Now here is what to expect: within one to two decades you will be able to alter the biological nature of the human species, or you may leave it alone. Genetic evolution will soon come under control of humanity and this will usher in a new epoch in the history of life.

Human evolution is a slow process: observable changes take most of a million years. The situation is about to change profoundly—thanks to advances of genetics and molecular biology—

hereditary change will soon depend less on natural selection and more on social choice.

Before too long, we will be able to select a new direction in our evolution. We will be able to decide what to do about our own heredity. The Harvard biologist E. O. Wilson, has said:

> This will present the most profound intellectual and ethical choices humanity has ever faced. We will be able to modify how our genes interact with the environment to produce a human being and tinker with the products at any level—change them temporarily without altering heredity or change them permanently by mutating genes and chromosomes. Humanity will be in a position to take control of its ultimate fate. If we choose, we can alter not just the anatomy and intelligence of the species, but also the emotions and creative drive that compose the very core of human nature.[5]

If these possibilities—no, *certainties*—are not enough to generate a huge priority for popular science literacy, I don't know what will.

We will need more popular consensus in this awe inspiring twenty-first century. Is it a surprise that we say we need to radically improve science education? We need popular understanding about so many things, such as global climate change, ozone depletion, air and water pollution, toxic and radioactive wastes, acid rain, loss of biodiversity, global oil spills, massive industrial accidents, exponential population growth, or the increasing susceptibility of society to electronic mischief or terrorism. The role of technology in widening the gap between rich and poor must be understood. Our society and government must also decide on drug safety, product liability, the need for benign and inexpensive electrical power, the legality of tobacco, and the proliferation of nuclear, biological, and chemical weapons. But also government must and will set policy on education, on abortion, on fetal tissue transplants, on how much to spend on research and on what kinds of research, and on the regulation, or not, of the new abilities in genetic engineering.

In so many of the seemingly beneficial advances that science-based technology has given us, there are almost always dark sides that require wisdom and courage—even the courage to forego or postpone certain applications if the technological assessment so indicates. The sword of science is double-edged. We are often torn between alternatives.

Steering science to a future which enhances human welfare and human potentialities and which minimizes social, technological, and even cultural catastrophes is not easy. It raises a fundamental issue of how we manage our nation so as to permit average citizens to wisely exercise their participatory rights bestowed upon them by democracy.

Citizens live lives that are far removed from the political, economic, cultural, and technical centers that give direction to society and when the issues that drive policies crucial to our futures are not within the comprehension of the citizen, crucial decisions on public affairs cease to be public and they fall into the hands of our leaders who too often make disastrous decisions.

Thus, to preserve democracy, it is not nearly enough to fix the voting machines, pass campaign finance laws, and to elect wise leaders; it becomes as essential to have some grasp of the scientific issues as it is to be able to read and write.

CONCLUSIONS

The invention of science and scientific thought emerged out of myth and magic in the Greek civilization around the rim of the Mediterranean Sea. We must recall that we owe to this period much of our literature, art, and philosophy, which we collectively call the humanities.

There is no question but that science has been the driving force for change in the way humans think and behave. The increase in our knowledge of the physical and biological world has been tremendous, far beyond any predictions. This knowledge has increased longevity, physical comfort, and potential for vast human advancement. But wisdom is another requirement;

wisdom tells us how to use our knowledge. Without wisdom, knowledge is dry, even dangerous.

To be educated in the twenty-first century is to be comfortable with all elements of our culture, with knowledge of fact, principle, and philosophy, but also with critical attitudes and with opinions. To be educated takes much more than staying in school, even in acquiring advanced degrees. It is to participate in all the opportunities offered by books, magazines, newspapers, museums, theater, even (choke!) television. It is to know history. This kind of learning has a name—it is called liberal arts education and it must connect the enormous power of scientific knowledge to the wisdom of the humanities.

After this long introduction we must return to our scientists, the practitioners of this activity called science. Science is what they do. It becomes clear that so many of them showed an early interest in the world around them. But we know that children, *all children*, are curious about their world. Carl Sagan, in many talks he gave, used to stress that all children are born scientists, but most (good for job security!) are cured of this dangerous attribute by parents and teachers too busy or too impatient to cope with endless "whys" and by the insensitivity of this complex system we call "school."

It is the rare teacher who encourages the curiosity of children, who fans the sparks of their interest in the world into the raging flame that drives them into a scientific career. The lesson from this is that we must train teachers to appreciate the value of encouraging the curiosity.

Out of such patient encouragement will become science literate citizens who can function intelligently in this new century of science, and from time to time there will emerge the future scientist who may solve some major problems and advance the welfare of all humankind, such as the lesson of our biographees.

CHAPTER 1

CLIFFORD GEERTZ

NOAH C. LAURICELLA

T wo young Americans walked unhappily through the village square. They had been in this remote Indonesian village for two weeks hoping to make contact with the residents, but they were slighted or ignored at every attempt.

What were they doing here? They were anthropologists intent on learning all they could about the geography, customs, history, politics, daily activities, ceremonies, and religious influences of this area. These were things that required detailed communication with the residents; thus the anthropologists were discouraged. Then Hildred Geertz, one of the anthropologists, noted a small crowd behind a larger hut on the edge of the square. Excited noises and shouting emanated from the assembled group.

The Americans, a married couple, sauntered over, mildly curious. But the activity in the center of the crowd drew them closer. "A cockfight!" whispered Clifford Geertz. The natives were clearly fans of the event, supporting each of the cocks with words of encouragement. Near the center of the ring were small piles of the local currency.

As the Geertzes got closer, they were startled by a shout from someone outside the crowd. They recognized the Balinese word for police—*pulisi!* Cockfighting was illegal here, and the crowd began a feverish dispersal. What should they do? Clifford quickly reasoned that they need not fear these police, as he and his wife were legal tourists and would not be implicated, but something urged him to join the fleeing crowd. He grabbed Hildred's arm and they ran with a small group of natives. After about five minutes of running, he felt a tug on his arm. It was one of the natives urging him toward an alley between two village houses. He followed his new guide, who found a gate in a fenced enclosure and urged the Americans inside. Soon they were seated with a group of the natives, one of whom was carrying a cock from the recent combat. The group, still catching their breath, was now more relaxed, laughing and joking about how they had eluded the police.

Although the Geertz's command of the local language was limited, it was now clear that he and his wife were included in the escapade. The locals started questioning the Americans as to why they were there and if they had a problem with the police. As they found out later, the social, political, and economic role of cockfighting turned out to be a key to the way these villagers lived. It was as significant to them as attending a baseball game or going to a movie theater would be in America. Clifford used this story to show how participation in local activities helps anthropologists understand native residents and be welcomed by them.

This is an example of the kinds of experiences that have become commonplace to the working anthropologist. The Geertzes were in Bali to study the people, and the people came to trust them and interact with them. The Geertzes wanted to learn how people lived their daily lives, how they communicated with one another, and what their surroundings were like. They were interested in marriage customs, the temperament of the people, their clothing styles, and their view of the world. Being extremely inquisitive, they both participated in the Balinese culture and observed everything around them.

G.I. BILL PROVIDES EDUCATION

One of the most prolific anthropologists of his time, Dr. Clifford Geertz, known as the ambassador of anthropology, has dedicated his life to research, discovery, and understanding. Geertz was born in San Francisco, California, on August 23, 1926. As a child he lived in rural California during the Great Depression. After completing his public education he entered the United States Navy. He finished his tour of duty in 1946 and drifted around San Francisco that summer. Uncertain of what career to choose, he asked a former high school English teacher for advice. At that time, Americans were starting to appreciate and realize the true value of a college education. The teacher suggested that he go to Antioch College in Ohio. The college had a system in place where one could work half of the time and study the other half of the time. He had not truly considered a college education during his childhood years, but as a former member of the navy, the G.I. Bill was available to financially support his studies. It provided college tuition for more than two million individuals who had served in the U.S. military.

Antioch College appealed to Geertz in part because he was ready to move away from California. Upon his acceptance, he was determined

Young Geertz at Antioch College, 1949
(*Courtesy of C. Geertz*)

to become a famous writer. Antioch College, located in Yellow Springs, Ohio, was a small, rural liberal arts college with fewer than one thousand undergraduate students on its campus. His time in Yellow Springs was a serious period of study. He was older than many of the other students and had been in the navy during World War II, so his perspective was much different from students experiencing college life for the first time. But this was also the period of his life in which he was truly finding himself. He was able to experiment with and evaluate different lifestyles until finally, identifying a path that seemed right for him.

Geertz used Antioch College's flexibility in selecting academic course loads to the fullest and explored a wide variety of academic disciplines during his four years at the institution. Because he wanted to be a writer, he thought he should major in English. For the work portion of his work-study program, he took a position as a copy boy at the *New York Post*. This cured him of his desire to enter the field of journalism. He eventually found English too constraining, and switched his major to philosophy.

Geertz married Hildred during his time at Antioch. She majored in English. After four years Geertz was a college-educated man, with a bachelor of arts degree in philosophy, who didn't know which road to travel down next. He had no job prospects, and neither did his wife. He made the decision to continue his education, but he had no idea where to go.

Once again, one of his teachers helped him make the decision. This time, however, his philosophy professor George Geiger advised him more about what to study rather than where to study. Geiger suggested anthropology, a field Geertz had never even considered since Antioch College didn't offer anthropology classes. Geiger warned against further philosophy studies because of that field's sorry state and unpopularity, and said he considered anthropology a much safer bet. Also, Geiger had a good friend, Clyde Kluckhohn, who was a Harvard anthropologist, influential in the new Social Relations Department.

Geertz still had no formal plan for entering graduate school or how to pay for it. He had used up all of his funding from the G.I.

Bill for his undergraduate education. Luckily, Geiger also had the clout to be able to offer Geertz a generous fellowship to attend graduate school. Geiger was in charge of deciding who was the most promising student who deserved this fellowship, ultimately choosing Geertz. The fellowship stipend supported the Geertzes for two years. It was a turning point in their lives. From that day on, Geertz could devote his life to learning, studying, and sharing his knowledge with others. Consequently, he has become one of the world's foremost cultural anthropologists.

The graduate school program in which Geertz enrolled was, at that time, in its experimental stages. Harvard University was trying to create a new department of study that tied together cultural anthropology, psychology, and sociology. The name of the department was social relations, and its stated purpose was to look at society from a new, previously untapped perspective. Until then, the late 1940s and early 1950s, cultural anthropology had generally been grouped with archaeology and physical anthropology in school departments. The Social Relations Department created an innovative combination and a new way of viewing this branch of anthropology.

Geertz conducted his first research project, Rimrock, while in graduate school at Harvard. This project focused on five distinctive cultural subpopulations located in the Southwestern United States—the Navajo, Zuni, Mormon, Texan, and Spanish American peoples. Geertz did not travel to the region, but spent his time in Cambridge, where he conducted research by working with reports and field notes of other researchers. He focused his attention on responses to death and to drought in the area and on the effects of alcohol on the region's cultures, two problems that all of the cultures shared. In comparing the reactions and solutions to the problems, combined with the success of those solutions for each of the five cultures, Geertz was able to gain a better understanding of each specific culture. When he completed his research, Geertz wrote an unpublished article called "Death, Drought, and Alcoholism in Five Southwestern Cultures," which is on file in the Peabody Museum Library at Harvard University. This was

Geertz's first foray into anthropological study and would serve to help develop good research skills for his subsequent work, most of which would take place with Geertz out in the field with the people he wanted to better understand.

EXPERIENTIAL INVOLVEMENT

In a very broad sense, anthropology is the study of human beings. The word derives from two Greek words, *anthropos*, meaning human, and *logia*, meaning study. But one piece of the definition is still lacking. Anthropology is not simply the study of humans at the present time nor is it about humans simply as idiosyncratic individuals. It is the study of human cultural diversity over the course of history.

Trying to describe exactly what it is that anthropologists study is more difficult. They study people, but they focus on what is interesting and important about how particular people or groups of people invest their lives with culturally specific meaning. An anthropologist might concentrate on societies as a whole or the role of one person within that society. A study might incorporate minute details about our own or foreign cultures or it might encompass the interactions of people in different societies. Some anthropologists examine the writings of ancient civilizations, and others look at the cultural complexities of modern nations. Anthropologists believe that you must understand human history in order to understand human beings at the present time and to make predictions about the future.

These questions concerning people can be viewed through a wide variety of lenses. Geertz has chosen the lens of a cultural anthropologist. Cultural anthropology is the study of the characteristics of different cultures and their interrelations. Cultural anthropologists try to understand the distinctive cultural meanings and values within a society. To do this, these researchers interview people within the societies, observe the activities and interactions of society members, and try to gain a feel for the inner workings of the communities they are studying by participating with them in everyday activities. These findings may then be used to describe the society as a whole or to explain a certain aspect of that particular culture. In either case, it is imperative that a substantial amount of time be spent experiencing life within the society. Within the world of anthropological study, nothing can be a substitute for hands-on, experiential involvement.

Cultural anthropology requires a flexible and diverse researcher. In doing anthropological research, one must be skilled in looking at problems while in a classroom setting and analyzing them. But the researcher must also be able to immerse himself into a culture firsthand and do hands-on field research in order to gain the clearest vision of a society's strengths, weaknesses, and defining characteristics. Highly refined field research and observational skills are very important because physically living in the midst of the people one is studying helps the anthropologist understand them better. The researcher must not allow the prejudices that he or she brings from his own culture to bias opinions and taint observations.

The problem is that anthropological researchers (just like the rest of us) aren't always aware of all their own, often taken for granted and quite subtle, cultural biases, beliefs, and values. Luckily, these do become increasingly clear after deep, disciplined exposure to other ways of life. One's own cultural presuppositions also become "visible" when one reads about other cultures, moving back and forth between one's own experience "at home" and others' experiences "elsewhere." So, over the course of long-term, firsthand experience with a peoples' thoughts, beliefs, fears, and reasons for each, a researcher learns to take into account many of his or her own cultural presuppositions. Gradually he obtains a fair appreciation for and knowledge of their society *at the same time as* obtaining a much better understanding of his or her own society.

Thus, one of the goals of cultural anthropologists is to learn more about their own culture by developing an understanding of the cultures of other people. By viewing the decisions, customs, and opinions of foreign cultures in a nonjudgmental way, anthropologists are then able to view their own culture in a fresh way and reevaluate their own decisions, customs, and opinions.

Geertz reinvented cultural anthropology by promoting a "hermeneutic" (interpretation-of-meanings or literary) approach to cultural phenomena. Instead of studying cultures "as if" they were like biological organisms (e.g., focusing mostly on the structure and function of social institutions like leadership or kinship), Geertz argued that cultures should be studied "as if" they were more like literary "texts" (e.g., focusing on meanings). This approach is illustrated in his interpretation of the Balinese cockfight.[1] It is not simply a duel between two roosters, but paints a picture with deeper significance. Unlike some other cultures where there are large distinctions between male and female activities, Bali is very much a "unisex" culture. One notable exception is that cockfighting is a male sport. Men who engage in it are described as being obsessed with the birds. The birds are well fed and well cared for, as if they were children. In a way, the men themselves are fighting, as the name "cockfight" may imply.

Geertz argued that anthropologists could think of themselves as reading over the shoulders of the people they were studying. What's more, they could think of those people as "authors" of the texts of their own lives. Geertz suggested that anthropology should not be about describing timeless social institutions and homogeneous "peoples." If cultures were like literary texts, then that implied that their authors were themselves reading, interpreting, disagreeing about, and even rewriting those texts all the time. The anthropologist's job was to try to capture some of this dynamism, this active, living quality of cultures, in his own (literal) writing. Geertz explained the goals of the field best when he wrote, "Most important, we [anthropologists] were the first to insist that we see the lives of others through lenses of our own grinding and that they look back on ours through ones of their own."[2]

This eloquent statement describes the challenge posed by any field that aims to make sense of human cultural life. That is, all cultural experience is inescapably *specific* (cultures are historically *particular* systems of meanings), including the experience of social scientists. It is impossible to find a culturally neutral (outside of culture) vantage point from which to describe it. Consequently, despite the discipline involved in anthropological training and research, there is a profound parallel between the researcher and the people being studied (be they Javanese or Americans): we all view the world through cultural "lenses" that need to be specified and understood.

In addition to cultural anthropology, there are three other branches of anthropological study: linguistic anthropology, archaeology, and biological or physical anthropology. Linguistic anthropologists focus their attention on one aspect of cultures throughout history—language. Language, the organization of sounds into meaningful units (phonemes, morphemes; distinctive systems of sounds and words and ways of combining them), has played an enormous role not only in assuring the long-term survival of societies but also in shaping their distinctive cultures. Language is not limited to speech. Linguistic anthropology also incorporates the study of the written word. Cultures are completely dependent upon language as a means not simply of practical com-

munication but also of artistic, philosophical, and religious expression (values and beliefs) and political power. Through language, one generation passes on its knowledge, hardships, successes, and wisdom to succeeding generations. Lacking written language, how can other cultures learn from those that have ceased to exist? Language is a building block of civilization, without which cultures would be unable to adequately adapt and progress. Linguistic anthropologists study human languages with particular atten-

Street peddlers in a Javanese village
(*Courtesy of C. Geertz*)

tion to history, structure, and change over time. They try to understand and explain the varieties of verbal communication between humans. Researchers in this field attempt to comprehend and clarify connections among the brain, human behavior, language, and cultural conduct.

Archaeologists study skeletal remains, human artifacts (like tools, buildings, cave paintings, storage jars, religious statues), and other fossil remnants of societies of long ago. Archaeologists use everything from simple tools to multifaceted machines to better understand cultures. Biological anthropologists trace the biological beginnings, development, and changes of *Homo sapiens*. In similar fashion to cultural anthropology, linguistic anthropology, and archaeology, biological anthropology seeks to answer questions regarding the origin, development, and current state of human existence. Professionals in all of these disciplines are curious about how people lived in the past, how they live today, and how they will live in the future. The scientists are curious about how the people communicate, raise their families, worship, earn a living, and view the world.

DISTANT COUNTRIES, DIVERGENT WORLDS

After Geertz completed his first study, Rimrock, he and his wife were given the opportunity to do research in Indonesia. This expedition, funded by the Ford Foundation, took them to the Brantas River plain in central Java, an Indonesian island located south of Borneo. Geertz and his wife, along with an interdisciplinary team of other Harvard graduate students, went to the country to study families, religion, and many other facets of the Javanese culture in what came to be called The Modjokuto Project. Hildred went to study family life, and Clifford focused on religion. For two and a half years they lived with a railroad laborer's family during politically difficult times in Java. In many ways and to the best of their abilities, they became Indonesians. Their ethnographic studies (describing and interpreting a group of people within a society) focused on a small group of subjects and their environment.

The Modjokuto Project was one of the earliest attempts to anthropologically study an entire civilization. The name "Modjokuto" means "Middletown" and it was a name that was

Village food vendor, Jozia, Java (*Courtesy of C. Geertz*)

made up for their field site. It is a common practice among anthropologists to disguise the actual places where research is done to protect the privacy of the people. The "Middletown" translation is sly. It is an allusion to a famous U.S.-based sociological field study by the same name.

Prior to the Modjokuto Project, most anthropologists had written their ethnographies as if the communities they studied represented small-scale, relatively homogeneous cultures. Geertz returned to Massachusetts after completing his research to compile a 700-page doctoral thesis detailing his findings on religion in Java. This earned him his doctorate and he eventually published *The Religion in Java* in 1960.

Geertz went on to become a professor of anthropology at the University of California at Berkeley from 1958 to 1960 and he taught anthropology at the University of Chicago from 1960 to 1970. In 1970, he became a professor of social science at the Institute for Advanced Study in Princeton, New Jersey, until his recent retirement. From 1978 to 1979, he was the Eastman Professor at Oxford University in England. Geertz has spent nearly his whole life as a teacher, researcher, and writer. He continues to do so today as emeritus professor at the Institute for Advanced Studies.

It should be noted that Hildred Geertz is a well-known anthropologist in her own right, with books on the Javanese family, Balinese art, and other subjects. While she and Clifford collaborated for many years, doing fieldwork together in Java, Bali, and Morocco, and even coauthoring papers, they eventually divorced. Hildred recently retired from a long teaching career at Princeton University (where she was one of the first three tenured women at that university and helped to found its Anthropology Department). No longer teaching, she is still very happily active in research and writing.

Geertz is best known for his fieldwork in Java, Bali, and Morocco. But he has written about cultures throughout the world. Geertz worked in Java from 1952 to 1954, followed by a trip to Bali in 1957. In Bali, he focused on village structure, kinship, the laws, and cockfights. Geertz and his wife immersed themselves in the tribal behavior of the people they were studying. Geertz used the cockfight as a symbol of Balinese society as he described how familial and societal bonds are created and tested, and how they evolve. In his article "Deep Play: Notes on the Balinese Cockfight," Geertz describes in detail what happens during a Balinese cockfight and why it is significant. Hildred Geertz focused her anthropological studies on the interconnections of art in Bali and its development and evolution over the course of human history. Clifford and

Hildred returned from Bali in 1958. During the 1960s and 1970s, while teaching, Clifford also did field research in the North African country of Morocco, where he studied city design, the monarchy, social identity, and marabouts. (Marabouts are Muslim monks, or holy men.) Throughout his career, Geertz has strongly emphasized how important symbolic things are to the development of a culture.

Geertz in Bali in 1957 (*Courtesy of C. Geertz*)

Geertz was never satisfied with simply learning new things for his own enlightenment. He wanted to record his newfound knowledge in order to evaluate it and offer the results to anyone who was interested. In *Agricultural Involution: The Processes of Ecological Change in Indonesia*, Geertz described the two most important approaches to agriculture production in Indonesia and their effect on the lives of the Indonesian people. These two methods are known as "swidden" and "sawah." Swidden is a temporary agricultural plot developed by cutting back and burning off vegetation. Sawah is a wet or irrigated Indonesian rice field. Geertz later returned to Java for further study during more times of political unrest and politically motivated acts of violence. His published work about this part of the world also includes *The Social History of an Indonesian Town*, *The Interpretation of Cultures*, and *Peddlers and Princes*.

INTERPRETIVE ANTHROPOLOGY

Over time, Geertz developed a way of thinking about and looking at different cultures and peoples that soon influenced people not only in the sciences but also in the humanities. People in many fields of study have benefited from Geertz's interpretive anthropological approach to research, discovery, and human thought. Geertz takes a literary approach as he looks at a situation's anthropological significance. He has argued many times that cultures and their survival methods should be analyzed and interpreted as literature. Geertz has argued that cultures are not just useful survival tools. Cultural behavior is certainly central to human adaptation, but what makes it different from other kinds of animal behavior is that cultures organize human experience into frameworks of meanings and values, frameworks that can be reflected on critically. While it isn't wrong to investigate the "functions" and "uses" of people's ideas and behavior, our understanding is incomplete without a complementary exploration of the "textlike" meanings people give to the world and to what they and others do. It was Renato I. Rosaldo Jr., professor of anthropology at Stanford

University, who called Geertz the "ambassador from anthropology" because he appears to be the most cited anthropologist by scholars in other fields. In that sense, Geertz may be contrasted with and compared to two widely acclaimed female anthropologists—Margaret Mead and Ruth Benedict—both of whom also achieved a certain popularity outside of anthropology.

Mead did field research in Samoa, New Guinea, and Indonesia on childhood, sex roles, and other subjects from the 1920s through the mid-1970s, publishing books like *Coming of Age in Samoa, Growing Up in New Guinea, Sex and Temperament*, and *Culture and Communication*. Throughout much of that time, she gained enormous popularity writing a regular feature in the popular magazine *Redbook*. She gave advice on every manner of predicament ranging from sex education to juvenile behavior to the race for technologically advanced nuclear weapons. People who had had no exposure to other cultures or anthropological research were intrigued by Mead's work in far off places, and its implications for Americans. By sharing her insights about cultural similarities and differences, she enabled people to relate to—and gain a better understanding of—other cultures.

But Geertz, more likely to focus on anthropology's stance with regard to issues of social and ethical philosophy than popular cultural dilemmas, does not fit the same mold as Margaret Mead. He seems more akin to another great female anthropologist—Ruth Benedict. Benedict did research with Native Americans and others in the United States. Like Geertz, she wrote superb essays about a wide variety of cultures throughout the world. One of her comparative studies, *Patterns of Culture*, is still assigned in anthropology courses today. Her ethnography of Japanese culture, *The Chrysanthemum and the Sword*, (based partially on research in Japanese internment camps during World War II), was influential when it was written and is still read today both in the United States and in Japan. Although their styles have been similarly literary and readable and their subject matter similarly "interpretive," Geertz and Benedict reached different audiences. Geertz's main audiences have been more academic than popular, but they have been remarkably broad. Geertz has broken down barriers between the social sciences and the humanities by consistently demonstrating that human social interaction is inescapably a matter of making cultural meaning. In so doing, he helpfully blurred the polarized distinction between the social "sciences" and the "humanities."

What lies ahead for Geertz? "Well, I am not going back into the field anymore, at least not for extended stays," he wrote in *Available Light*.[3] "I've enjoyed fieldwork immensely (yes, I know, not all the time), and the experience of it did more to nourish my soul, and indeed to create it, than the academy ever did. But when it's over, it's over. I keep writing, I've been at it too long to stop, and anyway, I have a couple of things I still haven't said."[4] As an ambassador from anthropology, Geertz has reached out to an audience that even he may never have imagined. The leaders of other academic disciplines such as ethics, philosophy, and literature have embraced his writings.

During many periods of his life, he did not know precisely where he was going or what he would do next. He simply allowed life—its blessings and hardships—to come to him. Even when the future seemed bleak and it seemed possible that his career had

Hildred and Clifford Geertz (*center front*) with natives of Bali (*Courtesy of C. Geertz*)

come to an overwhelming and insurmountable obstacle, Geertz waited for his chance. He chose a field of study, anthropology, which seems to be continually reinventing itself. He has however, been very much a part of the process of reinvention. As he wrote in his autobiography, *After the Fact: Two Countries, Four Decades, One Anthropologist*, "Other fields change as well of course, some of them more rapidly or fundamentally: but few do so in so hard to locate a way as anthropology."[5]

Clifford Geertz entered the field of anthropology through sheer luck, but his lucky choice strengthened the field enormously. This is attested to not only by authorship of sixteen books and almost one hundred scholarly articles, but also by being the recipient of numerous honorary and scholarly awards. Honorary degrees have been awarded from such notable institutions as Harvard, Yale, Princeton, and Georgetown Universities, to name only a few (he has received fourteen). His awards include the Social Science Prize (Talcott Parsons Prize) from the American Academy of Arts and Sciences (1974), the Sorokin Prize of the American Sociological Association (1974), the National Book Critics Circle Prize in Criticism (1988), and the Fukuoka Asian Cultural Prize (1992).

Noah C. Lauricella

CHAPTER 2

MARY-CLAIRE KING

PIONEERING GENETICIST

KELLY S. McARDLE

Imagine the future. You are a new parent. In the delivery room you and your spouse are anxiously awaiting news about your first child. A geneticist steps in, clipboard in hand, and informs you that your daughter will grow to be about 5'8" tall and have blue eyes, auburn hair, and an athletic body frame.

The ability of men and women to predict, or even decide, the physical traits of infants before they are born may sound far-fetched, but it is a definite possibility for the future. The field of genetics has made tremendous advances in recent years. As is commonly known, geneticists study a branch of biology dealing with genes. These genes code for many of a person's characteristics. Limited technology and lack of understanding about most genes prevents the above scenario from occurring—yet.

In the year 2001, researchers working on the Human Genome

Project[1] produced a rough draft of all the human genes. Though this may sound simple, the Human Genome Project began about fifteen years ago, cost billions of dollars, and involved tens of thousands of scientists from all around the world. It is estimated that humans have thirty thousand genes making up their genome (the collective name for all of an organism's DNA). Aside from mapping all the human genes, scientists soon hope to be able to identify all of the genes and to study how a particular gene, or combination of genes, may cause diseases, like cancer or heart disease, determine characteristics, such as eye or hair color, or contribute to conditions, like deafness. One of these illnesses, breast cancer, is of particular concern to women. Statistics say that for a girl born this year, if she lives to be ninety-five years old, she has as high as a 1 in 9 chance of developing some form of breast cancer within her lifetime.

A leading researcher in the field of breast cancer genetics is Mary-Claire King. In 1990, King showed that a gene for familial (inherited) breast cancer, called BRCA1, existed by determining its approximate location on chromosome 17. Not only has she been extensively involved with research on breast cancer, King also applies her knowledge of genetics to help people identify missing relatives; one outcome is that orphaned Argentinian children have been reunited with their grandmothers. Currently, she is also conducting research on an inherited form of deafness, research that may eventually lead to a treatment or cure as well as information about the cause.

MUSIC SERVES AS AN ENTRÉ

Mary-Claire King was born in Wilmette, Illinois, a Chicago suburb, in February of 1946. Ever since she was a child, King enjoyed puzzles, problem solving, and playing her flute. When asked about her childhood, King said, "I spent enormous amounts of time from the ages of ten to eighteen playing the flute. I did bird watching. I did not grow up in an academic family at all, so my brother and I would go out and watch birds, hike, and play music."

When King was in middle school, her family moved to Florida because of her father's health; he suffered from Parkinson's Disease. "That [grades 5, 6, 7, and 8] was a time of upheaval in my family as my father was sick. We moved from Chicago down to Florida. The place we moved in Florida did not have an academic type of people. . . . We moved there because it was warm, for my father's health. My father and I were unhappy there. I spent most of that time doing a lot of work with a local church and trying to understand what life was like in this really rural part of American . . . in the middle fifties.

"We came back to Chicago when I was in sixth grade [in Florida] and I jumped to seventh grade [after we moved] and started junior high back in Chicago. It was great to come home. It was very difficult for me to make the transition though. By having been away and by jumping a grade, I missed out on all my former friends. So I entered the new school and had to get to know people from scratch. But by being in band and orchestra, I got to know people and I met everybody that way. Obviously, I was a smart kid so school work was easy. But mostly, I remember those years as being very tough. I think that they are tough for everybody. I think the best thing a parent can do for a child is to take good care of them, for that time is trying, and to provide a stable place for them to live. I think it is very hard on a kid from the ages of nine to fourteen to have to move schools."

King did not have any particular scientific role model until high school. "I went to New Trier High School, and I think it is a phenomenally good high school. There I met, for the first time, women who were doing math and science really well. The best role models, I think, are actually people who are only a little older than oneself so you can actually visualize being in that role. Those teachers were a whole generation older, but they could do it. Obviously the concept of role model wasn't an active concept yet. But it did strike me that women could be paid to do math properly. . . . It was great and it completely changed my life.

". . . Don't forget, I grew up before any kind of feminist movement. I assumed I would go to college and have something to do with math, because I was so good at it. It is the sort of thing you could do by yourself, even if the school that you attended was horrible, which the one in Florida was. But it never occurred to me that I would have a scientific career. I don't think I even knew what it was. I assumed I would be a housewife and not anything more. Of course, I became a wife and a mother, but I also became a scientist. I only learned of that [the possibility of a scientific career] when I started high school."

King completed her undergraduate work at Carleton College in Minnesota. At Carleton, she studied math and received her bachelor of arts degree at the young age of nineteen. She was drawn to graduate work at the University of California at Berkeley (UC-Berkeley), thinking that she would combine her mathematical talents with biology in the field of biostatistics. A genetics course, given by Dr. Curt Stern, who included a challenging scenario each class, reawakened King's love of puzzles and helped put her on the path to becoming one of the top geneticists in the country.

The climate on many college campuses, during the late 1960s, was one of unrest and political protest and UC-Berkeley was no exception. Besides having a good academic program, King was attracted to UC-Berkeley because of its political activism. King, who rallied against the Vietnam War, was also once tear gassed by the police while simply walking across campus on the way to her laboratory. At one point, the National Guard closed UC-Berkeley on instructions by then Governor Ronald Reagan. This prompted King to take a leave of absence from graduate school and she worked for Ralph Nader, examining the effects of pesticides on farm workers. Because of her empathy for the underdog, she considered a more permanent job with Nader in Washington, D.C.

Finally, however, King returned to graduate work in the laboratory of Dr. Allan Wilson and decided to pursue a project that examined the differences in human and chimpanzee genetic material. She did this by comparing their proteins and found that humans and chimps actually have many more similarities than differences. In order for King to be granted a Ph.D., she had to write a dissertation on this analysis. By the time she was done, she concluded that the nucleotide base sequences (the sequence of the four chemicals that makes up DNA) for human and chimpanzee genomes were about 99 percent identical.

Scientists were surprised by King's findings, but publication of her research landed in the well-known and well-respected scientific journal *Science*. The research was so revolutionary that *Science* even featured it on the cover when it was published. Her work has inspired many researchers to pursue related types of experiments and sparked spirited discussion and controversy regarding human roots and human evolution.

During graduate school, King met her husband-to-be, Robert Colwell. They married after she completed her degree and moved to Chile to teach science on a Ford Foundation exchange program. King had briefly returned to the United States and was on her way back to Chile when a military coup occurred. Because of the civil disorder, King's flight was rerouted to Buenos Aires, Argentina. She did not know what had happened to her husband and their students who remained in Chile. Argentina was having similar problems and was in such unrest that King had to stay in her hotel room for almost two weeks.

Eventually, King made it back to Chile and was reunited with her husband. She found that many of her students and friends had been murdered or abducted. Together in Chile, King and her husband waited in their hotel room until the airports reopened and they were finally able to return to California. She has never returned to Chile.

DNA, GENES, AND PROTEINS

At the time when King began her groundbreaking genetic research, the structure of DNA had only been known for about twenty years. James Watson and Francis Crick had "cracked" the double helical structure of DNA in 1953. Few genes had been identified at this time. Even fewer genes had been associated with illness. The Human Genome Project had not been conceived. King believed, however, that some cases of breast cancer were due to the presence of a faulty gene. This belief was not widely shared in the scientific community at that time.

What exactly are genes and proteins and how are they related? All living things are made of cells, the smallest units of life. Each eukaryotic[2] cell, by definition, contains a nucleus, that is the control center of the cell, and holds the instructions for what to do, much like our brains tell different body parts what to do. The nucleus contains DNA, which stand for deoxyribonucleic acid. DNA is so tiny that it can be seen only with an electron microscope, which can magnify the tiny components found inside a cell up to 200,000 times their normal size.

DNA is made up of four possible nucleotide bases (carbon-based molecules), adenine (A), cytosine (C), guanine (G), and thymine (T).[3] Each gene is a specific number of the four bases, chemically linked together in a specific sequence. These four bases combine, in different sequences, to make all of the possible genes. This is similar to the way in which a limited number of musical notes can be put together to make an almost endless number of different songs. The cell then translates the DNA base sequence, or genetic code, into a protein. The cell uses proteins to give you your characteristics (eye, hair, or skin color, for example) or to help you perform vital functions (digest sugars or synthesize insulin.) DNA in a human cell, in total, is about three billion bases in length. It is divided into physical structures within the cell—twenty-three pairs of chromosomes. Barring genetic anomalies, specific genes are usually located on the same chromosome, at the same location, in every individual.

Occasionally, however, the sequence of bases changes in a gene. Sometimes this mutation has no effect. Other times, a single base change can be devastating to an individual. (Think about hearing a wrong note played in a song.) The result of a base change in a gene can result in an incorrect form of the protein being made, so that the protein doesn't function properly. In the case of the BRCA1 gene that King identified, mutations in the DNA sequence can actually lead to breast cancer.

MAPPING THE GENE FOR BREAST CANCER

In 1974, upon return from Chile, King accepted a post-doctoral position at the University of California at San Francisco (UCSF) Medical Center. There she began her work on breast cancer epidemiology—the field of study that tries to find and link certain risk factors to a particular disease. This was King's first look into whether breast cancer could be genetically inherited in family members.

King recounted her serendipitous move to pursue breast cancer research in this way, "With breast cancer work, I had finished graduate school and my Ph.D. was in genetics from Berkeley on a project in human evolution, not on cancer at all. Right after I finished school I went to Santiago, Chile, to teach on an exchange program that the University of California had. While I was teaching in Chile the military coup happened and I left. I came back to Berkeley where I had been living and I needed a job—abruptly. I hadn't figured I was coming back exactly then. There was a job available at UCSF in the Cancer Center. The directors of the center wanted to try to introduce genetics into cancer biology. So I started working there in early '74 and quickly realized that there was a real possibility to use human genetics or tools of human genetics to address the question of human breast cancer. I postulated that genes that lead some women to be at a very high risk for breast cancer might exist and spent the next seventeen years proving that they did."

After two years at UCSF, King returned to UC-Berkeley as an assistant professor. She juggled marriage, raising her daughter, Emily (born in 1975), and her career. "The major issue for success of women in science, that we still haven't solved, is how to set up a situation so a woman can have children at a time in her life that makes biological sense to have children, and still maintain a career. That is very difficult. Fortunately, there are a lot of guys now that are very active in taking care of small children. But it is still incredibly hard, even with both parents committing enormous amounts of time [to child raising]. There are still only so many hours in the day. The major impact for me when she [Emily] was small was just how to have the time. I don't know how people do it and I don't know how I did it. Being a parent of a young child and having a young career are philosophically incompatible and yet we have thousands of people pulling it off." Juggling marriage, family, and career took its toll, however, and King and Colwell later separated.

At Berkeley, King continued her studies on breast cancer and her quest for BRCA1. She undertook a study aimed at tracing family histories in order to correlate the presence of a DNA marker with the expression of breast cancer. This means that she was trying to find a specific piece of DNA that was found in patients with breast cancer, but absent in those without breast cancer; this piece of DNA would not necessarily be the gene associated with the cancer, but could be located very near to it. King believed that there was a genetic basis to some forms of breast cancer—a mutated gene that could be passed from parent to child, thus causing some families to have higher occurrences of breast cancer than others have. Epidemiological data seemed to bear this out, but other scientists were very skeptical. King and her partners began looking at over a hundred large families with high numbers of cases of breast cancer. They collected blood samples, from which DNA was isolated, then began searching all of the chromosomes for a specific marker, found in breast cancer patients, but absent in their healthy relatives.

The first step in pinpointing the location of an unknown (or sus-pected) gene is finding a marker. Markers are genes or pieces of DNA that have previously been identified and localized to a specific region of a particular chromosome. If a marker is always found associated with a disease, cancer for example, than it may be the cause of that disease or it is located very near the gene that causes the disease. King's determination of the existence of BRCA1 came after system-atic and tedious testing of hundreds of markers. When King found a segment of chromosome 17, a locus called D17S74, that appeared to be linked to a gene for breast cancer in most women diagnosed with breast cancer, she was not sure what to conclude. These latest find-ings suggested that this region contained a gene associated with breast cancer; the result that she had been searching for.

How did King persist, for so long, in a hunt for a gene, when many others didn't believe it even existed? She said, "Because the big 'ah ha's' come so rarely, you have to enjoy all the little ones along the way. I have also learned that it is really important to follow your ideas even if everybody thinks they are nonsense. There is objective proof out there. One of the great things about doing science is that you are looking for objective reality. It is unlike a lot of other fields of endeavor in that way. There really is a true answer that can, in principle, be revealed. In math, that is self-evident. It is also true in biology, just more indirect to get at. So if you have an idea, you can follow it out and there will be evidence for or against it. If there is evidence against it, you go on to another idea or change your idea so that you have a chance of one that is correct. But following an idea that is far fetched is perfectly legitimate because eventually if you are right, the evidence will point that way. In the long run the evidence always wins out in science and that's to me an enormously important reason to do it. You don't have to rely on other peoples' opinions in the long term. In the long term it is the evidence that matters."

Additional analysis of the data proved that King had found the general location of the breast cancer gene—the short arm of chromosome 17. Mapping an unidentified gene is like searching for a needle in a haystack and King had proved that the "needle" existed, although it hadn't been found yet. She gave an unscheduled talk at the American Society of Human Genetics convention in Cincinnati, Ohio, in 1990 and announced the news publicly for the first time. To many in the scientific community, the news came as a shock, since they had doubted that a single gene could cause an inherited form of such a complex disease as breast cancer. Celebration of this success did not last long—her discovery started a new race to find the exact location of the gene, to sequence it (determine the order of the nucleotide bases), and to determine just what the normal function of this gene was. Scientists around the world began looking for the next piece of the breast cancer puzzle.

THE RACE TO FIND BRCA1

King's determination that a breast cancer gene existed on chromosome 17 was confirmed by Gilbert Lenior's laboratory at the International Agency for Research in Cancer in Lyon, France. It was estimated that instead of being somewhere in the three billion bases of the human genome, BRCA1 was now localized to a mere twenty to thirty million bases. A gene can be only a few thousand bases in length. Finding it was not an easy task; there was still a lot of DNA to sift through to find BRCA1. Lenoir, as well as researchers at the Cancer Research Campaign Laboratory in Cambridge, England, the Imperial Cancer Research Fund in London, the Tokyo Cancer Institute, McGill University in Montreal, and the University of Utah all decided to search for the actual gene. The race was on.

One might think that King, having generally mapped BRCA1, would have an advantage in actually finding and cloning the gene. This, in fact, was not the case. Over the course of her search many scientific advances had occurred, and spurred by the genesis of the Human Genome Project in 1988, new techniques and markers for mapping and sequencing DNA were being developed. Having localized BRCA1, researchers began looking at all of the already known genes found in the same area. Perhaps the gene causing breast cancer was a gene that had already been isolated. After three years of work, most known genes had been eliminated, but the location had now focused on a region of DNA only one to two million bases in length. Genetic research was rapidly progressing. Another gene, BRCA2, associated with a different form of inherited breast cancer was found on chromosome 13.

Finally, in the fall of 1994, Mark Skolnick, of Myriad Genetics, announced that BRCA1 had been discovered. Myriad Genetics had been founded in 1991 to capitalize on gene discovery for the development of therapeutics and screening tests for diseases such as different types of cancers. One advantage that they had was the extensive family database of Mormons in Utah. The church kept extensive and detailed family pedigrees that to a geneticist, trying to find patterns of gene inheritance, was invaluable. Families were also very willing to donate samples for DNA isolation and to participate in health surveys. A private company, such as Myriad Genetics, was also able to devote significantly more resources to the search than government-funded laboratories.

BRCA1

The familial breast cancers that King was examining showed tumor growth. In normal, healthy breast tissue, cells maintain their place and don't leave the breast. Tumor cells, however, may migrate to other parts of the body. Tumors are a clone of cells (identical copies) that grow at an uncontrolled rate, ignoring and overtaking the surrounding normal tissue. This is how cancer grows. Generally it is thought that between three and seven genes in a cell either change or lose function through mutation to cause the cell to become cancerous. The genes involved are those that function in normal cell growth. Some of the genes promote cell growth while others put the brakes on growth, especially if something goes wrong in the cell. As it turned out, the BRCA1 gene was shown to be a tumor suppressor gene. BRCA1 functions in normal cells to stop cell growth when problems arise, but the gene has an inheritable mutation that eliminates this function in familial breast cancer.

You are probably wondering why there is no cure yet for such a devastating disease now that we know what the gene defect is. King had this to say: "The fact is the disease [breast cancer] is so complex. There are so many different things that go wrong with a cell between the time it is a normal cell in the lining of the breast duct (this is the same duct that produces milk) and the time that it is malignant, invasive cancer. The fact that we cannot pick up these lesions earlier on means that by the time we do pick them up there are a lot of steps that have gone awry, there are lots of mutations that have accumulated, and the cell is headed on a path of uncontrolled growth. When women die of breast cancer they don't die of cancer in the breast, they die of cancer cells that started in the breast and have moved elsewhere. By the time those cells get lodged elsewhere in the body (bone, brain, liver) we are much more limited in what we are able to do about it. So what we need to be able to do to cure breast cancer is to be able to detect it much, much, much earlier, before that invasion has occurred. That means we have to pick it up before all of the genetic changes have occurred, which means we also have to pick it up before the tumors are as big as they are now. And even tumors that are very small can already have sloughed off cells that go on to invade other parts of the body. There is not a single magic bullet that will cure the disease. It will take a whole arsenal of different kinds of approaches."

BREAST CANCER

The latest results were remarkable. But why the big deal? Cancer of the breast is different from other cancers. Breasts are often considered part of a woman's femininity and sexuality. They are also used for nursing children. Breast cancer is almost solely a woman's disease; 98 percent of the diagnoses are made in women. In earlier times, cancer of the breast was treated by swift, surgical removal of the breast. Consider how terrifying this must have been for the individual—facing surgery, facing the loss of a breast, facing cancer. Until recently, it was considered almost taboo for women to speak out about breast cancer. With Shirley Temple Black's and Betty Ford's encounters with breast cancer, the issue finally received much-needed publicity. Since then, there has been a rise in the number of women diagnosed with breast cancer as a result of the increased awareness.

Breast cancer comprises almost a third of all cases of cancer in women. Of this, inherited breast cancer accounts for 5 percent of the diagnoses. This amounts to about 1 in 200 women having inherited breast cancer sometime within their lives. But, someone who has inherited a defective copy of BRCA1 has a 1 in 2 chance of having breast cancer by about the age of fifty. Breast cancer causes more deaths than all other cancers in women except lung cancer. Five times as many American women died of breast cancer during the Vietnam War than soldiers who died fighting. Women who have died of breast cancer outnumber all deaths attributed to AIDS. The statistics for breast cancer are staggering.

King offered this advice: "For girls that are in families that have had a lot of breast cancer it will become important when one is in their twenties, but it is not an issue before then. It doesn't have any impact on one's life and there is nothing one needs to do differently if one is predisposed to breast cancer versus not." Monthly self examinations and regular follow up visits to a physician, combined with a healthy lifestyle, help ensure that cancer of the breast is prevented or caught in its early, more treatable stages, whether one is prone to breast cancer because of genetics or not.

No one is entirely sure about what causes breast cancer, either spontaneous or inherited. Diet, age, race, and climate among other factors have all been considered and all may play a role. A certain number of women will inherit a defective copy of the BRCA1 gene and never be found to have breast cancer, even if they live to be eighty or ninety years old. The number of American women being diagnosed, however, is increasing, as is the number of deaths.

Breast cancer is an issue that needs to be dealt with. According to King, "There has been a lot of public support for research. This has been tremendously important. The women's advocacy movement for breast cancer research has been a great help. The support for having confidence that science can eventually come up with a solution for this problem and putting a great deal of money into the hands of individual independent investigators to try to find such solutions has been an enormously important, favorable development. Breast cancer research, or medical research in general, is one of those rare areas in America where people, regardless of their political background, have been very supportive. We are enormously lucky as scientists to have that support. It has also been very helpful that women that have been through this disease and their families have been willing to participate in research studies, both in clinical trials of new compounds, and in basic research like the kinds I do. So both participation of patients and families, and general public support for research in the public and private sectors has been terrific."

THE GRANDMOTHERS

During her search for BRCA1, King was also drawn to another project. In Argentina, a sudden government change caused major problems for the citizens. The military captured thousands of individuals claiming they were working against the government. The arrested people became known as "Los Desaparecidos," or the disappeared. As a result, over two hundred babies and children were left parentless. The government claimed the orphaned children. As the grandmothers found information regarding the whereabouts of the arrested parents and their captured children, they discovered that all the adults had been murdered. The children, however, had been sold to childless families or given to members of the Argentinean military. The grandmothers of the orphans organized a protest movement and actually hoped to force the military into returning their grandchildren.

In 1993, a group of the grandmothers traveled to the United States and met with the American Association for the Advancement of Science. The challenge of matching the kids to their respective families was offered to none other than King. She was willing to take on this challenge and possessed the necessary skills to see the project through to its conclusion. King had lived in Chile in the early 1970s and taught genetics in Spanish. She was a leader in genetics work and she had a passionate desire to help underdogs overcome the unfair obstacles placed in their paths.

Scientists did not have a clear idea as to how these kids were going to be identified and matched with their families. King thought that maybe by matching DNA sequences (genes and markers) of the children to the genes and markers of the grandmothers, clues would be offered as to which kid belonged to which family. King decided to go to Argentina and take samples. Since then, King has brought together over fifty pairs. Following up, King also agreed to supervise the court battles and investigations that would take place. "The work with the grandmothers is remarkable, both because of the grandmothers themselves, who are now in their seventies and even older, and because of the stories of their grandchildren who were found and are now themselves in many ways picking up where their grandparents left off. These folks are now in college and some have finished and gone on to careers. So it has been a terrific experience to get to know these folks and see their lives unfold after they learned who they are and were returned to their families. It is just great."

OUR GENETIC FUTURE

Perhaps by this point a career in genetics sounds very interesting. An average day for King, who is a professor at the University of Washington, is busy with many different responsibilities to which she attends. She said, "I spend most of the day in my lab interacting with my students and my post-docs. I come in between eight and nine [in the morning]. People in my lab work whatever hours they like. Some of them start very early and go home earlier and then some don't start until late in the morning and stay until all hours. This morning I had an undergraduate lecture to give. Many days, I go to either departmental seminars or journal clubs . . . that are given by the students."

Geneticists usually require four years of college followed by graduate work. Besides a career as a clinical research geneticist, one could become a genetic engineer, genetic counselor, or clinical geneticist, for example. Of course, King did not know she was going to be a geneticist, especially one working on breast cancer.

"I think the most important thing is that [a career] be fun, that it be the sort of activity that the person enjoys. You cannot do anything for a long time if it isn't fun. In order to know if it is fun, one has to have some good training and some good practical experience. The best training for someone who is in high school is just to do all the math and all the science that they can. A lot of people my age, who now do genetics, came from math and biology. Biology has changed radically in the last generation. It was pretty descriptive when I was in high school, now it is very analytic. One doesn't use advanced math in what I do at all, but certain kinds of thought processes that one goes through to become good at math, recognizing the idea of hypothesis, developing a proof, and making a proof operational are important."

King has had much success as a geneticist, but what types of obstacles has she faced in her career? She had this to say: "There are all kinds; they fall into different categories. One of them is the boundaries of what one can do—boundaries of creativity and just overcoming the obstacle of taking an idea that one has and not being afraid to go with it—even if it is wrong. And most new ideas are wrong. . . . From the point of view of external issues, the questions of how to have enough time to take care of a child and have a career and having structures which permit that to be possible [can be an obstacle]. Until recently that [child care] was a huge issue. There are daily issues that all of us in science confront. [They are] How to maintain in an environment where it is very expensive to do science? How to maintain enough money in the lab to actually do it? . . . How to try to keep a laboratory alive and active and vital?" These obstacles have obviously not been insurmountable for King to overcome. She runs a laboratory with almost thirty people in it. She is a well-known and well-respected scientist. Her daughter, Emily, attended law school.

Because of the Human Genome Project, in the future, an individual's predisposition to diseases will be predicted before they are born. Today, through prenatal screening, a fetus can be screened for a limited number of inherited diseases. With the entire genome decoded, someday all genetic predisposition and diseases may be able to be detected before symptoms develop. With gene therapy, healthy genes could replace faulty ones in an attempt to cure illnesses before they begin. These wonders also make genetics a very controversial area in terms of ethics. For example, if genetic screening reveals that a baby is at high risk for developing a fatal disease at a young age, should the parents abort the baby? In cases where parents may have difficulty getting pregnant, they may choose to use fertilization techniques. If each embryo is tested for disease before implantation in the uterus and only the most healthy is used, then are humans "playing God" by not allowing natural selection to occur? Is there any benefit to testing adults for diseases that are not treatable? Individuals who test positively for an illness may be denied health insurance, life insurance, and sometimes—even a job. Geneticists will assist people with understanding these complex issues related to health.

How will you know if a career in science is right for you? King said, "Do things that one really enjoys and has some substance to them, regardless. Bear in mind that I didn't know anything at all about the field I was in. I never even heard the word 'genetics' when I was in middle school. I think our society does not take middle school students seriously, yet these are some of the most honest people in the world. Twelve year olds have a way of seeing the truth. If a person at that age can find something that they really like to do, that has some content, some creative element to it, regardless of what it is: sports, music, or science [they should pursue it]. Bird watching is what I did because that was what there was in Florida. Whatever it is that you get into, ideally do it with someone else that likes it, too. It makes a huge difference in how you see yourself and how you see the world and helps you in getting over the tough patches. When one gets to the age—to being in high school—the capacity to find something that is worthwhile and fun is enormously important. Quality of high schools differ too much. Sometimes it [school] is laid out before you like a candy store. Some high schools are so good that you have lots of opportunities. Some are not so good so you really have to make them [opportunities] for yourself. But the capacity to find something and go with it is tremendously important. The generation my daughter's age, people now in their twenties and thirties, have clearly demonstrated that you can learn new things quickly if you know how to learn new things. Learning something new and being excited and doing something creative is what I think matters the most. It will ultimately be science if that is the right thing for you."

HUMAN PATRON

When asked about her most meaningful work, King had trouble choosing only one event. She said, "I think there are two or three different kinds of very rewarding things that have happened [so far in my research]. From a purely scientific curiosity point of view the most rewarding times are those times that you say, 'oh, right' and something has really fallen into place that you have been working on for ages. Those events at that level are very rare, maybe once in every ten years, where something works out just beautifully. That is just great. From the point of view of doing research that is based on what really happens to people there is a lot of reward that comes much more frequently, when the work we have done for a long time infiltrates somebody's life. The kind of breast cancer work that we do has that kind of impact. Not easily, because people learn that they are at high risk and they take actions that will keep them from getting cancer in the long run. But, nevertheless, it is life saving and that is terribly important. The third kind of rewards that are common is when people that work in my lab have things work out for them. Just on a day to day basis this sort of thing happens all the time. They see how nicely experiments can fit together and how little pieces can be a lot of fun to sew together and watch a story develop."

King modestly said, "I have been involved with breast cancer and still am. Breast cancer genetics has been and remains an interest of mine and has been since the mid-1970s. I am also interest in inherited hearing loss, and a variety of other complex traits in people, and how genetic and environmental factors interact to influence those traits. [My colleagues and I] are also interested in using genomic approaches to tackle human rights questions."

In a career spanning almost thirty years, King has helped reunite families and has led the search for a cause of breast cancer as well as pursuing AIDS research. King joined the University of Washington faculty in 1995 as the American Cancer Society professor of Medicine and Genetics. She has received the American Association for Cancer Research Clowes Award for Basic Research, in 1993 *Glamour* magazine named her one of "The Women of the Year," and in 1994 King was named the first Walt Disney-American Cancer Society Professor for Breast Cancer Research; her work is partially funded from a $1 million endowment from Disney's widow. She is a woman who is truly a pioneer and leader in her field.

Kelly S. McArdle

CHAPTER 3

MARVIN MINSKY

MARGARET J. ANDERSON

"All right Pentheus, let's continue with your testing. I'll start a sentence and you have to complete it appropriately."

"Certainly."

"First sentence: A chair is used for . . ."

"Sitting in."

"Excellent! Let's keep going. A house is where . . ."

"People live."

"Very good. And also? A house is where . . ."

"People sleep."

"Yes, great. Now then, string is for . . ."

"Tying things together."

"And what else?"

"Turning lights on and off."

"Interesting point. What kinds of lights do you mean?"

"Ceiling lights, like those you might find in a closet."

"Wonderful! Now, what else is string for?"

"For dinner."

"Hmm. What do you mean?"

"You eat string!"

The researcher sighed and leaned back in her chair. "No," she said. "No, that isn't quite right. Never mind, that's enough for today. I'll see you again tomorrow." She made a note in her laboratory notebook: 'String? String cheese? Reanalyze food algorithm.' And then she switched him to the sleep setting. The glowing, green eyes of the android went dark and stared impassively ahead.

This example illustrates one of the possible problem scenarios that a researcher in artificial intelligence (AI) might face. Marvin Minsky is one of the founding fathers of AI, along with Allen Newell, Herbert Simon, and John McCarthy. AI combines elements of mathematics, linguistics, psychology, and computer science, to attempt to model and understand the workings of the human mind, recreating thinking activity in an inorganic, mechanical system. The applications of such a model are as boundless as the power of thought itself. Most AI researchers focus on writing computer programs and algorithms that try to mimic the intelligence of the human brain. This includes making complex decisions about the world by observation, understanding spoken language, playing games of strategy against a human opponent, or any of the other complex tasks that the we undertake everyday with relative ease. Replicating the functions of the human brain, however, is not a simple task.

Minsky began designing robots and intelligence systems back in the early days of computers when an intrepid, budding mathematician could count the number of computers on the planet on his fingers and toes. Since that beginning, in the late 1940s and early 1950s, Minsky has devoted himself to forging innovative ideas that do more than restate or reorganize the old. He is an outspoken advocate of encouraging people to stick to doing things that lead to fresh ideas and new ways of understanding the world. While he is extremely opinionated and dismissive of some fields of study that he believes are irrelevant, Minsky also possesses a winsome sense of humor and a heartfelt devotion to his work that is hard not to find inspiring. His interests range from artificial intelligence to mathematics and physics as well as the psychology of humor, which he once examined in an article titled "Jokes and the Logic of the Cognitive Unconscious."

SCI-FI FAN

Born in New York City on August 9, 1927, Minsky enjoyed an excellent education and supportive parents. His father, Henry Minsky, was an eye surgeon and an artist and his mother, Fannie Reiser, was active in the Zionist movement. He has an older and a younger sister, neither of whom are involved in science. "They [my parents] encouraged anything I did. I did a lot of music when I was a little kid. [I played] piano, the only instrument where you can play a lot of things at once." He enjoys the music of Bach, Beethoven, and Brahms. He said that he sees their work as a continuous stream of development. He stated, "Most music is just local fads that don't develop very much, but classical music is people trying to solve new problems in the same field."

Minsky is quite nonchalant about his education and passion for science. He said, "My father was a doctor doing research on eyes and I went to good schools and had great teachers and exceptional friends. They had gifted schools in New York and laboratories that kids could work in and things like that. So when I got to college it wasn't any different." He added, "To me it [science] was the only interesting thing. Everything else is repetitive and doesn't change."

Minsky's elementary education came from The Fieldston School in New York City, a private school noted for its emphasis on teaching ethical decision making and sound moral and leadership skills, while encouraging independent thought and critical thinking. He attended the Bronx High School of Science, but graduated from the Phillips Andover Academy, located north of Boston, in 1945.

He said of his experience at Andover: "That was mixed because it had a lot of bright people and an enormous [number] of athletic jocks. I was only there a year and there were two great teachers that I hung around with. One was a mathematician who taught wrestling and an English teacher, named Dudley Fitts, who was a Latin and Greek scholar."

Minsky credits this penchant for connecting to bright, academic individuals as one of the reasons for his successes. "It wasn't deliberate, but the way I got to be a good physicist and a good mathematician and a good psychologist and biologist is by 'attaching' myself if I met somebody who I thought had good ideas. I hung around with Warren McCulloch (a founder of cybernetics)—but not just to learn what he had to teach. (He had been a neurologist.) It was more because he had good new ideas—and I wanted to learn 'how to think that way.'

"If I would ask a question and he [McCulloch] would reply in a certain way, I would say, 'What kind of thinking would it take to look at it [a problem] that way?' [To see their perspective] you attach yourself to people, and like a vampire, try to suck their methods out of them. You don't go to them to get knowledge because there is plenty of knowledge in books and on the Net now. . . . If you take fifty years you can do a lot of things and I think every couple of years I would attach myself to someone to try and understand how they think." It is not surprising, therefore, that Minsky's advice to others is to do the same thing to stretch their own boundaries of success.

Minsky admits to studying languages as a child, but said, "I did a little Latin because we had to and I did French in high school, which was OK. But, I was never very good at them. And if you can't speak perfectly, it's not worth speaking at all. . . . I think that what happened was that they taught too much grammar and too little reading. In Greek, which I wish I had done instead, you could read Aristotle, who is a fantastically bright guy, and a few others. . . . Aristotle is a science fiction writer; he makes theories of everything."

And Minsky thinks that science fiction is the only really interesting literature. "If you read novels, it's the same people facing slightly different mixtures of the same problems and ending up with the same nonsolutions to them. . . . I read science books and science fiction from when I first started to read. Science fiction had a lot of influence. In those days, there was only H. G. Wells and Jules Verne. Then later, I ran into Isaac Asimov and actually became friends with him. . . . If you read a science fiction writer like Greg Egan, every year he has a novel with fantastic new ideas that maybe nobody ever had before." Clearly, he sees science fiction as innovative and everything else as being boring and repetitive.

This interest and fascination with science fiction has lead Minsky to coauthor his own science fiction novel, *The Turing Option* (Warner Books, 1992), with Harry Harrison.[1] This thriller, set in 2023, is about an AI researcher saved from death when he becomes a hybrid with a computer. Shot in his own laboratory, the rest of his colleagues murdered, he searches for the killers, all the while becoming less and less human.

As for books, in general, Minsky hopes that we'll soon see the end of them. "I don't see the point of books now. . . . The trouble with a book is, you can't search it." He finds the Web much more convenient than a library, particularly with search engines such as Google. Minsky also doesn't believe in intellectual property, that is to say, patents on ideas or theorems, such as genetic codes or computer programs. He thinks copyrights should be abolished for everything except humanist literature. He hopes that science journals will soon disappear because he believes they limit the flow of ideas. He doesn't publish anything in journals unless he retains the rights to it.

Minsky views both athletics and the humanities as fairly futile and uninteresting. When asked if he was athletic as a youth, he said, "I could run faster than the bullies." He admitted to playing golf "once." Then said, " I can shoot a basket with my left hand, but I wouldn't do it very often, because it's silly. Have you ever seen a cat? It's much more graceful than any human athlete; one should give up right at the start."

While he dismisses his lack of language fluency and athleticism with good humor, one also hears a lack of tolerance in himself for anything that is less than perfection. He clearly feels more comfortable among the academically advanced. "I went to schools where people were smart. There was a year when I was in a 'regular' school and it was pretty unpleasant. Bronx High School, Harvard, Princeton, and MIT—I regard those as civilized environments." Part of this attitude toward the "common" folk was also due to the year after high school (1945) was spent in the Navy, which ended his desire for association with nonacademics.

He also believes that history, as he has seen it taught, ". . . is bunk, as Henry Ford put it. What they [historians] emphasize, is the politics, and that's the same as social affairs and there is no depth to it," he says. "I am interested [for example] in how come mathematics stopped after Archimedes for 1,500 years, but the historians don't tell us that," he points out. "I don't think they [historians] have good ideas about how to explain human behavior.

"Consider how much history there is and that psychology only started in about 1880. How come it wasn't until 1930 that Piaget discovered that five-year-old children don't conserve quantities the way seven year olds do? . . . If you pour water from a small, fat glass into a tall thin one, then the five year old thinks there is more water because it looks bigger. . . . The seven year old will say it is the same amount. The interesting question [to me] is, why wasn't that discovered until 1930?

"That's why I don't think very much of people like Virgil and historians and the humanities in general," he continues. "They keep rehashing it. Shakespeare had a lot of psychological observations, but he's not that much better than Euripides. There's no progress in that field. I don't see it [history] as a respectable human activity until they get better ideas."

Minsky received his undergraduate education at Harvard University, obtaining a bachelor of arts in mathematics in 1950. "I was a physics major and then I switched to mathematics. Mathematics is the only way you can understand simple things, but it is not very good for understanding very complicated things. I got interested in how the mind works, more or less, in my college days."

Minsky also continued his practice of bonding with role models. "There were several people that I attached myself to for

several years. There was Andrew Gleason, who was a great mathematician at Harvard. I would spend a lot of time with him. There
was George Miller, who was a young psychologist and I hung
around with him. There was great philosopher named Warren
McCulloch, who (as mentioned earlier) was one of the founders of
cybernetics. I spent a few years talking to him." While Minsky only
mentioned these three individuals in conversation, over fifty
people are important enough for him to list on his Web site
(www.ai.mit.edu/ people/minsky/minsky.html) as mentors or as
individuals who influenced his thinking. Some of these people he
continues to work with, to this day. Gleason went on to solve
Hilbert's Fifth Problem, one of the oldest and most important
problems in mathematics. Miller went on to become a founder of
the modern field of cognitive psychology. McCulloch, among his
many achievements, is best known, however, for being one of the
founders of cybernetics and (with Walter Pitts) wrote the first
important paper about neural networks.

Cybernetics is considered the "bottom-up" approach to artificial
intelligence. Cyberneticists attempt to model neural networks and
other systems that adapt to their environments. This approach led to
many useful kinds of machines, but never was very successful at the
kinds of higher-level thinking that could solve complex and difficult
problems. Another approach, the "top-down" method of artificial
intelligence, which Minsky supports, focuses on writing computer
programs to think intelligently, like people. Rather than adapting,
these programs mimic human thought processes. These two approaches can also be defined as being natural, mirroring the brain,
or artificial, starting with computer systems.

MYRIAD ACCOMPLISHMENTS

Minsky's formal education was completed in 1954 when he received
a Ph.D. from Princeton University. His dissertation was about
neural network learning theories, which he would later become critical of as a way to successful artificial intelligence. He also built a

stochastic neural-analog reinforcement computer (SNARC), the first randomly wired neural network learning machine.

Neural networks use a system that is designed to be physically similar to the way that the human brain is laid out to store information. A neural net, in its simplest form, takes input and produces some sort of output by analyzing the input data. For example, a neural net might take four digits as input. Each one has a separate "node" which transmits a signal into the network. Each of the nodes is gathered and the inputs are prioritized according to relatively determined weights to produce an answer. The network "learns" by adjusting variables in ways that produce better results. This permits the networks to work with new inputs in unique ways. (Minsky now believes that these low-level neural network machines are too limited, because they can't learn enough about themselves. Neural nets are fine for recognizing objects and beginning to store complex information about the categories into which the world fits— so brains use them in many places. But they're useful, he thinks, only at rather low levels, and other parts of the brain must use structures that are better suited to more reflective kinds of thinking—such as for making models of themselves.)

Upon completion of his Ph.D., Minsky accepted a three-year Junior Fellowship at Harvard University that allowed him to pursue his research with few other obligations or demands on his time. During his fellowship, he invented and patented the confocal scanning microscope; a microscope providing significantly improved resolution of images.

Following his Harvard fellowship, Minsky moved to the Massachusetts Institute of Technology (MIT), where he remains today. In 1959, he and John McCarthy cofounded the MIT Artificial Intelligence Laboratory. (McCarthy, a founder of AI, is credited with coining the term "artificial intelligence" at the first AI conference held at Dartmouth College in 1956.) Minsky served as the AI Lab's codirector (1959–1974) for fifteen years. He then accepted the Donner Professorship of Science (1974–1989) at MIT and today is the Toshiba Professor of Media Arts and Sciences, which he was awarded in 1990.

Minsky helped design and develop some of the first robotic arms and hands and, with Seymour Papert, the LOGO "turtle" (1972). LOGO, invented by Papert, is a children's computer programming language. The LOGO turtle allows children to program the movements of this turtlelike robot. Minsky is also a founder of LOGO Computer Systems, Inc., an enterprise that supports the constructivist approach to learning[2] and is a proponent of students having early and constant access to computers.

One gets the idea that there are probably very few topics that Minsky hasn't thought about. Certainly, if he can apply ideas about psychology to an area or program a computer to try something in a field, he does. And so, Minsky has taken on the challenge of music—both making it as well as analyzing people's reactions to it. In 1970, he and Edward Fredkin invented a synthesizer, MUSE, which composes variations of musical themes. In "Music, Mind, and Meaning" he asks, and attempts to answer, the most basic question, "Why do we like music?" Many of Minsky's writings can be found on the Web (www.media.mit.edu/~minsky/).

About his many accomplishments, Minsky said, "I never had a plan [for my life] and that's why I ended up doing so many different things." He added, "A plan is the way to narrow yourself and not get anywhere." He clearly credits his flexibility and interest in many fields as another reason for his success in diverse areas.

HUMAN CONSCIOUSNESS

There is no harder problem in artificial intelligence, indeed perhaps in any science, than that of human consciousness. Since he was an undergraduate, Minsky has focused a great deal of his research energies to tackling this problem. To understand this mystery, scientists have to solve the problems of how our brains automatically acquire and understand fantastically complex information. One should also understand that Minsky considers consciousness a "suitcase" word into which we lump all of our concepts and understandings and misunderstandings about our minds. His method is to take the mind apart into its components; he considers the brain to have "four-hundred different kinds of computers in there."

Consider, for example, a person trying to decide what to eat for lunch at a salad bar has to first identify everything there is to eat using his vision. This, you might think, is very easy. People just look at what is in front of them. But what do people really see? We see a large swatch of colors—reds from tomatoes, green leafs of lettuce, and blurs of salad dressing that could be any color. In an instant, our brain makes sense of this painting of colors and decides where the lines between different objects go, how far away they are, and what precisely each object is. But what if the dimly lit salad bar contains a bowl of cherry tomatoes and a bowl of strawberries? Both are similar in size and round-shaped. Both are reddish in color. A defining feature is that the tomato is smooth, while the strawberry has a pitted surface. How does one program a computer to visually identify the difference?

Thus, the brain must reason about the world around it in complex ways. We make split-second decisions all the time, taking into account a huge number of details that, when you stop to think about it, aren't really very obvious or simple. It is fairly easy to teach a computer some general facts about the world such as 'there is a way into and out of every room.' However, knowing something and understanding what it means are rather different ideas. The problem of building a computer model, which can speculate about a world that *might* exist, is intriguing and difficult. How do you build a program that can think about the question "What would happen if you were put in a room with no doors and no windows?" Or even harder, a truly conscious system would be able to think about itself: What is it doing? What has it done? A conscious machine might, while pondering the question of a doorless and window-less room, answer the question 'What are you doing?' by remarking that it is thinking about being caught in a complex but impossible situation, since a room with no doors and no windows could not exist.

In Minsky's opinion, "Consciousness is easy to put into a

machine. The hard thing is getting anything like commonsense reasoning [out] and being able to [get computers] to understand complicated problems. What people call consciousness is about ten different things, and none of them, by themselves, is very complicated. For example, just being able to remember what you were doing recently [is easy to program into a computer]. If you write a program in the computer program LISP, you can turn on a thing called *trace* and it keeps a record of everything the program did and you can write parts of the program that can look at that. So that if something went wrong, the LISP program can look at that and say 'Why didn't this work?' and 'What can I change in what I did?'

"I don't think consciousness is much of a mystery. It is a mystery to the public and most scientists because they think it is one thing. But as soon as you see that it is a dozen different things, different ways the machine can reflect on what is happening inside, or what recently happened inside rather than what is happening in the world, then there is no mystery at all. But what no one has been able to do is get a high quality of commonsense reasoning into a machine." Minsky put it succinctly: "If you know a million things, and a million things about those things, how do you sort which to think about?"

Another aspect of consciousness, according to Minsky, is the ability to build a model of oneself. "It may be a very bad model, but it's already the beginning of self-awareness and reflection," he explains. "It's easy to make a machine that will make grand plans, but unless it has a model of what sorts of things it's likely to do in the future when problems come up, it might get stuck on some bad plan that doesn't work. So consciousness is partly remembering what you have been doing recently and partly about making generalizations about the kinds of things you do, so that you have a model in your mind about what you are likely to be able to do." Once one can picture what they can do, they can begin to narrow down choices based on what else they know about the world and what might be sensible based on how the world might react.

To obtain commonsense reasoning, Minsky says that one needs about a half dozen different ways to represent knowledge in order to make artificial intelligence work. Then one needs to figure out how to make some knowledge generate other knowledge. For example, if you know that camels are nasty and often bite, then you may also know that llamas are unfriendly based on the fact that they look and behave in a similar manner to camels. This kind of inference to create new information is much different from other kinds of inference, such as reasoning that a glass of water three times as tall as another glass probably has more liquid in it.

Minsky puts his ideas this way, "The main thing is not to get trapped into thinking 'I know one magic way [of putting information together].' You have a big population of people who think it [machine intelligence] should be done using mathematical logic. I think that is a big mistake because mathematical logic is designed to avoid contradictions and be consistent." Minsky interprets Kurt Goedel's famous "incompleteness theorem" as showing that a consistent mathematical system won't be able to think about itself because it won't be reflective enough. Instead, consistent systems can only prove things about things within the system such as numbers and variables in mathematics. One can't use mathematics to prove something about mathematics itself, only parts of it. "So in my theory, half of your knowledge is negative knowledge about things that you shouldn't do and things that you shouldn't think about."

So again, we're back to the brain containing many different kinds of computers and, in Minsky's opinion, most artificial intelligence experts are all looking for "the trick" that will do everything. "So my theory is 'the trick' is to find management systems that can handle dozens or hundreds of kinds of inference machines [systems of organizing knowledge and making decisions]. In order to do that, it [a machine] has to have a lot of knowledge. There isn't going to be a simple formula for it."

GENETIC PROGRAMMING

Minsky authored the groundbreaking book, *Society of Mind* (Simon and Schuster, 1985). In it, he tries to define intelligence by pulling apart its attributes and writing a page-long description of each. He believes that intelligence is made up of many, many smaller parts, each of these parts in and of themselves, all mindless. He covers topics including memory to space recognition and such ideas as ambiguity. A basic tenet of *Society of Mind* is that intelligence is the careful orchestration of the mindless parts, cunningly meshed and melded together. (His daughter, Juliana, illustrated the book.)

Minsky is working on a new book, *The Emotion Machine.* "It is a sequel in the sense that it has theories that alter things that were not in the other book. And a few of them [theories] have changed. It has more topics. It explains a lot of psychological behavior that wasn't touched in the other book. . . . It has theories about various emotions. But they are each different. . . . Each emotion is a somewhat different mental organization or way of thinking, and there is some machinery to switch these. The book has a lot of suggestions about what they might be like. There are a lot of things that might have escaped people."

One topic that Minsky will be writing about in *The Emotion Machine* is genetic programming. A system that he considers to be inefficient. Genetic programming, in terms of AI, is modeled after the evolution of life on Earth. It essentially takes several computer programs and runs them. Each of these programs is generated randomly, and they are all rated on how well they perform a particular task. Then the most successful ones—those that most effectively accomplished what they were designed to do—are recombined in different random ways and tested again for effectiveness. The most successful of the next batch are then crossed together once more, and so on. In theory, this process of eliminating ineffective program strategies and combining effective ones in new and unique ways produces highly efficient programs in a way similar to how evolution produces increasingly well-adapted organisms through generations of natural selection.

This method might be used to create a program that guides a mechanical mouse through a maze. The first batch of programs might very well result in only a few programs that get anywhere at all. One mouse might move straight ahead all of the time.

Another might constantly turn in circles. These programs, while not even able to solve the problem, would be a good start. These different programs are then crossed together to produce a new batch of programs. Upon testing, we might find that we have slightly smarter programs that walk and turn once in a while. Some of these crosses would, of course, fail completely. They would be eliminated by the next generation of new programs. Eventually, this method of recombination would produce a mouse which would have "learned" how to get out of a maze (perhaps by always following the right wall).

Minsky thinks this method produces good results but with no record of the errors it corrected. In this context, he sees people's admiration of evolution as a huge mistake. Genetic programming doesn't allow for people to learn from mistakes. This is because every time a mistake is made, it simply gets eliminated from the electronic gene pool, and there's no record of it. The people in favor of this method don't realize that evolution is an inefficient system because it doesn't remember why the unsuccessful attempts weren't successful. Almost everything that could be learned from the evolution gets scrapped because there's no record of what the mistake was that caused it to be eliminated. Minsky is on a campaign to get genetic programmers to realize that they're imitating something that's imperfect. He's convinced that there's no way the evolution method can avoid large numbers of rare mistakes. "If they start out from scratch every time, they will probably not get there," he said. "Somehow, these people have no perspective."

CRITICAL THINKING

Minsky's faith in science and the potential of the human mind seems unshakable. But it's obvious that he feels that society would progress faster and farther if more people thought like he did. Another area where he "goes against the flow" is in his spiritual beliefs. As far as religion is concerned, he's a confirmed atheist. "I think it [religion] is a contagious mental disease. . . . The brain has a need to believe it knows a reason for things. So if somebody with a beard comes along and tells you that they know [where we came from], then you're sunk. So it is very contagious." He continued, "I don't believe the world exists. This is just one of a number of mathematically possible worlds, so the question of who created this world is a silly question." He points out that there's really no way to tell whether we've been simulated or not.

Minsky thinks the people who sit around wondering about existence are making a mistake. "It makes sense to say, 'Is there a red table in this universe?' To say that a table exists is to say it is in this universe. To say that the universe exists, is to say that it is in itself—and that doesn't mean anything." The argument is circular. "It doesn't actually mean anything. To say that it came from somewhere else, then you would have to ask about the somewhere else. But the religious people say, 'Oh, God made himself.' But what does it mean to say 'made'? It is all a little technical mistake. People aren't trained in critical thinking well enough. Most scientists haven't ever thought of this. They think this world exists and there is something special about it. But in cosmology there is another theory, the 'all possible worlds theory.' They just haven't applied it to themselves."

Definitely outside of the mainstream of what most people believe, he does approve of SETI, the Search for Extraterrestrial Intelligence, studies that survey the universe for evidence of other inhabited planets. "You should listen to the stars and figure out what extraterrestrial life might be like, but you certainly shouldn't pay any attention to anyone who says they are coming to earth for sex. If they could get to Earth, they would have sex machines by now!" (This is in reference to individuals who believe that they have been accosted by UFOs.) He pointed out that the budget for SETI is very inexpensive. "It is a thousand times less then the lipstick budget. SETI is just a few million dollars and [the budget for] lipstick is twenty billion. Golf is forty billion."

Minsky is not just controversial when he talks about issues of history and religion, but can be a bit of a controversial figure in his own research field of artificial intelligence, especially when he is quite open in criticizing the methods of others. However, in a career spanning more than fifty years, he has helped lead and shape the field into what it has become today. His colleagues have honored him with the Turing Award (1970), the Killian Award (1989), and Japan Prize (1990) to name a few. He has also been elected to both the National Academy of Sciences and the National Academy of Engineering. He has formally served as mentor to nearly one hundred students who pursued their graduate work with him and countless others, most of whom he probably has never met.

On a personal note, Minsky is married to a pediatrician, Gloria Rudisch. They have three children, Margaret, Henry, and Juliana. He is also an animal lover.

Minsky's advice for students is clear—make your own opportunities and probe the minds of good mentors—like he did. "If you're interested in something, don't wait for school to tell you about it," he said. "I know people who say 'Well, I'd like to learn some biology, but I don't have time for a course in it until my junior year.' They should learn how to read a book. My advice is, if you read a book a day, you can't go wrong, unless they're real bad. If you are interested in something, you should do it. And find somebody who knows about it and make friends with them. If you want to learn about computer programming, then get to know some good hacker and you will learn fifty times faster than in a course." And of course, his advice is to also attach yourself to people who have good ideas and learn to think like they think, as he did.

Will we soon see computers that meet the gold standard, the ultimate test for true artificial intelligence? The Turing Test was devised in the 1950s by British researcher Alan Turing. It basically says that a computer is intelligent if it can deceive a human. A few programs have been able to do that already. There are programs that play chess and checkers quite well. There have been several programs that could hold their own in conversations, keying off input to respond with comments and questions of their own.

It's 2001. Is the real version of Hal, the independent computer from *2001: A Space Odyssey* on the horizon? Not quite yet, but Marvin Minsky is certainly trying to lead the field of artificial intelligence toward an ideal version of this rogue computer.

Margaret J. Anderson

CHAPTER 4

STORY MUSGRAVE

SPACE DOCTOR

M. BLAINE EUBANKS

Being a doctor means being prepared for anything. And Dr. Story Musgrave faced one of his greatest challenges when he encountered of on the most unusual patients in history. This patient was the Hubble Space Telescope, one of the costliest, most intricate, and most important scientific instruments ever built. On December 2, 1993, Musgrave and a team of astronauts aboard the space shuttle *Columbia* set forth on the ultimate doctoring mission. Their primary task was to correct a flaw in the curvature of the telescope's mirror—a flaw that was narrower than one-fiftieth the width of a human hair. It would be the challenge of a lifetime, and the culminating adventure of a journey that began in eastern Massachusetts and ended in the stars.

A TURBULENT CHILDHOOD

Musgrave spent a lifetime getting ready for this mission. He was born on August 19, 1935, on a 1,000-acre dairy farm in eastern Massachusetts. His name, Story, is a family name. "It was a last name from two generations ago on my mother's side. It was a last name. It's a fun name. There was a U.S. Supreme Court justice that had the name Story. There are some other fairly well-known Storys." His name was probably one of the best gifts that he received from his family.

Musgrave spent much of his free time as a young man wandering around the huge farm, watching the stars, kayaking, and repairing farm machinery. He said, "At the age of three, maybe younger, I'd go in the forest in the middle of the night and be at home and comfortable. I had my own little kayak to go in the rivers, at that very young age. I was really rooted in the soil. That was where I found myself, out in nature. I was out in the earth. I was driving farm machinery by the age of six or seven or eight. When it broke down, I would have to learn how to fix it, because they would leave me out in the field, it was a remote field. They would come get me at sunset, so if it broke, I would have to fix it on my own. . . . I became 'self-reliant,' in Emerson's words (his essay). My own self-identity, my own sense of 'self' is what carried me forward. It's what carries me forward today. I always look back at that child back then, and that's what propels me today. That is my rock today as well. I look back there and see where that child brought me—to where I am today."

Nature was an anchor for Musgrave and an escape from a turbulent life at home. Both of his parents committed suicide, as did a brother, and these weren't the only generations of his family affected by psychological illness. Musgrave's great-grandfather and grandfather had also taken their own lives. It was not a childhood that seemed likely to produce a great astronaut or a world-renowned space doctor. He said, "I did not have difficulties, they did. Probably, nature played some role in that. I escaped to the sanity of nature. That was my rock."

If anyone ever had an excuse to fail, and if anyone ever had a background that would justify a defeatist attitude, it was Story Musgrave. Astonishingly, the proud astronaut credits some of his success to his dark past. Despite being surrounded by a family full of alcoholism and having abusive parents, he describes many of his childhood tragedies as positive events that brought him to where he is today. "Without those things," he said, "I wouldn't be here."

The future doctor's first "patients" were the tractors and farm equipment that he learned to repair. For Musgrave, a tractor isn't that different from a space telescope. "I learned the skills of being able to look at a drawing and totally understand how things functioned and how it worked. I had learned visually on the farm. So I could see it, and I knew how it worked, and I knew how to fix it. I got that skill as a child."

At eighteen, Musgrave joined the marines. Over the course of his long military career, as both a soldier and test pilot, Musgrave flew 17,700 hours in hundreds of different kinds of aircraft. As a volunteer parachutist, he completed more than 600 scientifically studied free falls. His skill with machinery grew. "When I was in the Marine Corps, where I was a mechanic and I got [to work on] more machinery—introduced to military aviation—even though I'd soloed an airplane prior to the military. Military aviation certainly grew those seeds as well. And so, even though space is nowhere near on the horizon yet, it is going to be a long time still coming, those seeds continued to grow, and I started getting an appreciation for books by reading manuals on how to fix airplanes. I needed to be able to read them and I learned how to interpret drawings and schematics, which I used, of course, for my entire thirty year career as an astronaut and then some." His natural abilities in the operation of machinery and in technical analysis served him exceptionally well, and they caught the attention of his superiors.

As a young man growing up on a farm, Musgrave had little exposure to books, which were considered kind of a luxury. "Books were not 'part of the equation.' It was farming and books didn't get the cows milked. I had no books then and I did not even really know what a book was, if you get down to it. Obviously, I

had my school courses, which I never finished. I never did graduate from high school."

"You never did graduate from high school?" I probed.

"No. So I was not really compatible with books. And yes, they
were there and I used them for courses," he replied. His focus was
on the family farm and nature. "It [my focus] was out in nature. It
was the earth, it was the sky, it was the heavens. It was the soil. It
was the animals and the machinery. It was the physical world. So,
it turned out I was internally motivated toward that world, but I
had no choice either."

After his experience in the military, Musgrave gradually came
to develop a passion for learning and for books. He said, "The limitations of not having a high school diploma presented themselves
to me. That led me off to college. But then, I got education in different sciences, math, computers, chemistry, medicine, physiology,
and biophysics."

When the opportunity to study and learn finally came through
the military, Musgrave wasn't content with expertise in any one
discipline. In fact, that's probably an understatement. Starting in
1958, he earned a degree in mathematics and statistics from Syra-
cuse University. The next year he earned a master's degree in business administration, operations analysis, and computer programming from the University of California at Los Angles (UCLA). In
1960, Musgrave added another bachelor's degree to his collection—
a degree in chemistry from Marietta College. In 1964, he earned an
M.D. from Columbia University, followed by a master's in biophysics and physiology from the University of Kentucky in 1966. In
1987, he earned a master's degree in literature from the University
of Houston, and in 1997, Musgrave was actively engaged in writing
theses for two more degrees: psychology and history. These two,
when completed, brought his total number of degrees to nine.
Thanks to the opportunities provided by the military, Musgrave
was able to fulfill his dreams of a broad education. Even today,
Musgrave's library contains thousands of books. He is an eternal
student, continually reading and writing poems and stories.

Musgrave's motivation for all of this academic achievement

was an inquisitive nature. He said, "It was just basically curiosity. . . . But it was the courage to change paths or to combine paths or to want to bring this discipline into the current discipline. It is very creative, and it is a very powerful thing to do." Story has always sought to bring many levels of expertise to his undertakings. In any endeavor, he is equal parts scientist and philosopher, psychologist and historian, poet and doctor. His ability to combine the perspectives of a scientist and a humanist has been a signature of his career as an astronaut. "For me, it is all the same, but it is just different paradigms. But, they are human paradigms. There is nothing about that out in nature. [In nature] there are not those divisions. Those are human divisions. They are purely human divisions. We love to pull things apart as humans and we like to separate the body and the mind—like Decartes. And then we have to spend the next century trying to put it back together. We have not succeeded yet. We pull apart science and religion because we have what we call a science paradigm. We have people that do that. We have people that do religions. Those are only human categories. . . . [Religion and science] are all the same thing. They are only human categories that function in our culture. That is the only reason there is any separation. The physical cosmos is also spiritual, which sounds a little strange. However, I am a spiritual person—that cannot be denied. That humanity is spiritual, the presence of spirituality, cannot be denied. Yet it is the cosmos that is physical, biological creation and evolution, which produced this spirituality. So, within that context, they are all the same thing. They came from the same source."

A "JACK-OF-ALL-TRADES" AT NASA

The National Aeronautics and Space Administration (NASA) recruited Musgrave in 1967 from the U.S. Air Force, where he had just completed a postdoctoral fellowship. While he was recruited as a scientist/astronaut, Musgrave's initial role was to design mission-related equipment and to learn mission control procedures, instead of going into space. His reputation within NASA grew as his expertise and ability became known. Musgrave, knowledgeable about aerodynamics, was an experimental test-pilot as well as an M.D., so he was selected for many projects in the emerging space program. Musgrave served as communications advisor for Skylab's second and third sojourns into space, and his innovations and expertise were essential to the Skylab missions.

His first chance to go into space came on April 4, 1983, on the maiden voyage of the *Challenger* space shuttle. On this expedition, he and fellow astronaut Don Peterson conducted the first space shuttle extravehicular activity for the purposes of testing new spacesuits. The tests put new modifications in spacesuit design into the vacuum of space, and monitored their performance. Musgrave's next trip would come in 1985, again on *Challenger*, where he performed important experiments in astronomy, astrophysics, and the life sciences. (He was lucky not to be on the ill-fated voyage of *Challenger* when it exploded in 1986.)

Despite all of his other achievements, Musgrave will probably be best known by most people for mission STS-61, the mission to repair the Hubble Space Telescope. He had been involved with Hubble since its inception in the 1970s. Congress and the public had gradually come to understand the benefits of a telescope above Earth's atmosphere, which could view deep-space objects without having to look through the atmosphere. The reason why stars twinkle at night is because of atmospheric interference that distorts the view of stars and distant galaxies much in the same way that heat rising from a desert plain or sun-drenched highway can create blurry mirages. While this may be lovely for poets and star-crossed Casanova wannabes, on a more practical level it makes viewing deep-space objects a difficult experience for ground-based telescopes. Astronomers think of Earth's atmosphere as being composed of "seeing cells," blocks of distortion (blobs) that bend starlight many times before it reaches the ground. Any image that reaches even the best ground-based telescope is still hopelessly twisted and turned by these "seeing cells." The concept of a space-based telescope goes back to an idea of astronomer Lyman Spitzer in 1946.

The light that our eyes can detect makes up only a very small part of the entire electromagnetic spectrum. Volumes of information about the universe is recorded in other forms of energy invisible to our eyes, including ultraviolet radiation and X-rays. These differ from visible light in that they have a much shorter wavelength. Additional problems arise for astronomers who want to use information besides just the visible light that we see to study stars. For example, nearly all stars are virtual factories of X-ray radiation. The ability to determine what kind of X-ray radiation is being produced, and how much, is a great clue to understanding how a particular star works. For example, a certain star might produce a light of only a particular wavelength, which can then tell us information about the star's type, temperature, and location. Some of the light that astronomers need are absorbed in the atmosphere and never reaches the ground. This is a good thing for humans because without this protection from dangerous X-rays we wouldn't be able to survive. (Dentists put that lead apron on you when they take X-rays of your teeth for a good reason.) Astronomers, therefore, must fly expensive, heavy satellites above the Earth's atmosphere to collect and study some of the precious light emitted from stars.

PLANS FOR HUBBLE

A telescope perched above Earth would be able to solve both of these problems. First, it would be permanently perched above all the seeing cells of Earth's atmosphere. Stars that appear fuzzy and faint and are hard to distinguish because of atmospheric distortion from Earth would theoretically be crystal clear when viewed through Hubble.

Hubble would also help astronomers further their research. Valuable studies would be able to be conducted with Hubble's powerful telescope, which uses detectors sensitive to infrared through ultraviolent starlight. Going from a ground-based telescope to Hubble is like suddenly going from getting only one station on your radio to being able to tune in to half a dozen. Instead of being able to use only a narrow band of wavelengths (visible light) to study stars, with Hubble, scientists could tune in to a very broad array of wavelengths without the atmosphere getting in the way. Scientists estimated that Hubble would be able to see stars fifty times fainter at distances seven times greater than ground-based telescopes.

From day one, Musgrave had been a supporter of the dream that would eventually become humankind's first, large optical telescope in space. Twenty years of planning, hard political lobbying, and fund raising by scientists and lobbyists around the globe went into the realization of the Hubble dream, one of the most scientifically complex and ambitious projects ever attempted. Those who wanted to make Hubble a reality had to contend not only with an incredible scientific challenge, but also with a public and a Congress reluctant to spend money on large scientific projects. Even some scientists were opposed to Hubble. Such an expensive, elaborate telescope meant a great shift of funds from the pet projects of many scientists. Some critics saw Hubble as an elaborate propaganda tool, a show-off telescope designed to bolster NASA's public image. Millions of dollars and countless human-hours were dedicated to convincing the scientific community, the government, and the public that an Earth-orbiting optical telescope was worth funding.

On April 25, 1990, the over twenty-year-old dream of the Hubble Space Telescope became a reality, as it was released from the space shuttle *Discovery*. Scientists around the world cheered what was initially seen as one of the great triumphs of the space program, but the elation was short-lived. By June of that year, scientists anxiously observing the images returned by the Hubble Space Telescope were beginning to notice serious flaws in the images. Pictures that should have been crystal clear were fuzzy and grainy, still better than those from Earth-based telescopes but nowhere near the clarity scientists had expected.

A public outcry quickly ensued. The telescope, which had been in production for nearly twenty years by the time of its release, had been sold and resold to the public until expectations had reached almost unrealistic levels. The public and Congress had been forgiving of the telescope's immense budget and design delays, but had also been prepared to receive immediate positive results. When the images returned were blurry, despite the fact that they were better than images from ground-based telescopes, the public, the government, and even members of the scientific community cried foul. The problem was gradually diagnosed. A major error in the fabrication of the telescope was the cause of blurry images. In an attempt to salvage some of its reputation, NASA quickly utilized computers to enhance the images. This helped to eliminate some of the distortion and bought the space agency time. Looking to the future, however, the scientific community agreed that a repair mission of some kind would be necessary if the telescope was ever to live up to its potential.

THE MISSION TO REPAIR HUBBLE

The idea of a manned mission to fix Hubble was not an outrageous idea. NASA had planned on sending astronauts on periodic servicing missions anyway. Musgrave played a role in the then controversial decision to make crucial parts of Hubble serviceable by humans. "I wasn't necessarily responsible for the momentum that led to its being serviceable, but I was there amongst the group who was going to make that decision, [the decision] that it would be serviceable by humans. [This is] opposed to satellites, which you park out there [in space] and if they break, they're broke. . . . Making it friendly and compatible, there isn't much downside. There really is a nice halfway that means 'space walking friendly.' . . . There are specifications that I helped develop back then for what makes it absolutely 'certifiable friendly.' . . . Hubble is fantastically 'friendly.' " Many of Hubble's parts were modular and could be slid in and out of place like massive dresser drawers.

Any manned mission to fix Hubble, however, would not be routine. Technicians estimated the process would require five

Musgrave is tethered to the end of the Remote Manipulator System as he prepares to install protective magnetometer covers to the Hubble Space Telescope during its repair mission (*Courtesy of NASA*)

space walks, more than any repair mission ever attempted. Although much of Hubble was friendly to human repair, as Musgrave put it, some of the parts that would have to be changed were not. The one hundred-inch mirror had a curvature error near the edge measuring nearly one-fiftieth the width of a human hair. This doesn't sound like much, but in terms of such a precise instrument it is an unacceptable one, an error capable of causing terrific distortion. The flawed mirror itself, unfortunately, was built into the telescope and could not be replaced. Solving this problem would require the installation of new mirrors, properly calibrated to refocus the light from the main mirror to produce a clear image.

Hubble's mirrors weren't the only problem. Musgrave said, "Well, it had thirteen major failures, when I went to repair it. The mirror was number one. Wrong curvature in the large mirror (100-inch), which of course is part of [the] structure—it could not be replaced. We had to install instruments that had their own correction for atmospheric collaboration and also an optical bench which had pairs of mirrors that would intercept the aborated light [light that has been reflected incorrectly], correct it, and then reflect it into the other instruments. So those five pairs of mirrors corrected for five other instruments." Other major failures had helped to cripple the telescope. Problems with photographic chips, directional controls, and other systems left engineers and scientists scratching their heads.

What went wrong? Why did the instrument have so many flaws? After the mirror problem was discovered, it was determined that the large mirror of the telescope had never been tested. The polishing machine that ground the mirror incorrectly was the same instrument used to check the mirror curvature. No mistake was detected because the machine was checking its own work. In Musgrave's own words, "Well, there was no checking on the large mirror, it was never tested, [not] even once. And that was the design from the start. The problem was the polishing machine, which was going to do the final polish, was also the machine to check the result. So you in fact have not run a test. It is absolutely faulty thinking. You are not measuring light, you are only measuring curvature. There was never a light shown down through the barrel to see that it would be focused at the point where the instruments pick off the light. There was no end to end test."

In the pressure to get such an important and exciting instrument off the ground, basic checks of accuracy had been skipped because of a tight budget and limited time. Many scientists knew that not everything was being done to ensure the success of Hubble, but faced limited options when confronted with a reluctant Congress and a tight budget.

The committee assigned to investigate the problems found disturbing evidence of just how many corners had been cut to bring the telescope into the air. One device that was designed to test the mirror, called the reflective null corrector, was found to be the wrong size for the lens in testing. In their haste to finish the job, technicians charged with fabricating the mirror, used three household washers to bridge the gap, and they told no one. Had anyone discovered it, the use of household washers in an instrument so precise should have been a red flag signaling disaster. Yet in the haste to make Hubble fly, it was ignored until Hubble failed in space.

The optical flaws were in part blamed on the complexity of the mirror system. NASA officials pointed out that the combined testing of the mirrors using artificial stars would have required several hundreds of millions of dollars. Furthermore, there was danger of contaminating the optical surfaces—not to mention the technical difficulties of testing such a huge instrument, expected to work in the weightlessness of space, on the ground. Nevertheless, not testing the mirrors was a major mistake.

The media was quick to pick up on the mistake, and the results made NASA face serious public criticism. On their front cover, *Newsweek* magazine called the telescope a "$1.5-Billion Blunder."[1] In 1990, Gary Larson, creator of the "Far Side" comic strip, drew an image of two aliens waving and smiling from the window of a UFO. The picture is blurred and shaky, and the caption reads, "Another photograph from the Hubble Space Telescope."[2] South Dakota Congressman Robert A. Roe was even less subtle. "What is wrong with the system we are following," he asked, "that failed to identify this flaw until the bloody thing was up in the air and we had spent a billion-and-a-half dollars?"[3]

It would be up to a space doctor and his crew to see if the enormous patient could be made well. The stakes were far higher than simply the need for better photographs of distant stars, although those were on NASA's wish list. The sharpness of photographs taken using the Hubble telescope would serve to provide details of such extended objects as quasars and galaxies. If NASA could not successfully keep a functioning telescope in space, many wondered how the agency would be able to keep living beings in space on a long-term basis. Hubble was not a complete failure because scientists were able to get new and exciting images from the telescope, but it remained a floating monument to what many saw as corner-cutting scientific research. The future of space science and of NASA rested on the hope that Hubble could be fixed quickly and cheaply.

STS-61, the mission to fix Hubble, was the culminating mission for a man with many abilities and many passions. Musgrave led a team of highly trained and experienced astronauts, all of whom had to function seamlessly and cooperatively. Fixing Hubble and bringing this team together was the full realization of Musgrave's philosophy, the idea that poetry, art, science, and technology are inseparable parts of the same whole. A task of this complexity would require more than a simple knowledge of how to fix the telescope. The machinery and the incredible sensitivity of the parts involved were simply too complicated to be fixed with a rudimentary mission. One faint thumb print on the main telescope mirror would be seen in every image taken from that point forward. One miscalculation could turn Hubble's already flawed vision from bad to worse. One misstep could make the barely usable telescope unusable, and perhaps irreparable. And the repair had to be made in space! The tremendous precision required in the Hubble repair would demand an astronaut who could bring equal parts science and ballet to the mission. Musgrave, with his broad background and multiple interests, was an excellent choice for such a demanding task.

BALLET IN SPACE

To many, a thorough understanding of the systems and machinery aboard the telescope and a basic understanding of what to do would have sufficed as preparation for the Hubble repair. But that was merely the beginning of the preparation process for Musgrave. For eighteen months, he and his team relentlessly planned, practiced, and rehearsed the movements of each finger, toe, and wrench turn. "This may have been the most rehearsed space mission since the moon landing," Musgrave said.

To Musgrave, preparing for the Hubble mission was like rehearsing for a dance performance. He said, "It's like choreographing a ballet. I think ballet is as close as you can get except you add 300 tools. And so you have 300 tools and you have a body that is in a spacesuit. A body in a spacesuit means it's rather bulky, cumbersome, loss of tactile [sensations], not great range of motion, and all those kind of mobility things—in an environment in which everything is free to move. So it's a little different work environment but you take that work environment, with 300 tools and you choreograph the work and the tools—the body and the tools. That's as simple as it is."

"Like you are trying to do it as an art form, almost?" I asked.

"Oh, it *is* an art form! I can tell you who's a great space walker by sitting in my window and looking at the parking lot," he said. "You can watch how someone picks up a tool and how he or she relates to it and how they handle it. You look at how someone changes a tire and there you got it. . . . Which nut comes first? How many turns before you go to the next nut and how do you position the wrench when it first goes on. And you know, it's just all of those kinds of details—we do the same thing in surgery." Repairing a precision telescope in space is a good example of a task requiring a combination of art and science skills—skills that Musgrave had been perfecting his entire career.

For cost reasons, certain components of the satellite had been designed to work for only a few years, so routine servicing shuttle flights were needed to replace those components. Hundreds of tools and devices had been prepared so the astronauts would be ready for any problems. Many procedures were practiced on Earth using a huge water tank to simulate the conditions in space. If you are floating, submerged in water, you are technically weightless. Some training even went on during real space conditions on earlier shuttle flights.

The Hubble repair mission was far more ambitious than anything anticipated by the NASA experts. The mission had three major goals: (1) to correct the optical flaws in the mirror of the telescope as well as possible, (2) to prove NASA's belief that the

Hubble could be serviced in orbit, and (3) to increase the reliability of the entire array of instruments by replacing failed or poorly operating components. Among these was the solar panel array. Due to temperature changes, its interactions disturbed the precise pointing of the telescope and even threatened the entire structure of the telescope. Another part that needed to be replaced was the wide-field planetary camera. This device, as large as a grand piano, was actually four cameras. Instead of using photographic film, the light from the telescope was focused on light-sensitive charge-coupled device (CCD) chips. These are semiconductor devices that respond to light hitting the chip by emitting electrons that are collected and registered electronically. In the 1980s they were on the cutting edge of technology. Today they are found in digital cameras. In spite of all efforts to keep the chips clean, somehow they had become contaminated. They, too, had to be replaced.

The principal task of the astronauts was to fit the equivalent of glasses to the eye of the telescope, the main mirror that had been ground incorrectly. This mirror could not be replaced except by extensive testing on the ground and intensive computer calculations. Correction elements were debated, built, and—you can be sure—tested. Of course, when you go to your optometrist to have your glasses fitted to correct your vision, the doctor asks you how far down the eye chart you can see and then asks, "Does it look better this way or that way?" Your answers determine the prescription. In the case of the Hubble telescope, the only test of success after the installment of the new optical components would be the photographs of stars made after the repair crew had left. Many people saw the Hubble mission as a make-or-break effort for NASA. Embarrassed by the flaws in the telescope, a perfect operation could restore public confidence in the agency.

During the mission, the telescope's mirrors didn't cause the greatest difficulties for Musgrave and his colleagues; the telescope's solar panel array did. These very thin, huge panels provided power for the telescope. A design fault in the panels caused serious vibrations every time Hubble crossed the day-night boundary in orbit. This was traced to warping and distortion of the panels; the vibrations occasionally caused the telescope to lose its fix on the guide star.[4] The solar ray drive powering the solar panel array was supposed to provide the pinpoint accuracy needed for the perfect imaging of faint stars. It was as though our poor blind patient was trembling too violently to find what he was supposed to be looking at.

The contractors identified the design fault; the panels had to be replaced, as would the electronic controls that drive the solar arrays. Although many parts of the Hubble were designed to be replaceable in orbit during maintenance missions, this unit had not been designed that way. It's no mystery that tools designed for space work must be much different from those designed for use on the ground. Screws and switches that on Earth are simple to fasten and unfasten are almost impossible to use in a weightless environment. The telescope's solar panel array drive, for example, had been installed on Earth using screws similar to those on the back of any personal computer. But tiny screws could easily slip between the fingers of astronauts wearing bulky spacesuit gloves, and a lost screw can be devastating when you're floating hundreds of miles above the nearest Radio Shack.

Musgrave had initially told the mission planners that the task of replacing the solar panels and control grips was impossible to perform in space. Their solution had been to design a set of clips, large enough to be held easily in zero gravity, which would eliminate the need for impossible-to-handle screws. The plan was to attach these clips to the solar array drive in place of the screws, thus enabling the crucial panel's replacement.

One month before the planned launch, the clips came in. Much to the frustration of Musgrave and his team, it was discovered that they were the wrong size. What could be done? Clips that would not attach to the solar panel drive were useless. There was no time to produce new clips: the launch was four weeks away. Was the entire mission worth delaying? If the team waited, money would be lost and precious launch windows missed. Finally, the decision was made to go ahead and fly the mission without the useless clips. STS-61, the crucial mission to fix the Hubble space telescope, was launched knowing that Musgrave was going to attempt to do a job in the manner that he had considered to be impossible.

Musgrave describes the attempt to replace the solar panel, and especially the electronic controls for the drive, some of the hardest work he has ever had to perform. The outcome was also uncertain. Imagine replacing the circuits on the back of your personal computer while floating in space and wearing massive, padded gloves. After hours of meticulous, finger-numbing work, the box was at last replaced, and the ground team began to check the giant solar panels powered by its operation. Failure would mean the loss of crucial portions of the solar panel array, a critical area of the telescope.

At last the message from the ground team came through. Repairs, so far, were considered successful. Musgrave and his team had done what had appeared to be impossible. He said that he felt very good about that, but he refused to rest on his laurels. In fact, he and his team had too many other things to worry about, so there wasn't a lot of time for celebration. Even a functional solar panel drive did not necessarily mean a functional telescope.

The drive repair was a major victory, but how would the final images look? Would the effort expended to fix Hubble pay off? Would eighteen months of painstaking, precise preparation result in a successful repair? Scientists around the world waited anxiously for new data from Hubble, and once they saw sharp images appear on computer screens, they cheered. Not only was Hubble functional, but it was producing images clearer and sharper than its designers expected. The mission referred to by NASA officials as the most difficult servicing-and-repair mission ever attempted had become one of NASA's greatest successes. It was an incredible triumph and a long-awaited moment of glory for a farm boy from eastern Massachusetts.

A SPIRITUAL EXPERIENCE

Musgrave views himself as one in a long line of authors and independent thinkers including Henry David Thoreau, Walt Whitman, and Ralph Waldo Emerson. He said, "My belief system is similar to the American transcendentalists—the Emersons, the Thoreaus, the Poes, the Whitmans. And the English Romantics—Wordsworth, Shelley, Keats. People like that went into nature to have a spiritual experience; they went into Nature for direct revelation." Musgrave thinks of himself as following in their footsteps. Before every space-flight, be it in December, July, or some month in between, Musgrave immersed himself in the ocean of activity surrounding the rocket. Out in nature, near the spaceship, he absorbed the ambiance as the sun went down, regardless of temperature, preparing himself for flight. Watching satellites, he pictured himself in orbit, as they were. He was making and absorbing the spirit of spaceflight.

Being an astronaut is not a 9-to-5 job to be done for a pay-check—at least, not to Musgrave. For him, it is a spiritual experi-ence, an adventure into nature not unlike Thoreau journeying into the woods or Whitman extolling the beauty of the open road. Just as their America was unexplored, wild, and uncertain, so is the expanse of space yet laid out before us.

Musgrave's eccentricity may cause him his share of contro-versy. Yet the man and his dream of bringing art, science, and phi-losophy together to those of us still stuck on Earth lives on, despite the fact that his days with NASA ended in 1996. "I have no official involvement [with NASA]. I was back there visiting. I was in Mis-sion Control during the last Hubble servicing mission, just a small support. They call me up and ask me questions. We exchange ideas about things. I do educational programs at the Kennedy Space Center, but my entire life right now is dedicated toward the 'expres-sion.' Moving spaceflight into art. One hundred percent of my life is that." He has worked on several PBS videos as well as consulting with Disney. "Whether its resorts or pavilions or rides or other ways to capture what spaceflight experience is. . . . I am writing three books. I am writing a book of poetry. I'm painting. I worked on *A Mission to Mars*, that's a Brian DePalma film. . . . I spent four months on that—[doing] technical consulting, but also as an artist."

TO CONTENTMENT FROM TURBULENCE

Musgrave is an explorer, first and foremost, both of the human mind and of outer space. He is an adventurer into the final frontier of space, a pioneer whose curiosity and determination have allowed him to explore places that many of us will only dream about. If anything, it is his ambition and life's work to bring the wonders of space into the lives and dreams of people on Earth.

Does Musgrave think that we should travel back to the Moon? "Yes, but we should also go further out. But we need to balance the programs. Currently, we have no exploration. We send a small craft to Mars every couple of years, but there's no exploration. Exploration means doing things in which people are able to help define their own selves and to get meaning. In other words, 'How do you define what the human meaning is?' Things like Hubble are real exploratory. You are defining the universe, so it's: 'What is the universe?' 'What's our place in it?' 'What does it mean to be a human being?' "

Musgrave credits his own success to hard work and self-reliance. "Somehow, I was blessed with the survival instincts. You can throw out the usual things—nature, nurture, genetics, and the environment that formed you—your constitution. But somehow, I came into the world with real survival instincts. I guess a sense of 'self' is what it is. When you come into a world that all around you is far from perfect, you realize you are not the problem. You realize you need to survive the problem or distance yourself from it, or find another anchor. There are a lot of people that may be immersed in things that are not good, and you know that they somehow blame themselves for it, or they somehow think they're part of it, or they've caused it, or they get wrapped up in it. They do not understand that it is beyond their control and they really need to use themselves as the anchor and not the external world. Somehow, as far back as I can remember, even at the age of three, I said, 'My goodness, what a world I have come into!' I looked at it from afar, and said, 'This ain't so good.' "

The world that Story Musgrave entered wasn't so good. But instead of letting that world shape him, he confidently discarded it to create one that suited him better. A world that produced an astronaut, a physician, a poet, a writer, a philosopher, an artist, and educator—all in one man. A man that performed a ballet in space to help repair the Hubble Space Telescope.

M. Blaine Eubanks

CHAPTER 5

STEVEN PINKER

LANGUAGE'S BAD BOY

SUSAN E. JOHNSON

Imagine two rooms: one of them completely overrun with rats, the other totally filled with mice. Now fill in the blanks: "The first room is _____-infested. The second room is _____-infested." You likely described the first room as "rat-infested." You might have chosen either "mice-" or "mouse-infested" for the second. Why only one choice for the first room? Why would you have never said the first room was "*rats*-infested?" We'll get to that answer a little later in the chapter. The cognitive scientist and linguist Dr. Steven Pinker asks himself these and similar questions in order to discover the way the brain functions.

A HIPPIE INTELLECTUAL

Pinker was born September 18, 1954, and raised in an English-speaking household in Montreal, Canada, a province in which most residents speak French. Since French was so commonly spoken, he grew up studying that language, in addition to the Hebrew he learned at his Jewish Sunday school. He said, "I studied French because it was the other official language in the province, and studied Hebrew in Hebrew school. I was exposed to Yiddish from my grandparents and also studied Spanish in high school. The mathematical beauty of the grammatical constructions impressed me. . . . Working out the derivations was like solving a puzzle in combinatorial mathematics. This was especially true of Hebrew. Later on when I learned there was a field called psycholinguistics that actually worked out the logic that human brains follow when they learn and use languages. I was tremendously excited."

Little of Pinker's early science education came from teachers in school. "I had the disadvantage that the school I went to was ignorant of science and I got little science education. In those days, most elementary school teachers had received little training in science," he said. "I spent most of my time cutting out colored squares and pasting photographs from *National Geographic* into geography projects. It could have been better."

When he was in middle school, the teacher realized that math and science projects were lacking from the curriculum and she gave a number of the students workbooks. "She didn't have to teach it, but, we could teach ourselves. That's how I learned about probability and plane geometry." From this experience, he realized that a lot of learning comes from personal inquiry and independent work. "That taught me that most learning is learning that you do on your own. You can't rely on your teacher to teach. That's certainly an important lesson for being a researcher or a scientist; that there's so much knowledge out there and those few hours spent in a classroom will only expose you to a fraction. For the rest, you have to go out to the library, the Web, or books and magazines, and educate yourself."

Despite the weaknesses of Pinker's early academic classes, he got quite a bit of intellectual stimulation at his synagogue Hebrew school. "I was stimulated in the Jewish Sunday school that I went to. We were stimulated with moral dilemmas. Such as: [W]as [it] right to drop the atomic bomb to end World War II? Would it be right, if a scientist made an invention in a company, for the head of the company to take credit instead of the scientist? Is capital punishment justified? Should the economy be redistributed so the rich have to give their money to the poor? I think that helped give me an appreciation of logic and precise succinct argumentation."

In high school, Pinker got the chance to appear on a Canadian television quiz show *Reach for the Top*. This show offered smart kids a way to get prestige without having to be on the football team. It gave him a sense of his own identity. He recounted it this way: "[I was] definitely not a jock, because I was always a bit small for my age. I wasn't terribly coordinated. I'm not athletic. I was definitely not a nerd either. I tried to be rather inconspicuous through much

Pinker and classmates on *Reach for the Top* (*Courtesy of S. Pinker*)

Pinker at 20 years of age (*Courtesy of S. Pinker*)

of my childhood. I think I came into my own late in high school. Where I grew up in Montreal there was a television quiz program for teens called *Reach for the Top*. I was selected for the team. The team did well. We went on television. We won a number of games and won the city championship. That increased my status in high school, but, not in a nerdy way, because this was in 1970 and 1971. It was the hippie era, and we were hippie intellectuals. We had the best of both worlds in the status department, without having to be either a jock or nerd. We were the first team to go on television not wearing shirts and ties, but wearing sweaters, and one of us wore a bandana. I was lucky that niche existed. I was not in the ham radio club or astronomy club."

Pinker grew up during the 1960s, a tumultuous time in which many political and moral issues were being discussed. Many of these debates involved questions about human nature and he attributes this as one of the reasons that he chose to pursue research in psychology. "Even though I was too young and I was certainly not a student radical, I read all the arguments [about the great debates of the 1960s]. Many of the political debates of the age were really questions about human nature. For example, if you believed that people were basically generous, you would be a Marxist and believe in the slogan 'From each according to his ability; to each according to his need.' If you believed that people are basically selfish you would subscribe to capitalism and agree with Adam Smith that it isn't the generosity of the baker that causes him [to] give us bread but his own self interest. Those are two different ways of organizing society, much debated in the 1960s, but ultimately questions of the mind, of human nature. Similarly, if you believe that humans are basically peaceful and cooperative, you might find anarchism appealing as many of us did in the '60s and '70s. [The idea] is that all corruption comes from property, the armies, and the police. On the other hand if you think that people are basically nasty and aggressive you would want a police force and an army there to protect people from one another. So there again a political question hinged on your view of psychology."

After high school, Pinker went to Dawson College, a two-year public college that was part of the Quebec educational system. His career plans were vague; his parents wanted him to become a psychiatrist, but he thought he might become a high school math teacher, or else be hired by a "think tank," though he really didn't know what a think tank was. When it was explained to him that university professors both teach *and* do research (which includes a lot of thinking), he knew that was the career for him. However, he was still unclear about which field interested him the most. While at Dawson, he read an article in the *New York Times* about the linguist Noam Chomsky.[1] This work had a tremendous influence on Pinker's upcoming career decisions. The idea that language wasn't just an assemblage of words, but a natural expression of a deep structure organized by an instinctive force was intriguing to Pinker, who had already become fascinated by the mystery of language in his Hebrew studies at his synagogue.

LANGUAGE AND THE MIND

According to Chomsky's theories, there's an underlying structure to language. The brain stores a finite number of grammatical rules that are then able to produce an infinite number of sentences. Your brain works somewhat like a computer program, able to process an unlimited amount of information with only a limited number of commands. For example, there is a rule in the English language that says that when making a past tense out of a regular verb, such as "walk," you simply add an "-ed" to the end. So "I walk" becomes "I walked." But this rule applies not only to this one verb, but also to *all* regular verbs in our language, as well as all verbs that will enter the language over time. This one simple rule therefore has huge significance. The importance of this theory lies in its implications: if someone could find out exactly what these rules were and how they were learned, one could come that much closer to understanding exactly how our minds work, still one of the greatest mysteries in science.

The connection between language and the mind, which Pinker learned from Chomsky's work, removed any interest he may have had in the medical practice of psychiatry and turned it to the scientific research into the principles that lay beneath both cognitive psychology and language itself. He realized that his talent and interest lay in research rather than in medicine and that he was therefore meant to do research in psychology, rather than to practice medicine as a psychiatrist. During his senior year as an undergraduate at McGill University in Montreal, Pinker worked on a project about auditory perception, the sense that allows you to walk along a busy street, for example, and separate the sounds of cars driving by from the sound of someone talking to you. While plotting the points for this experiment, fifteen of his data points lined up exactly as the theory had predicted. Pinker was excited and knew at that time that research was for him.

The switch to cognitive psychology, however, also made Pinker and his family a little nervous. "They [my family] viewed it with skepticism. [They were] worried that I would be unemployed. This was in the 1970s when the job markets for academics crashed. There were articles in the *New York Times* about Ph.D.s in philosophy who were driving taxis and becoming assistants to sheriffs. Being a psychiatrist was a guaranteed job, whereas, going into academics was the equivalent of playing jazz trombone or joining the circus. I was young enough. . . . At worst, I could always retrain myself. . . . As it turned out, I did get a job right out of my training. It was a happy ending."

He decided to apply to graduate school at Harvard University right after he finished his undergraduate studies, both because there was nothing he wanted to do more than continue his studies, and so that if the worst happened and he wasn't able to find a job, he could always retrain himself. Fate smiled and Pinker was admitted to Harvard. His initial experiences at graduate school, however, were discouraging. His advisor was a mathematical psychologist who thought that science always needed to be represented mathematically, with equations, formulas, and other mathematical terms. According to Pinker, this advisor discouraged his interest in studying thinking and language, telling him that the study of those subjects wasn't real science because they couldn't be captured in mathematical equations.

Uninspired by the work encouraged under the guidance of his advisor, Pinker said that he floundered around, doing experimentation dealing with children's memory, not finding anything that seized his interest. He wrote a long paper in which he reviewed literature on mathematical and computer models of children's language acquisition, only to have it rejected twice from scientific journals.

Things started to get better when Harvard hired a new faculty member, Stephen Kosslyn, who became Pinker's advisor and friend. Kosslyn encouraged him to do the kind of research that he wanted to do and Pinker's work thrived under his new mentor. He ended up writing his graduate thesis about mental imagery, which is the kind of thinking you do when asked to imagine a three-dimensional object or space, your bedroom, for example. While still a graduate student, he published three papers about mental imagery in scientific journals. He also persisted working on the language acquisition paper, and after his third revision, it was accepted. He ended up expanding this twice-rejected paper into the material for his first book, *Language, Learnability, and Language Development,* published in 1984.

Pinker's persistence in his work paid off; he was getting his ideas published. Yet he still had the worry of what to do if he couldn't get a job. Perhaps he would "apply to twenty-five jobs and get none of them." He didn't have to worry too long, though. After a year as a postdoctoral fellow at the Massachusetts Institute of Technology (MIT), he was hired by his alma mater, Harvard, to be an assistant professor in the psychology department. He left, however, after a year to pursue an opening at Stanford University, lured by its top-rated psychology department. After a year of life near the Pacific Ocean, he came to miss the East Coast and decided to move back to Cambridge. In 1982, he returned to MIT to teach and do research and has stayed there ever since.

THE EVOLUTION OF LANGUAGE

One of Pinker's most important ideas is his theory of how the mind is structured and how it came to be what it is. The theories of evolution and natural selection play a large role in his work, and although these theories are accepted in the scientific community, they are controversial in popular society. People who believe in the theories of evolution and natural selection think that life is constantly changing, and organisms eventually adapt to their environment, or they can't survive. Every living organism has DNA, which controls how the organism is made and influences most of its traits. DNA is able to make copies of itself, and after it does so, some of the mother's DNA and some of the father's DNA combine to make their offspring. Sometimes, however, there is a mistake in DNA replication, so that maybe one tiny chemical is added or left out. This change, or *mutation*, sometimes gives the offspring a certain trait that is different from all the others of its species. (Mary-Claire King, profiled in chapter 2, is a geneticist who studies DNA mutations that cause breast cancer.)

Imagine if this process of mutation were happening over billions and billions of years. Tiny changes in DNA result in tiny changes in the new organism. Certain changes might allow the organism to survive longer and give a selective advantage to its offspring. Because of the increased ability of these individuals to reproduce and survive, these changes eventually become widespread until a whole new species is formed. More and more mutations happen all the time, and more and more beneficial changes occur. Eventually, the world is covered with millions of species that have evolved and are still evolving to adapt to the fluctuating environments caused by the changing conditions of the Earth.

Pinker believes that cultural attitudes reinforced with ritual practice over long periods of time could become as binding as physiological mutations in the genetic structure, so that our minds develop characteristic preferences or inclinations to instinctive processes. This touches on controversial issues, but then a lot of Pinker's work is very controversial, and these ideas are definitely no exception. Some people have problems with the basic theory of evolution. For cultural and religious reasons, they believe that all life was created just as we find it now rather than evolving over a long period of time. Others who don't have a problem with the idea of physical evolution react with strong opposition to the theory of the evolution of the mind. People have difficulty accepting, for example, that the love they have for their children might originally have evolved as a protective measure for the parents' genes, so they could be passed down to succeeding generations. Pinker believes that all the activity in the mind is the result of the chemical processes going on in your brain, and they are occurring for reasons that were important for the survival of our ancestors millions of years ago. Many people reacted with uneasiness to these theories, which he described in his 1997 book called *How the Mind Works.* Although his book won two awards, was a finalist for the Pulitzer Prize, and earned much critical acclaim, Pinker was the target of many bitter and often personal attacks as a result of it

Pinker reflected on how people accept his work: "There is still controversy and hostility [about my work]. . . . There are political implications as well as scientific ones. People get excited about that. Also, I think they [people who criticize my work] have a knack for choosing controversial topics. Even if it [my theories] were to get resolved, they would pick the next one to get emotionally upset about. . . . I suspect I am always going to be at the center of some controversy." He added philosophically, "In the long run, the truth comes out and if you were right, you may be called wrong, but you'll be proven right in the long run. And if you're wrong, it's good that you're proven wrong, because you want to find the truth. But, there is a lot of anxiety when you stick your neck out and people take shots at you. You think it's the end of the world at the time, but things always work out in the long run."

NATURE VERSUS NURTURE

Another great debate that Pinker has found himself in the middle of is the nature/nurture debate. This debate revolves around what exactly makes us what we are. The nature advocates believe that we are born with information in our genes about who we are. An *extreme* example of nature's influence says that if someone were able to look at your genes when you were a baby, they could give your parents odds on whether you were going to be a violent person or an even-tempered one. Your genes might predict, at least statistically, whether a person would prefer horror movies over comedies or maybe even what your opinion might be about the death penalty.[2]

The nurture people say that the information in our genes does not play a large role in how our personalities develop. They say that other factors including our parents, neighborhood, friends, and education determine who we are. The people on this side of the debate say that if you grew up in a violent home, you would pick up on the violence around you and would grow up to be that kind of person.

As you might guess, Pinker is on the side of nature. He writes about studies done on identical twins that were separated at birth. Identical twins, as opposed to fraternal twins, share the exact same DNA. Because of this identical DNA, if the nature theory is correct, these separated twins should be strikingly similar. When inter-viewed, in fact, the twins obviously shared similar physical charac-teristics, but they also had similarities in personality, shared opin-ions, and even common tendencies to do such strange things as always walking into the ocean backward. Pinker takes this as evi-dence that our genes, during development, help to mold our minds, shaping how we will later work and learn. He doesn't, however, believe people are immune to the influence of their own social expe-riences. So, although our genes shape how we feel and learn, there is always important shaping by culture and environment.

When we are conceived and our genes begin to form what will later become our brain, the genes build it into an organ that does computation, a bit like a computer. The brain works by receiving information from its environment, processing this information with built-in hardware, and then generating some sort of response. Pinker says that language is one of those things that is processed and fit together in what could be described as akin to one of the computer programs of the mind.

REGULAR IRREGULAR VERBS

Pinker describes the mind as being like a gigantic database. It stores not only things like memories and dates for tomorrow's history test, but also thousands of words along with rules to make these words join together to form coherent sentences. The brain is able to cut down on the number of words it has to store by memorizing the root words for things, not necessarily every possible form of each word, such as regular plurals, past tenses, and so on. The brain makes other forms by using a rule that it applies to all such words. For example, your brain, in its word memory, is right now storing the word "squish." It is probably not storing the words "squishes" or "squishing" or "squished." It doesn't need to. Instead, it has the rules for changing any regular verb into these other forms. This rule allows you to take in any new word you come across and be able to process it quickly. For example, as e-mail and the Internet became more widespread, someone came up with the verb "to spam," which means to send out unrequested junk e-mail. When this word came into the English language, people didn't have to wait for it to have an entry in a dictionary to use it. Without being told its different forms, people were able to manipulate it using the conjugation rules embedded in their brains, and thereby say and understand "spams," spammed," and "spamming."

Other words, however, don't follow these rules. Take the word "go," for example. It is irregular, meaning that its conjugation doesn't follow the normal rules. The correct form of its past tense, for example, is "went" instead of "goed." So because this particular word doesn't follow the normal conjugation rules that your brain stores—such as adding "-ed" to make past tenses—it has to store all the forms of this word separately. So although "squished" and "spammed" do not have to be in your mental dictionary, "went" does have to be there.

This may not sound very intriguing at first, but think again about the example at the beginning of this chapter. The words you chose to fill in the blanks demonstrate this principle. When your brain was presented with the challenge to provide a word to describe the room full of rats and a word to describe the room full of mice, it had to search quickly through its mental dictionary. Anyone familiar with Pinker's theory of the mind would have been able to predict that your choice for the rat room would be "rat-infested." Why? Because the word "rats" simply does not exist in your brain. "Rat" is stored in your brain along with the rule of adding "s" to make a plural noun. Because the word "mouse" has an irregular plural, both words would be possible solutions in the other case. Both "mouse" and "mice" are stored in the brain's lexicon.

You can test this theory of how the mind works by listening to younger siblings or neighborhood children who are just learning to talk. While they are learning the irregular forms for such common words as "do" and "go," their brains pick up on the normal rule for forming past tenses with "-ed." You've probably heard little kids say "doed" or "goed" before they've gotten completely used to saying "did" and "went." This is their mental word-making program in action. You can also do some experiments with these children. Make up some sort of nonsense word like "frib." Show them a picture of a person and say something like, "This person really likes to frib. He does it every day. So yesterday, he . . ." They will most likely say that he "fribbed." Although this word most assuredly was not stored beforehand in the child's mind, the program to manipulate it is.

This experiment is exactly the kind that Steven Pinker does to come up with his theories about the mind. One of his current experiments, with Dr. Jennifer Ganger, involves the study of language development in identical and fraternal twins. This project, called the MIT Twins Study, is a long-term study that began in June 1995 and involves more than five hundred families of twins across the country. Pinker and Ganger have asked the parents to track their children's language development starting at ten months of age—everything from their first words to how they form past tenses. They are trying to see if identical twins develop language in a more similar manner than do fraternal twins. If they do, this would suggest that some of the pacing of language development occurs because of one's genes. "We are looking at thousands of twins. We are seeing if identical twins are developing language on a more similar schedule than fraternal twins. If so, because identical twins have the same genes, and fraternal twins have half the same genes, then some of the pacing of language development occurs because of a genetically influenced maturational timetable. That would explain why some children develop language earlier or later than others." Although this project depends on parental observance of their children and compliance to collect data in specific ways, it contains more detail than any other study of its kind done before.

Another project Pinker is working on employs the use of the new technology called magnetoencephalography (MEG). "It measures magnetic signals that are emitted from people's brain as they are thinking. I am using it to see what parts of the brain are active, and in what sequence, when a person does a simple language manipulation such as when they change a verb into the past tense. We flash 'break' on the screen, and they have to say 'broke.' We flash 'walk' and they convert it to 'walked.' . . . We hope this will shed some light on how language processing unfolds in the brain.

"Past tense was not only simple, but it has been what my work has been centered on for the last ten years. In fact, I just wrote a book called *Words and Rules* about these ideas. For most verbs in the language, like 'walk,' we change to the past tense by adding 'ed.' That is an all-purpose handy-dandy rule we can use for any verb. We don't have to be taught every one individually. For example, to form a past tense for 'spam' you can just use the mental rule to get 'spammed.' It is a very simple rule allowing for creativity; it allows you to say things that you haven't memorized like a parrot. A controlled group consists of irregular verbs like 'break'—'broke,' 'come'—'came,' 'sing'—'sang.' [They] don't follow a rule and have to be memorized. In science, it is good to compare things that are almost identical except for one difference. Irregular and regular verbs are both simple and both convey the same meaning, but one of them needs a mental rule and the others you need to look up from memory. That is why it is such a good way to study language scientifically."

Pinker is studying the areas of the brain that are used when past tenses are formed from verbs, with the hope of discovering more about the process of language formation. Pinker believes that as the role of technology in our society continues to increase, questions about the language abilities of computers will become more important. (Marvin Minsky, featured in chapter 3, is a founder of the field of artificial intelligence and is working on these types of questions.)

Our minds share some characteristics with computers. But while computers usually have just one processor working very quickly, human brains have hundreds of billions of processors working more slowly. Because of these numerous processors, our minds are much better at sorting out complicated patterns instantly and storing huge amounts of information. The most powerful supercomputers have only as much power as the nervous system of a snail. That is why the challenge of building a computer system with the conversational abilities of the average human four-year-old child is so difficult.

TAKING INITIATIVE

For those interested in this field or other scientific fields, Pinker recommends that you don't look up answers to your questions in an encyclopedia. That's too easy. He said, "Read science magazines like *Discover* and watch shows like *Nova*. Do as much as possible. Think up your own experiments. If you have a hunch about something, figure out some way to see if you're right or wrong. Figure out a way of doing it yourself. So if you're wondering whether aluminum rusts or not, don't go to the encyclopedia, put aluminum in a glass of water and after a couple of weeks, see what happens. Try to think like a scientist. Instead of always going to an authority, think of how you might find out the answer yourself. Ask yourself, 'How would I design an experiment to test the idea?' You could do that for not just rusting metal, but for how the minds of children work. Go to your younger brother or cousin and think up a test that would prove to you mental rules of language."

How does Pinker's own inspiration come to him? He said, "It's a slow, long process. In fact, people have studied how ideas come to people. This research contradicts the stereotype of the artist or scientist saying 'eureka' and having a fully formed solution to a problem or work of art, occur to them in an instant. People often think that great ideas just pop out of the unconscious. It is especially popularized in the movie *Amadeus*, about the ingeniousness of Mozart. However, scholars that have looked at the process of creativity find that inevitably thinkers think in small steps. What seems like a eureka at the time, turns out to be a fairly minor tweaking of an idea they had before, which was a minor improvement of an idea they had before that. If you look at people's diaries, lab books, or correspondence, imperfect versions of that problem are found for quite some time before. I think that's true for me as well. I ruminate, I obsess, I worry, I try out ideas that are either wrong or it takes a lot of time to realize they're wrong. There's a huge amount of trial and error and mental play, and direct disconfirmation by experimental data, that go into the shaping of any idea."

Although truth is a slippery thing and can never really be fully grasped by any scientist, Pinker still strives for it. During his experiments, he manufactures models that are not based on radical conjecture or quasi-scientific theorizing, but on hard evidence. Sometimes people are puzzled as to why Pinker wants to understand some of the greatest mysteries of the human mind.

Pinker's long hair and colorful ties confuse some people at MIT. With his passion for wearing boots and jeans and listening to rock music, he doesn't look or act like many of other professors there. But he insists that his lifestyle is pretty conservative. He is married, voluntarily childless, and he spends a lot of time reading, writing, doing research, going to conferences, and jogging. He says that he and his wife enjoy each other's company too much to allow children to intrude.

Pinker has been described as "language's bad boy." He commented, "I am actually a good boy. I write with a sense of humor. In some ways, I am unconventional. I have long hair and they describe me as looking like a rock musician. I do not look like a typical MIT professor. But deep down I am pretty conservative."

Pinker is currently a professor of psychology in MIT's department of Brain and Cognitive Sciences. He has written hundreds of articles and book chapters, while writing and editing eight books. His research on visual cognition and on the psychology of language has received the Troland Award from the National Academy of Sciences and two prizes from the American Psychological Association. His books have received numerous awards; *How the Mind Works* was a finalist for a Pulitzer Prize. *Newsweek* named him as one of the One Hundred Americans for the next Century. These achievements are only the start of what "language's bad boy" and its "intellectual hippie" will accomplish in his search for the origins of our language.

Susan E. Johnson

CHAPTER 6

SALLY K. RIDE

FIRST AMERICAN WOMAN IN SPACE

ERICA L. RUDDY

Space, the final frontier. These are the voyages of the starship *Challenger*. Its mission, to test a new robotic arm and to conduct scientific experiments in space; to bravely take Sally Ride where no American woman had gone before.[1]

If the exploration of space parallels the expansion of the Wild West, Sally Ride is like Laura Ingalls Wilder, who wrote *Little House on the Prairie*. Instead of traveling by covered wagon with the simple necessities of life, Ride traveled in a fast and highly sophisticated space shuttle, equipped with cutting-edge technology. While Wilder explored with her family and close friends, Ride traveled with a highly selective and expertly trained National Aeronautics and Space Administration (NASA) team of astronauts. Both were pioneers of their time, exploring new terrain where very few had gone before. Facing many difficulties and an uncertain future, they pushed forward and traveled far into the unknown.

In 1961, the first Americans were launched into space. Twenty-two years later, in 1983, Dr. Sally Ride became the first American woman to follow in their footsteps. This was a major accomplishment not only for Ride, but also for all women in the United States; she became an instant role model. During her career with NASA, Ride flew into space twice and investigated the *Challenger* explosion. She left NASA in 1987 for academic pursuits at Stanford University and served as Director of the California Space Institute at the University of California at San Diego (UCSD). Most recently, she has been devoting much of her time and efforts to science education. This includes authoring four children's books and helping develop and guide EarthKAM (Earth Knowledge Acquired by Middle school students), a UCSD, NASA, and TERC (a not-for-profit educational group in Cambridge, Massachusetts) -sponsored program that unites students in the classroom with spaceflight.

AN ATHLETE AND A SCHOLAR

Ride was born on May 26, 1951 in Encino, California. When she was young, Ride showed an exceptional talent both as an athlete and as a scholar. Her father, a professor of political science at a local college, and her mother, a women's counselor, always supported Ride's curiosity, but didn't push her in one direction. Ride said, "Neither of my parents were scientists. They weren't the original impetus for me in pursuing a career in science. Once they saw that I was interested in science, they encouraged me to pursue that interest. . . . But had I not expressed an interest in science myself, it wouldn't have occurred to them to suggest that."

During her years in junior high, Ride did realize, however, that she wanted to become a scientist. "I probably knew that by seventh or eighth grade. I knew that my interests in science were there. I do not know whether I would have been able to verbalize them then. . . . I was reading *Scientific American* and science classes and math classes were my favorite classes. I knew pretty early that I was interested in science."

Ride realized how important her education would be to her future. Her interests in math and science put her at the top of her class, but two people played a key role in nurturing her passion for science. "I had two mentors that encouraged me, and [they] are probably responsible for me going on in science through high school and college. They were two high school teachers that I had. One was my trigonometry and chemistry teacher, believe it or not, and another one taught physiology. [Elizabeth Mommaerts] had a Ph.D. in physiology and had taught at UCLA before she started teaching at my high school. Both of them spent a lot of time with me and encouraged me to pursue science." Mommaerts remained friends with Ride until her death; Ride dedicated the book *To Space and Back* to her and the astronauts killed in the *Challenger* explosion.

This bright, attractive, and lively young woman was also an avid tennis player. She was a nationally ranked amateur, among the top twenty on the junior tennis circuit and had a scholarship to attend the Westlake School for Girls in Los Angeles. How did Ride manage to play competitive tennis but still do well in school? She recounted it this way: "I am not sure. I spent a lot of time playing and practicing tennis, and I also spent a lot of time with my school-work. I guess it is just a matter of finding time for things you enjoy."

After graduation from Westlake, Ride was torn between tennis and academics. Twice, after high school and during college, she thought that she might pursue a career in tennis instead of physics and astronomy. "Once, it happened when I left high school and went on to college. I made the decision that I was going to be very serious about tennis and pursue tennis." She began to devote much of her time to the game, but eventually, academics won out and she enrolled in Swarthmore College. However, after three semesters Ride decided once again to return to tennis. "In my sophomore year in college, I had a change of heart and decided to give tennis a serious try, and fortunately, that lasted only a couple of months. I went back to school, and that was pretty much it." (Ride no longer plays tennis, but has taken up golf as an adult.)

Ride switched colleges, moved closer to home, and enrolled in Stanford University. Interestingly, she graduated from Stanford University in 1973 with both a bachelor of science degree in physics and a bachelor of arts degree in English literature. She considered graduate work in English, but finally settled upon graduate research at Stanford in physics and astronomy, dealing mostly with X-ray astronomy and free-electron lasers.

In the early 1970s, Stanford University's Physics Department was in an exciting state due to the invention of the free electron laser (FEL). A standard laser, described in chapter 11 about Dr. Charles Townes, organizes a population of atoms in which one band electron is in an excited state. This "pumped" population is stimulated to emit photons by the presence of just that kind of photon that is radiated when the atomically bound electrons return to their ground states. In the FEL, the electrons, injected into the laser at high energy, are not bound to atoms. In one form of FEL, the electron beam is passed down a series of magnets that "wiggles" the beam transverse to the direction of motion. This encourages the creation of an electromagnetic wave, which is further encouraged by a mirror system. The interaction of the newly produced electromagnetic wave, the wiggler magnets, and the energetic electron beam manages to convert significant amounts of the electron's energy into electromagnetic energy—hence, it is a laser.

The advantages of the FEL are its ease of covering the short wavelengths beyond the visible into the short X-ray region. It is easily tunable over its range of wavelengths by changing the electron beam energy.

Ride's interest and research in FEL's is not unconnected to her interest in astrophysics. The domain of "empty space" is far from empty. Light of all wavelengths criss-crosses the intergalactic region, the "vacuum" over the long distances of viewing have significant numbers of atoms, especially of the light elements. Near planets are plasmas—clouds of electrically charged particles. Thus, tools for understanding their complexity are needed. Understanding is also needed about how the short wavelength radiation, X-rays, would be absorbed on their way to being viewed by Earth-based astronomers. The FEL with its associated technologies provided Ride and her colleagues with intriguing challenges, both for their own interest and in the connections to space physics. The theoretical side of astrophysics fascinated Ride; that combined with the state of knowledge at the time provided ample opportunities to construct useful calculations.

In the years from obtaining her Ph.D. until entering the NASA program (1976–1980), Ride, with colleagues, published a number of papers, some of whose titles we list to suggest the kind of physics Ride was doing:

1. "Absorption of X-rays in the Interstellar Medium" (1977)
2. "The Interstellar Medium in the Direction of the Crab Nebula" (1977)
3. "A Free Electron Laser in a Uniform Magnetic Field" (1979)
4. "A Laser Accelerator" (1979)
5. "The Non-Linear Wave Equations for FEL Driven by Single-Particle Currents" (1980)

Astrophysics is a branch of astronomy that deals with applying the laws of physics to objects in outer space. It deals with the origins, the locations, and movement of celestial bodies throughout the universe. Astrophysicists today are conducting research to help us better understand and explain the origin and evolution of the physical universe. They do this by observing stars, planets, galaxies, asteroids, comets, dust clouds, and such cosmic events as nova (star explosions) and supernova. They also measure the properties of light, X-rays, infrared and ultraviolet radiation, neutrinos, and other particles. They apply the relevant laws of physics such as Einstein's general theory of relativity and, in the case of the very early universe, the quantum field theories and data obtained by particle and nuclear physicists. They are trying to understand our universe, especially how it began, how it evolved to its present state, and what will happen in the distant future.

NASA relies heavily on astrophysicists to design experiments for various space-based observatories and short term space shuttles. For each mission into outer space, scientists and mathematicians must gather and analyze massive amounts of data. Through careful calculations they must plan the exact task for each space mission. Some missions go to the moon, others venture to Mars, while still others may travel to study the moons of Jupiter or the other distant planets. The bulk of the research however is on satellite observatories in orbit around Earth, heavily laden with special equipment designed for the many research objectives. The Hubble Space Telescope, described in chapter 4 about Dr. Story Musgrave, is an example.[1] COBE, described in chapter 10 about George Smoot, is a satellite that carried three instruments for measuring cosmic background radiation in search of evidence for the big bang.

NASA

Since World War II, the United States, with a huge influx of scientist refugees from Europe, has been a forerunner in scientific discovery and research. Toward the end of the 1950s, the government decided to gather top scientists, and form an agency funded by the government and dedicated to space exploration. Initiated by President Eisenhower and the U.S. Congress, NASA officially began on October 1, 1958. The government defined NASA as the organization that would research flight in and above the Earth's atmosphere. They claimed NASA would explore space and promote peace. But one of the main reasons the government started NASA was that the United States was in an intensive "space race" with the Soviet Union. After World War II ended, the United States and the Soviet Union entered into a long and protracted rivalry, dubbed the "Cold War." The competition was in military power, but also spilled over into culture and science. Which society was more successful? International prestige would follow success, or so it was thought.

On October 4, 1957, the Soviet Union launched the world's first artificial satellite, Sputnik 1. By achieving this major accomplishment, the Soviet Union gained much prestige in the eyes of other countries. Sputnik was a blow to United States self-confidence and lead to frenzied efforts to improve United States education as well as scientific research. The United States also realized that the satellite posed a threat to their country because it could be developed and used as a weapon. This strongly motivated the United States to create its own program for space exploration.

From its beginning in 1958, NASA continues to lead the way in scientific exploration of our solar system and beyond. NASA has always been one of the leading pioneers in space exploration, its scientists and astronauts form an elite group of individuals dedicated to exploring outer space.

A "RIDE" IN SPACE

While finishing graduate school, Ride saw an advertisement in the newspaper encouraging people to apply for admission to the NASA training program. She applied and was selected from over eight thousand applicants (including one thousand women applicants) for the first astronaut class that would include women. "NASA was very clear that they were going to bring some women into the astronaut core. They brought six of us in together. It was a group of thirty-five astronauts. So, out of thirty-five, six were women."

The training process for astronauts requires both mental and physical preparation. Ride underwent parachute training, water survival, radio communications, and navigation training, all to prepare her to become an astronaut. She recalls that the female astronauts were trained side by side with their male counterparts. "We went through all the same training, all the same experiences that the male astronauts did, and were just made to feel that we were part of the astronaut pool, from which they were going to select people for flight."

Ride proved herself time and time again as a valuable member of the NASA team. One of her main projects was to develop a special robotic arm that could be used to deploy and retrieve satellites. Ride and her colleagues perfected a design that NASA could use

Ride on the flight deck during STS-7, monitoring the control panels from the pilot's chair (*Courtesy of NASA*)

in space. Little did Ride know that she would later be given the opportunity to actually test this arm in outer space.

Ride was selected as the mission specialist for the 1983 *Challenger* mission. She began an extensive training program that would prepare her for flight in outer space. As a mission specialist, Ride was chiefly responsible for conducting scientific experiments. Her main duties aboard the spacecraft involved supervising all the scientific equipment on board. It was her responsibility to oversee several experiments, and ensure that the on-board research was conducted properly.

On June 18, 1983, the space shuttle *Challenger* lifted off for mission STS-7 from the Kennedy Space Center in Cape Canaveral,

Florida. Led by Commander Robert Crippen, *Challenger* was soon launched outside of the Earth's atmosphere. On this mission, the astronauts deployed two satellites, conducted over forty scientific experiments, and performed tests of the mechanical arm that Ride had helped to design.

Ride described the experience as truly remarkable. The astronauts had to learn how to move around in space without weight. For hours they trained in weightless chambers to learn how to sleep, eat, and even exercise without the help of gravity to hold them down. "I think the thing that was most surprising was weightlessness. The training just cannot prepare you for weightlessness. Weightlessness is just plain fun. It is just something that is just different than anything you experience in the day to day training. It is one of the things that makes flying in space very special." Weight is defined as the push of the scale on your feet (on the floor) which cancels the pull of gravity when you are at rest relative to the Earth. In space, there is no stationary floor, the entire shuttle is in free fall with you, therefore you are weightless.

Six days, two hours, twenty-three minutes, and fifty-nine seconds after the launch, the shuttle landed at Edwards Air Force Base in California. People from all over the world witnessed the safe landing of the space shuttle and celebrated the importance of the mission. Scientists gained valuable research and benefited from data collected by the mission. And Ride completed her mission as the first American woman in space.

Feminists viewed the flight as a major accomplishment for women and hailed Ride as a role model for aspiring female scientists. The media extensively covered the story of Ride's first space flight because of the intense public interest. Ride said, "It [publicity] did not have any effect before my flight, because I was able to insulate myself from that while I was in training for flight. After the flight, it took over my life for a little while until I got assigned to another flight. It both created opportunities in that I got to do a lot of things I would not otherwise have had a chance to do. I visited the White House and a variety of things. But, it also complicated my life considerably because I thought of myself as an astronaut and a research physicist, and not as a famous person. It took some time for me to get to back to the life that I wanted." The intense publicity has contributed to Ride becoming a private person, not wanting to discuss personal issues with the media.

Roles at NASA have changed for women since 1983. Ride put it this way: "I think that the significant change is that there are more women in every part of NASA now. Even in 1983, when I went into space, there were not many women engineers at NASA. There were not very many women in mission control, if any at that time. And now, there are women in mission control, there are women engineers, there are women working on solid rockets, and there are women in every field. I think that is the main difference. They are visible in every place."

In our interview, Ride commented on opportunities for women in math and science. She said, "I think they [women] are given equal opportunities. It has not always been true, but now, I think they are given equal opportunities. . . . Twenty percent of astronauts, or more, are women these days. Women are still under represented in particularly physics and engineering disciplines. But, it is not because the opportunities are not open to women. There are a variety of factors, some of which are sociological. I think it is just going to take a while to overcome and get the numbers up. But, the opportunities are definitely there."

Ride would soon get another opportunity to fly in space. On October 5, 1984, *Challenger* mission STS 41-G ventured through Earth's atmosphere to further study outer space. NASA chose Captain Robert L. Crippen to serve as commander of the shuttle (his fourth mission in space). Jon A. McBride was pilot, Sally Ride, David Leestma, and Kathryn Sullivan were mission specialists, and Paul Scully-Power and Marc Garneau were payload specialists. Sullivan and Ride were the first two women to fly in space together. Sullivan became the first woman to walk in space and Garneau became the first Canadian citizen aboard a United States shuttle.

About nine hours after liftoff the *Challenger* crew deployed the first of three satellites designed to study the movement of energy on Earth. This satellite, called the Earth Radiation Budget Satellite

(ERBS), studied the amount of energy generated by the Sun and the amount of energy reflected from the Earth back into space. The crew of *Challenger* also operated the Shuttle Imaging Radar-B that photographed the Earth using a variety of advanced cameras. Ride's responsibilities on this flight were to operate the robotic arm to release one of the satellites into orbit and to assist with the earth science experiments that had been designed for the flight.

THE CHALLENGER EXPLOSION

After successfully completing her 1984 mission, NASA scheduled Ride for another flight. However on January 28, 1986, tragedy struck NASA when *Challenger* exploded just seventy-three seconds after takeoff. The explosion killed all seven crew members, commander Francis R. Scobee, pilot Michael J. Smith, mission specialists Judith A. Resnik, Ellison Onizuka, and Ronald E. McNair, payload specialist Gregor Jarvis, and Christa McAuliffe, the first teacher to fly in space. The explosion of *Challenger* was a great loss to NASA. From April 1981 through January 1986, NASA launched twenty-five missions in its four orbiters, *Atlantis*, *Challenger*, *Columbia*, and *Discovery*. Mission STS 51-L aboard *Challenger* was the only mission to result in the loss of human life. NASA shuttle missions after the explosion were halted for nearly three years.

People across the country were shocked to learn of the explosion of *Challenger*. President Reagan delivered a speech later that day to the American public in which he addressed the explosion. "Sometimes painful things like this happen. It's all part of the process of exploration and discovery. It's all part of taking a chance and expanding man's horizons. The future doesn't belong to the fainthearted; it belongs to the brave. The *Challenger* crew was pulling us into the future, and we'll continue to follow."[2] Just six days after the accident, President Reagan appointed a Presidential Commission that included Ride and Neil Armstrong. They were charged with determining the cause of the explosion and making recommendations for future spaceflights.

Investigations after the accident revealed that the explosion was caused by a mechanical failure in the boosters. The boosters are divided into several segments and held together by various mechanical pieces. Under normal conditions, devices called O-rings expand and contract to prevent fuel from leaking into different parts of the rocket. There is an incredible amount of gas pressure between segments of the rockets, and on the day of the explosion, the O-rings failed to stop the fuel from leaking through, causing the booster to catch fire.

There are several reasons why the O-rings failed to work. The primary reason is that the weather at the Kennedy Space Center at the time of the launch was extremely cold. The night before the launch, temperatures had plummeted to 18 degrees Fahrenheit and at the time of the launch the temperature was 36 degrees Fahrenheit (barely above freezing). The extreme cold temperatures made the O-rings expand and contract at a slow rate, thus making it possible for fuel to leak. Also the O-rings had been used on previous missions, so they had already acquired some minor damage and corrosion that could have contributed to their failure.

With the help of NASA, the Commission interviewed over 160 people and produced more than 122,000 pages of information on the accident. Over 6,000 people were somehow involved in the in-depth investigation of the entire NASA program. Many procedures were revised to improve safety.

The explosion of *Challenger* also affected Ride in many ways. On a personal level, Ride lost some close friends and people with whom she had trained for years. The intensive training at NASA bred extreme loyalty and camaraderie among the astronauts. The explosion of *Challenger* dampened the spirit of NASA astronauts. She said, "It was very important to me personally, because I had five very good friends who were on that flight. Four astronauts that came in the same astronaut class that I did, whom I had worked with for eight years. So, I knew them very well. The most important part of the accident to me is losing some very good friends."

On a professional level, Ride would never have another opportunity to serve on another spaceflight. She had been in training for her third spaceflight when she was reassigned to the Presidential Commission to investigate the accident. NASA would cancel all missions in the near future and reevaluate its future plans. She stated, "It had a very sobering effect on NASA, and it had NASA rethink its safety requirements and procedures. It put more focus back on safety, more focus on testing and reliability. And of course, there were not any space shuttle flights for almost three years after the *Challenger* accident."

Ride commented on what the public has been told about the *Challenger* accident: "I think there was

Ride on the middeck during STS-7, wearing headset and flight overalls (*Courtesy of NASA*)

a lot of publicity associated with the accident, and the media actually did a very good job of putting the story out to the public. So there was quite a good understanding of what went wrong, both technically and in the system that allowed it to happen. So, I actually think that people have a pretty good picture of that accident."

After the investigation was completed, Ride was assigned to work in Washington, D.C. at the NASA headquarters to assist NASA in long-range planning. She published a report entitled *Leadership and America's Future in Space* that became known as the "Ride Report," although many individuals had contributed. The purpose was to make recommendations about future plans of the space program. The report suggested sending astronauts back to the Moon, exploring Mars, and supporting NASA's Mission to Planet Earth program. Currently, there are no plans for a manned Moon mission, but Mars exploration is being continued via unmanned, robotic surveyors. Mission to Planet Earth is continuing; its overall goal is to understand our global environment, understand the changes that human and natural elements cause to it, and to improve and protect the quality of life on Earth through the global environment.

Ride retired from NASA in 1987 after logging over 343 hours in space. She accepted a fellowship in the Center for International Security and Arms Control at Stanford University, where she stayed for two years. In 1989, she moved to the University of California at San Diego where she became the director of the California Space Institute (CalSpace) and a researcher in astrophysics.

At CalSpace, Ride directed research on a variety of topics. She worked on different applied science projects, taking scientific knowledge and putting it to practical use for everyday life. It is important to note that scientific knowledge gathered from different space travel and research might be applied to problems here on Earth. For example, data gathered about the Earth's atmosphere could be used to monitor changes in the Earth's climate. Farmers or environmentalists might use the new climate data to help improve soil conditions. This data could also be used to track pollution, and help identify other problems in the future. Ride stepped down as director in 1997 to focus on her research and teaching.

Ride's scientific research bibliography resumed after her NASA service in 1990 with a remarkable vigor up to her current deepening involvement with science education. In the period of 1990 to 1997 she was author or coauthor of over twenty papers, mostly on the theoretical aspects of astrophysics. Many of these carry out themes of her Stanford interest in astrophysical topics involving electromagnetic fields to plasmas induced by solar wind (a strong "wind" of hydrogen nuclei, protons, emitted by the Sun). She developed an interest in X-ray generation by a unique process of scattering intense laser beams off a beam of very high-energy electrons supplied by a linear accelerator. The intensity of the laser light is so high that complex (nonlinear) mathematics must be used. Short, intense, and coherent bursts of X-rays are the staple of much research in the structure of complex molecules, viruses, and the structure of various other materials.

In her personal life, Ride fell in love with fellow NASA team member Steven Hawley and the two eventually became engaged. They took their marriage vows during an informal and private ceremony, Ride dressed in jeans and a rugby shirt, with only a handful of family members present. These two were the first set of NASA astronauts ever to marry. They later divorced just as quietly as they married, but remain good friends.

Ride is intensely private, perhaps because of being the first woman in space and gaining such notoriety. She will talk about her interest in science education, but downplays being an astronaut and doesn't like questions of a personal nature. Does she regret this, the intrusions into her personal life? She confidently stated, "I would do it all over again."

Personally, Ride will admit to being a Trekkie, and commented on the effects that science fiction has on students and the space program: "I think that kids are pretty smart, and they can separate reality from fiction. I personally love *Star Trek*. I watch it every week. I have also noticed that people are very, very interested in the space program."

EDUCATION EXPERTISE AND EARTHKAM

Ride has published four children's books, *To Space and Back, Voyager: An Adventure to the Edge of the Solar System, The Third Planet: Exploring the Earth from Space,* and *The Mystery of Mars.* In her books she shares her experiences as an astronaut and writes about several topics in astrophysics. Children who admire her as a scientist and desire to learn more about space often read her books. She believes that science can be an exciting field for all children, but that children are exposed to it in many different ways. "Some schools do a very good job of motivating students and getting them interested in science and presenting science as an interesting field to pursue. Other schools do not do it as well. Some parents see the value [of science] and see it as exciting and interesting and as a viable career. Other parents do not. So it very much depends on the individual situation." Through her books, Ride has encouraged children to continue with their interest in science.

In 1995, Ride also assisted with development of a project known as EarthKAM (www.earthkam.ucsd.edu), a collaboration of UCSD, NASA, and TERC. So far, EarthKAM has reached thousands of kids all over the country. EarthKAM links students with shuttle missions by using a digital camera that astronauts place in the shuttle window. Students are able to target and direct the digital images of Earth, based on where the shuttle is in orbit at the time that the camera is operating. Space shuttle maps are provided and computer software verifies that the target images will be available during flight. A computer on board the space shuttle is linked to the camera and downloads the images back to Earth. Images usually appear on the Internet within hours of when they are taken. School children have directed thousands of digital pictures of natural phenomenon all over the world. Through EarthKAM they participate in the space program (without ever leaving Earth!), design their own investigations to learn about the Earth, and gain Internet skills. The project is based at UCSD where college students also assist in monitoring images and links with the participating schools.

Ride has also served on the Board of Directors of Space.com, a Web-based company aimed at promoting the sharing of space and space-related information with the public. In September of 1999, she accepted the position of president, but resigned about a year later.

Sally Ride and Laura Ingalls Wilder have a lot in common, even if a century of time separates their lives. Both used their persistence and boldness to carve a niche for themselves as explorers. Maybe if Laura Ingalls Wilder was alive today she would trade in her calico dresses for a space suit. She might have joined Ride as an explorer on the frontier of space. Or maybe she would enter into business or emerge as a leader in medicine. Regardless of what she would choose to do with her life, her curiosity and courage would allow her to make an impact on society, just as Ride did.

Ride is often remembered as being the first American woman in space, although she states that she did not become an astronaut "to become a historic figure or a symbol of progress for women." Her colleagues at NASA remember Ride as a brilliant scientist with a practical approach to science, perhaps one of the best compliments she has been paid. The public has lauded Ride with a number of prestigious awards, which she modestly downplays. They include the Jefferson Award for Public Service, the American Woman Award from the Women's Research and Education Institute, the Lindbergh Award, the Lawrence Sperry Award, and two National Spaceflight Medals. Because of her brilliance and dedication to illuminating science for others, Ride will always be remembered as a truly extraordinary astronaut and science educator.

Erica L. Ruddy

CHAPTER 7

F. SHERWOOD ROWLAND

CONTROVERSIAL CHEMIST

MARGARET J. WAT

D r. F. Sherwood Rowland took a second look at a chemical most people thought was a wonder. The chemical, called chlorofluorocarbon (CFC), had been used in refrigerators, in aerosol cans, in car air conditioners, and in many other products and offered users what everyone thought was a safe, modern convenience. For years, scientists had been searching for a chemical for use in refrigeration systems and CFCs seemed to be the answer. Without refrigeration, foods were subject to bacterial growth and spoilage. CFCs, developed in 1928 by Thomas Midgley Jr., were used to remove heat energy from the interior of refrigerators and to dump this heat into the surrounding kitchen area, keeping the interior, and thus the food, cold. CFCs are known as halocarbons, the molecule carbon (C) bound to halogen atoms of chlorine (Cl), fluorine (F), or bromine (Br). CFCs were considered to be safe; they did not explode nor were they poisonous if they leaked out of their container. (During a demonstration, Midgley had inhaled CFC gas to show it had no adverse effects on his health. He also blew CFC gas onto a flame to show that it wouldn't ignite, like the hydrocarbons ethane and methane from which it was made.) CFCs were relatively inexpensive and changed from liquid to gas and back again under conditions of temperature and pressure that were simply and conveniently generated. The common uses of CFCs multiplied after World War II; in addition to its use as a refrigerant, it was used as a propellant in items such as deodorant, hair spray, paint, and insect repellant. At its peak, the economic amount of CFC use was estimated at over $1 billion annually.

However, as Rowland and his colleague Dr. Mario Molina discovered, this chemical is not harmless, but contributes to depletion of the ozone layer in the Earth's atmosphere, the layer that protects us from ultraviolet light. Use of CFCs was banned and Rowland and Molina eventually won a Nobel Prize in chemistry for their findings. However, publication of these findings did not come with instant acclaim for the scientists; rather, they were first accused of conspiracy against American industries.

ACADEMICS AND ATHLETICS

Frank Sherwood Rowland (pronounced ROW-land, with a long "O") was born on June 28, 1927, in Delaware, Ohio. Education was both valued and expected in the family and Rowland's was accelerated as the gifts that would lead to greatness began to appear. The Delaware public school system encouraged acceleration and he was fortunate to have excellent teachers. He entered first grade at age five, skipped fourth grade, began high school at twelve, and graduated from high school before his sixteenth birthday. His father, Sidney A. Rowland, was a mathematics professor at Ohio Wesleyan University (OWU) and his mother, Margaret Drake Rowland, was a Latin teacher. "I didn't think that much about what I was going to do when I grew up. I just assumed that I would do 'something.' Basically, I think from a very early age, I just assumed that I would probably teach at a university as my father did. I thought he seemed to enjoy what he was doing and so that just came to be, slowly, what I would do."

Like many successful students, he was an avid reader. "Our house had a very large number of books in it, so I read widely, with a lot of it [my reading material] being history. Naval history became something that caught my interest. There was a lot of mathematics involved in talking and thinking about ships." He spent many hours simulating naval battles with realistic scale-models, rating each ship and the effects of combat on them using mathematical models.

Rowland cites several teachers as having been influential. High school teachers of mathematics (whom his father had taught at Ohio Wesleyan), a Latin teacher ("Latin is a very useful subject to have taken for understanding how language works"), an English teacher ("a real stickler for grammar"), his science teacher who ran a weather station, and the basketball and tennis coach (one of the math teachers) who persuaded him to start playing sports. One gets the sense that Rowland enjoyed a wide and well-rounded interest in academics, which he took advantage of to its fullest.

For several summers during high school, his science teacher entrusted him with the operation of the local volunteer weather station. This was his first exposure to systematic data collection. Rowland said, "He just asked me if I would do it. But surely the reason he asked is that I was the best student in the class. . . . There were maybe 10,000 of these stations all over the country, each with a volunteer weather observer and, I presume, each of the volunteer weather observers had to find somebody to take it if they left on vacation because the weather bureau wanted daily measurements."

Complementing his accelerated academic progress in school, Rowland developed an interest in sports. Tall and athletic, Rowland enjoyed tennis, basketball, and baseball. Tennis was the first sport that he played competitively. He played varsity tennis his junior and senior years of high school, and was also on the varsity basketball team during his senior year. Throughout his life, sports have played an important role.

After graduation from high school, Rowland entered Ohio Wesleyan University. The United States was already in World War II, but he was only sixteen years old, so he was not subject to the compulsory draft. He triple-majored in chemistry, physics, and mathematics. "School was always easy. I have a good memory and at that time, probably even a better one [than now]. . . . I didn't have to read a book twice to know what was in it. That makes coursework very easy." He also played on the university baseball and basketball teams and wrote much of the sports page for the college newspaper.

Shortly before his eighteenth birthday in 1945, Rowland was ready to begin his final year of college. Instead, he enlisted in the U.S. Navy. Fortunately, the war ended while he was still in basic training and he spent much of his time playing sports for naval teams and did not have to face combat. After about a year, he returned to Ohio Wesleyan and graduated in 1948 with a bachelor of arts degree. He continued playing sports as well and was the basketball team's leading rebounder and third-leading scorer.

In the fall of 1948 Rowland was admitted to the University of Chicago's (UC) chemistry department for graduate studies. Both of his parents had attended UC, so the choice was really an obvious one for him. He was assigned to the laboratory of future Nobel Laureate Dr. Willard Libby. The assignment was a good one for both men; Rowland went on to receive his master's degree in 1951 and his Ph.D. in 1952 for research carried out under Libby's supervision. His Ph.D. thesis examined the chemical state of cyclotron-produced radioactive bromine atoms. In this process, radioactive atoms are created in very low concentrations. They can be studied and followed as they decay into a lower energy state. The experience of researching atoms in very low concentration was later useful during the CFC project when Rowland would examine chemical species in low concentrations.

Even as his education reached its most rigorous and intensive phase, Rowland balanced his academic and athletic interests. At the

University of Chicago, he played basketball and baseball. During two summers, he also played semiprofessional baseball in Oshawa, Ontario. One year, he took over management of the team and coached it to the semipro championship of Canada. At one point, he entertained thoughts of a professional sports career. Luckily for the environment and for Earth's future generations, academics won out.

It was during 1952, about the same time that he received his Ph.D., that Rowland married Joan Lundberg. They would eventually have a daughter, Ingrid, born in 1953, and a son, Jeffrey, born in 1955. When asked what he is most proud of, he replied, "I don't think I would rank order them. I'm very pleased with the way things have worked out in my marriage and with our children. I'm pleased how they [things] have worked out in what I do for a living. I wouldn't put one over the other." When probed about his biggest accomplishment, he said that certainly discovering the threat to the ozone layer is important. However, he also recounted that his son had a very bad automobile accident about twenty-two years ago. "I think that there were some things that happened in the early, first few days, just after he emerged from a coma. My being with him probably prevented him from having a much worse outcome than he did. We were able to communicate before he could speak. And in doing that, we found out a major physical problem that could have been a major paralyzing complication." It's obvious that his family and home-life is very important and satisfying to Rowland.

ROWLAND'S RESEARCH ACTIVITIES

Many years of research experience converged upon the CFC project. Rowland obtained his first academic position as an instructor of chemistry at Princeton University. Rowland's main research activities were in radiochemistry, the chemistry of radioactive atoms. In the summers from 1953 to 1955, he pursued tracer chemistry research at Brookhaven National Laboratory. Tracer chemistry utilizes a radioactive atom that labels or tags compounds in order to follow their synthesis or degradation. He mixed the sugar, glucose, and lithium carbonate and put the concoction into the neutron flux of the Brookhaven nuclear reactor, resulting in a one-step synthesis of radioactive glucose—glucose tagged with ^{3}H (tritium), the radioactive isotope of hydrogen. Glucose is an important compound in the chemistry of metabolism. Tracing reaction paths using radioactive tritium was to become a valuable technique in the developing science of biochemistry and the new subfield of tritium hot-atom chemistry was born.

Rowland remained at Princeton for four years before moving to the University of Kansas. He progressed to a full professorship, built a research group in radiochemistry, and gained an international reputation as a chemist.

In 1964 Rowland moved to the University of California at Irvine (UC-Irvine). This was an exciting time as UC-Irvine was a new campus in the California University system. Rowland was recruited as founder and first chairman of the chemistry department, hiring its eleven inaugural faculty members and teaching its first courses. He remained chair of the department for six years, before stepping down in 1970 to concentrate on his research. He extended his research efforts into photochemistry, the chemistry of processes that are sensitive to light, using radioactive tracers: tritium (^{3}H), carbon-14 (^{14}C), chlorine-38 (^{38}Cl), and fluorine-18 (^{18}F).

A NEW LOOK AT ATMOSPHERIC CHEMISTRY

Rowland had a standard practice in his research of moving into new and challenging areas of chemistry. He continually searched for innovative ideas and topics that would stimulate members of his laboratory as well as himself. He had developed a personal interest in the state of the environment, which had also become a significant topic of discussion by the general public in the early 1970s. The first "Earth Day" was held in 1970. His daughter Ingrid had a growing interest in environmental issues. He attended a workshop in Austria sponsored by the International Atomic

Energy Agency (IAEA) on the environmental applications of radioactivity. In a fortuitous meeting, after the conference, he shared a train ride with an individual from the Atomic Energy Commission (AEC). The AEC had been supporting some of Rowland's research activities for quite some time and this individual was trying to get chemists and meteorologists involved in collaboration with each other.

In due course, Rowland was invited to the second Chemistry-Meteorology workshop, which took place in 1972. While there, he heard a presentation about the work of James Lovelock who had recently detected atmospheric concentrations of manmade chlorofluorocarbons. The idea presented was that the chlorofluorocarbons could be used to trace mass air movements because they are stable molecules and their concentration would not change in the atmosphere. Although Rowland wasn't an atmospheric chemist, he knew that although the CFCs are stable on Earth, in the atmosphere it's a whole different story. Through his experience with photochemistry he knew that sunlight could break the chemical bonds of CFC molecules. If the CFC molecules don't remain stable, he thought, then what happens to them in the atmosphere? The question stimulated his interest in studying the atmospheric fate of the chlorofluorocarbons, so he included the idea into his annual funding proposal to the AEC. It was approved.

Dr. Mario Molina joined Rowland's research group as a postdoctoral fellow in 1973. Rowland presented him with several possible projects, including determining the fate of CFCs in the atmosphere. Though this project was not closely related to his prior work, this is the project that Molina chose to study.

At the beginning of the project, Molina said that he had no experience with atmospheric chemistry and had to do a lot of background research before he could begin. As often happens when new eyes take a fresh look at a body of knowledge, thinking about the work changes. The atmosphere had been regarded as a vast reservoir into which products of human activity could be dumped without producing significant, long-term effects.

Atmospheric chemists have traditionally been interested in

how the gases, liquids, and solids in the atmosphere interact with each other and with the Earth's surface. They have more recently focused on the interactions of the Earth's atmosphere with life, particularly in how human activity affects the atmosphere. They study the chemistry of smog, global climate changes influenced by the production of greenhouse gases, and toxicity of air pollutants. This recent emphasis is, in part, a consequence of the successful prediction by Rowland and Molina of the depletion of stratospheric ozone by chlorofluorocarbons.

The atmosphere is composed of four parts: the troposphere, stratosphere, mesosphere, and thermosphere (figure 1). The troposphere is the part of the atmosphere that begins at the surface of the Earth and extends up about 15 kilometers (km) above the ground. The stratosphere is the middle layer; it begins where the troposphere ends at 15 km and goes up to 50 km where the mesosphere begins. Ozone is concentrated at the boundary between the stratosphere and the mesosphere. We refer to this as the ozone layer.

Ozone (or O_3—a molecule with 3 oxygen atoms) occurs naturally in the atmosphere. It is created by a chemical reaction that combines the form of oxygen required for respiration, O_2, with single atoms of the element. Ultraviolet (UV) light from the Sun is absorbed by O_2. The radiant energy excites the molecule and an oxygen-oxygen bond breaks into two free oxygen atoms, monatomic oxygen.

O_2 is abundant in our atmosphere and easily reacts with the unbound oxygen atoms forming new ozone molecules. Ozone can also absorb UV light and breaks apart to O and O_2. This O atom also reacts with O_2 to from O_3 again. These processes have been a stable component of our planet's atmosphere for more than three billion years.

This chemical process, and the layer of ozone gas it produces, protects the Earth's surface from UV light. Like the chemical bonds in O_3, molecules important in life processes can absorb UV light and degrade. In particular, nucleic acids of DNA can be altered, causing the genetic code to be unreadable or incorrectly read. Without the ozone layer, increased levels of UV light at the surface

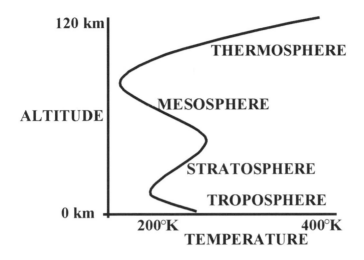

Figure 1. A sketch of how the temperature changes with height above the surface of the Earth.

of the Earth would cause skin cancers in humans, but more importantly, cause severe genetic damage to all species.

Rowland and Molina knew that the CFCs released into the air entered into the upper atmosphere. The question they were interested in was what happens to the CFCs once they are in the atmosphere? As they began to discover the answer to this question, their alarm grew.

CHLOROFLUOROCARBONS DEPLETE THE OZONE LAYER

The story starts innocently. After the CFCs escape from the squirt of a spray can or from the leakage of an air conditioner, they enter the troposphere where circulation insures that they spread out quickly. For example, CFCs released over North America can travel to Europe in a few weeks. Usually, unnatural substances that enter the atmosphere are prevented from contaminating the balance of the atmosphere by a cleansing mechanism in the troposphere. Unwanted substances, such as pollutants from factories, are often dissolved in water and washed down within several weeks. However, when CFCs enter the troposphere, they are not washed out in a few weeks by this mechanism, because unlike most pollutants, CFCs are so stable that they do not dissolve in water or become oxidized. Instead, they continue their diffusion up into the stratosphere.

When the CFCs are passing through the troposphere, the ozone layer shields them from the powerful UV rays of the Sun. But in the stratospheric ozone layer, the CFCs and the ozone molecules, can be zapped by the UV light like victims in laser tag. The ozone molecules absorb the UV light and shake like crazy and break apart, protecting our bodies from absorbing this light. The CFCs, on the other hand, get shattered into the individual atoms that make up the CFC molecule, like a tower of Legos breaking up into its separate building blocks. For example, one CFC molecule, CCl_3F breaks down into $Cl + CCl_2F$, in the presence of UV light. One of the resulting atoms, chlorine (Cl), is extremely reactive, and it searches for something with which to combine. Ozone is more plentiful in the stratosphere than anywhere else in the atmosphere, so it's easy for the chlorine to combine with an ozone molecule. These molecules undergo a chemical reaction; the chlorine becomes chlorine monoxide (ClO), and the ozone (O_3) is now gone, replaced by diatomic oxygen (O_2). Molecular oxygen, O_2, no longer has the UV light-absorbing capacities that ozone has. Consequently, the UV light can travel right through the oxygen, down through the troposphere, and onto the Earth's surface.

And things get worse. The newly formed ClO often finds and reacts with another molecule, monatomic oxygen (O), which is also plentiful in the stratosphere. After these molecules react, they pull apart as two separate molecules, this time as O_2 and the menace, free chlorine. Chlorine, as reactive as ever, can now combine with another ozone molecule, which again results in ClO and O_2. These reactions keep repeating themselves, forming a chain reaction. As a result, much of the ozone layer is destroyed.

"The key factor in converting [our project] from an interesting scientific problem into a major environmental problem," said Rowland, "was the existence of a chain reaction, a catalytic chain reaction."

This is a summary of what happens:

1. UV light + CFC → Cl (chlorine) + residual molecules
2. $Cl + O_3 \rightarrow ClO + O_2$

The objects to the left of the arrow are the ones present before the reaction; the ones to the right of the arrow result from the reaction. The arrow represents the chemical reaction. The UV light breaks the CFC into Cl and a residue. This Cl combines with O_3 in the ozone layer in a chemical reaction, which produces new molecules, ClO and O_2, with completely different properties.

Then ClO undergoes another chemical reaction with another common chemical, O, in the atmosphere. This is the reaction:

3. $ClO + O \rightarrow Cl + O_2$

The Cl that results combines with yet another ozone molecule through reaction (2), and the process repeats all over again, destroying another ozone molecule. The chlorine consumed in reaction (2) is released in reaction (3) and the process is repeated. This is called a catalytic chain reaction because the original Cl molecule reappears to destroy more and more ozone. Rowland and Molina's calculations indicated that a single Cl atom could catalyze the destruction of 100,000 ozone molecules! Eventually, with the CFC production skyrocketing and its concentration in the ozone layer increasing, the ozone shield would be punctured with holes, like openings in armor.

Rowland and Molina were stunned to see that according to their calculations, if the use of CFCs continued to accelerate, half the ozone layer would be gone in a matter of decades. CFCs were used in our air conditioners, deodorants, hair sprays, and cleaning sprays; the chemical made wide-scale refrigeration possible. The environmental consequences of what they visualized were overwhelming. They double- and triple-checked their calculations, but found no error. If CFCs continued to be used and manufactured at this rate, the ozone shield would eventually be filled with holes and could no longer protect us from the dangerous UV light of the Sun. As the enormity of the discovery overwhelmed the two researchers, they knew that this problem was no longer just one that was interesting and scientifically stimulating to them, but one that involved the welfare of everyone on Earth. Rowland says, "At that time, the world was putting one million tons of CFCs into the atmosphere every year. But the effectiveness of each chlorine atom, when it came to destroying ozone is multiplied by a factor of a hundred thousand. But multiply a million tons of CFCs by a hundred thousand and now you're getting on to the scale in which the natural system of the planet operates and that made it a major problem."

Three months into their research, Rowland and Molina knew that their study projected massive stratospheric ozone depletion. This was dire since ozone protects us from the dangerous UV light that can cause human skin cancer and cataracts. UV light also can inhibit photosynthesis, the way plants make food. A one percent decrease in ozone can lead to a three percent increase in skin cancer cases. Immune system damage has been traced to UV exposure. UV effects have been discovered in water at nine-foot depth levels, raising fears of damage to crucial plankton in the oceans.

The realization of the significance of the work of the team came shortly. Rowland described how the work progressed. "Mario was doing some of the calculations first but as soon as he found . . . that the fluorocarbons would decompose and [estimated] that they would last for 50 or 100 years . . . [it] was already an interesting piece of information. Then, as soon as the chain reaction popped out, both of us were working on it all the time."

ENTER POLITICS AND CONTROVERSY

Rowland and Molina published their findings in *Nature*, a well-respected scientific journal, in 1974.[1] Within months, their paper generated much discussion and attention. Some people were alarmed, and others doubted the findings. One of the biggest doubters was the CFC industry, the companies that manufacture chlorofluorocarbons for use in common household items. The industry insisted that the discovery was merely a theory, unsupported by real world evidence. These companies insisted that there must be other occurrences in the complex atmosphere that would partially absolve the CFCs. The basic issue raised by the aerosol industry was: "Is there sufficient data to warrant government interference in a very profitable and useful industry?" Occasionally, the criticism was personal. Rowland said, "The most intense personal opposition came from the aerosol industry. The CFCs were the propellant gases that were their favorites for delivering a wide variety of products. And something one could laugh about now, but wasn't so laughable then, was they even suggested that we (Molina and I) were agents of the KGB of the Soviet Union, trying to destroy American industry."

Throughout this opposition, Rowland and Molina proved their theory was valid. Their reasoning was sound and no one found holes in their logic. They had come to their conclusion based on sound scientific methodology. They trusted that additional scientific evidence would support their claim.

Meanwhile, the CFC industry insisted on more time for more evidence. Rowland, Molina, and their supporters among scientists and environmentalists recognized that a wait-and-see approach to the environment wasn't enough. If everyone waited several years to be 100 percent sure that the ozone depletion occurs, by then, it would be much too late to take action. Rowland, Molina, and their supporters tried to convince the scientific community and the public that people have a responsibility to act immediately to ensure that humans and other living things will not be severely affected by one chemical that humans made for their own convenience.

The U.S. government listened to this advice, and in 1976 it enacted the first ban on the use of CFCs in spray cans. Other countries were slower, preferring to wait for more evidence. Meanwhile, researchers were busy collecting more data. Scientists sent up hot-air balloons to take measurements, and planes were sent to collect samples of air from the Arctic, Antarctic, and Brazil. The commercial stakes in CFCs were very high. Whereas aerosol products could find substitutes (by 1978, the use of CFCs was already diminishing), there was still the investment in the coolants for air conditioning and refrigeration. Also undiminished was their use for foaming agents in foam insulation and packaging, solvents that clean solder from electronics and grease from sheet metal, and in sterilization of medical instruments. The public protest began to wane and when the Reagan administration came in, the Environmental Protection Agency (EPA) vigilance was reduced dramatically.

Then in 1985, a dramatic finding stunned the scientific world. An ozone hole had been found over Antarctica. An ozone hole is an area of extremely low ozone concentration—so abnormally low that the British researchers who made the measurements initially figured their machines were malfunctioning. But those low measurements were accurate. Environmentalists had to decide whether the hole was natural or manmade.

People knew that legislation could not wait for the answer. After this evidence, it was clear that there was something seriously wrong with the natural balance of the atmosphere, and we could not wait to fully confirm that CFCs were the only cause. In a united effort, environmentalists from twenty-four countries and legislators from around the world met in Montreal to draft a proposal to significantly limit CFC production. The treaty, which came to be known as the Montreal Protocol, was completed on September 16, 1987. According to the treaty, CFC production in signatory countries would be reduced to 1986 levels by the middle of 1989, and these levels would be reduced to half over the next decade. The Montreal Protocol signified the world's confidence in Rowland and Molina's findings; although there were still not direct measurements that CFCs caused the ozone hole, the public recognized the importance of the theory. These countries, with an increased sense of responsibility, realized that the prevention of further damage was the first priority, and they could not wait for further scientific confirmation. The CFC industry collaborated with scientific communities in placing the welfare of living organisms above economic interests and convenience. Drafters of the Montreal Protocol also took into consideration that the agreement would need to be even stricter if additional scientific evidence confirmed Rowland and Molina's theory. They agreed to meet again in 1990 to review the scientific progress and make necessary amendments.

Meanwhile, scientists zealously pushed to find the exact cause of the severe ozone depletion over Antarctica. Rowland said, "There were three [expeditions that played key roles]. The first was on the ground in Antarctica in 1986. They made measurements with ground-based instruments and they sent balloons up." From that expedition, "they found that there were chlorine oxides present in the atmosphere and in large quantities." Chlorine oxide is one of the compounds involved in the chain reaction decrease in ozone. "That same group of scientists came back the following year, also on the ground, and did more experiments," continued Rowland. "And a different set of experimenters flew in with a high flying aircraft. The flights would come from the tip of South America, because the airplane couldn't land in Antarctica. They also measured chlorine oxide and ozone and demonstrated that when there was high chlorine oxide concentration, they had low ozone. That was a very convincing explanation for most scientists." These studies confirmed the theory that the hole was caused by the chlorine destroying the ozone over the Antarctic.

Why a hole over the Antarctic? Antarctica is the coldest and most isolated place on Earth. Over Antarctica, ice particles form in the stratosphere during the winters. On the surfaces of these ice particles, reactions occur that change the bromine and chlorine from the safe form to the destructive form. Rowland said, "Droplets make up a cloud. And the first guess was that the droplets would be ice, and then it became that it was the ice mixed with a little nitric acid and a little sulfuric acid." When the sun returns to Antarctica in the spring, it catalyzes the reaction that causes the destructive halons to destroy ozone. The ice particles accelerate this destruction with alarming efficiency.

The Antarctic ozone hole had completely caught the scientific community by surprise, including even Rowland and Molina.

They knew that evidence showing reduced ozone levels would sooner or later appear, but even they did not expect such a large and severe drop, spanning the entire continent of Antarctica. In fact, the ozone hole actually had started forming in the late 1970s, with ozone concentration over Antarctica dropping lower every spring. The concentration levels would recover during the summer, but then dip again in the spring.

After the ozone hole was discovered, scientists began to wonder if there were global signs of ozone depletion. Teams working in the Arctic discovered the same reactive chlorine compounds as in the Antarctic. Around the world, researchers made measurements of ozone concentrations using satellites and ground-based equipment. By 1988, a consensus had emerged that global ozone levels had declined during the past decade. Other processes, in particular the solar cycle, could account for some of the variations, but could not explain the entire decrease.

The evidence of global ozone depletion caused by unnatural means began pouring in. An international panel discovered that ozone levels had dropped not only during the spring but also during the summer. This news was cause for concern because people spend most of their time outdoors during the summer, and they could be exposed to higher-than-normal levels of UV light.

With the deluge of supporting evidence of stratospheric ozone depletion by CFCs, delegates from around the world met to revise the Montreal Protocol. Even though the original plan mandated that CFC production would be cut by 50 percent, chlorine and bromine levels would still increase in the stratosphere unless production was totally eliminated. Knowing this, there was a strong move to strengthen the Montreal Protocol. The treaty was revised so that CFCs would be completely phased out by the year 2000 in developed nations, and completely phased out in developing countries several years later. To show their cooperative effort, developed nations pledged to create a fund to support developing countries that were purchasing substitutes for CFCs used daily. The scientific community now has no doubt that CFCs play a major role in the depletion of our precious ozone layer.

Rowland and Molina were awarded the Nobel Prize in chemistry in 1995 in recognition of the significant impact their work has had not only on science, but on all human lives. Paul Crutzen, a Dutch researcher, shared the prize that year for his work in discovering that nitric oxides, chemicals found in the exhaust of jet planes, also contribute to the depletion of the ozone layer. The Nobel Prize awarded to these scientists marked an important milestone in atmospheric chemistry; it was public recognition that rather than being a static expanse of blue sky, the atmosphere requires a dynamic balance and the achievement of that balance plays an integral role in our existence.

Rowland and Molina's work has advanced ozone research. Rowland said, "There's a huge amount of research going on now. The number of people who are investigating ozone or the compounds that react with it probably went from around 50 to 10,000, on a regular basis. So, there's an enormous amount that's known now that wasn't known in 1970."

"It's a matter of asking questions. The problem for any scientist wanting to do original research is how to get away from the crowd." By simply asking questions and trying to learn about the world around them, Rowland and Molina saved humanity from the dangers of severe ozone depletion. They have forever changed how we think of the atmosphere and our role in its protection.

Rowland has remained at UC-Irvine and is currently the Donald Bren Research Professor of Chemistry and Earth System Science. He is also Foreign Secretary of the National Academy of Sciences, a position that requires extensive traveling. He continues to do research in atmospheric chemistry and is active in the battle to understand the influence of CO_2 and other so-called greenhouse gases on the global climate. Through his role as Foreign Secretary, he is trying to unite scientists from around the world not only in problems of an environmental nature, but global issues such as population and education as well. Besides being awarded the Nobel Prize in chemistry, Rowland has received the Tyler World Prize in Environment and Energy, the Charles Dana Award for Pioneering Achievement in Health, the Japan Prize in Environmental

Science and Technology, the Peter Debye Award in Physical Chemistry from the American Chemical Society, and the Roger Revelle Medal of the American Geophysical Union. He has authored or co-authored nearly four hundred scientific publications, his peers have elected him to the National Academy of Sciences, and he has served as President of the American Association for the Advancement of Science. The one-time ball player is a leader in atmospheric chemistry, a field that barely existed before his research efforts. And, he has helped make the environment safer for future generations.

Margaret J. Wat

CHAPTER 8

VERA RUBIN

ANNE KATHERINE HALSALL

I f you live in the city or even a large town, you probably don't see many stars at night. This is because the glow from the buildings and streetlights washes out all but the brightest stars and planets. Now, suppose you take someone who has lived in the city their whole life and take them into the country, far from the light pollution of civilization. Imagine their surprise when they looked up to see the entire sky filled with stars—stars they had never seen before, that they never even knew were there. The moral of the story is this: when it comes to stellar matters, you can never be certain that what you're seeing is all that's really there.

You probably know that astronomes have long been observing starts, as well as planets, galaxies, and other celestial phenomena that most of us don't see. But did you know that some astronomers also study what they can't see? Now, wait a minute! How does an astronomer study what they can't see—even when they use the most powerful telescopes? Dr. Vera Rubin, astronomer, wife, mother, and thinker conducted a study on the rotation of galaxies. The data she collected soon became well known, for it lent proof to a theory from the 1930s; one that postulated the existence of an "unseen component" of mass. This dark matter, as it is called, does not radiate nor absorb any light, so astronomers can't see it through a telescope. But as Rubin's data showed, dark matter is present in the halos of individual galaxies. And the study of dark matter shows that its mass may make up over 90 percent of the mass in the universe.

HER EYES TO THE STARS

For Rubin, it all started at a very young age, when she was a little girl with an immense interest in the stars. As early as she can remember, she was excited about asking questions of nature. She fondly recalls one of her first memories, sitting in the back of a car wondering why the Moon appeared to move with her. Later, her family moved to Washington, D.C., and she got her own bedroom with a window facing north. Before she fell asleep at night, she would watch the stars from that window, which sparked in her a deep love for observing the sky. Even at such an early point, she knew what she wanted to do with her life.

Vera Rubin was born on July 23, 1928. "I was born in Philadelphia. My father [Phillip Cooper] was an electrical engineer, and my mother graduated from a girl's high school, but was employed at Bell Telephone Company, where she met my father. I have one older sister, [who is] now a retired judge." When asked about her relationship with her family, she admits to the joy of family life. She says, "I had a very close family and did things with my family. They were very supportive of all my interests. My father helped me build a pretty simple telescope. When I wanted to attend meetings of the Washington, D.C., amateur astronomers, he drove me, and stayed, thinking it was improper for a young girl to be at a meeting with mostly men." She admits that it was the support of her family that nurtured her interest in science and unfortunately, not school. "[I had] no mentor in school. My physics teacher ran the class like a macho boys' club. My parents supported me."

Rubin was always precocious, and though her favorite subject in school was math, the

Rubin at 17 years of age (*Courtesy of V. Rubin*)

stars held a special fascination for her. When asked about why she chose to go into astronomy, she responded, "My sister always said she wanted to be a doctor, and I never knew what I wanted to be, until my early teens. At about eleven, I started watching the stars from my bed, and just became captivated. Within the year or so, I had started reading about astronomy, and knew that I wanted to be an astronomer. I just could not imagine living on the Earth, and not trying to find out what all those things in the sky were doing."

Rubin did well in school. Yet despite her gifts, she was still in many ways just like every other teenager. She recounted school in this way, "I loved math, more than any other subject, and did well in school. I skipped several grades very early, and graduated from high school at sixteen. I had the usual interests. I edited our high school yearbook, belonged to a science club, and refused to join a high school sorority. I played the piano, did arty things, cooked, and sewed clothes. I had dates, but was not overly social. I sometimes refused a date because I thought I would rather stay home and read (or something). I did have a boyfriend or two. I was most attracted to the smart boys, and they were not very social. I sometimes felt left out, because I wasn't one of the 'popular' girls, but I recognized, even then, that my interests were really just a little different from most of the girls."

Rubin in the observatory at Vassar College (*Courtesy of V. Rubin*)

Rubin worried about college, which seemed like it might be something of a problem because of the cost. She wanted to go to Vassar College to study astronomy, one of the few women's colleges where it was taught. She was also attracted to Vassar because she knew Maria Mitchell had taught there. She had read about Mitchell as a child, and was inspired by her story. In 1847, at age twenty-nine, Mitchell had discovered a comet with the telescope her father had put on their roof. At age thirty, she was the first woman elected into the American Academy of Arts and Sciences, and later was appointed director of Vassar's observatory, while becoming a professor of astronomy. Rubin said, "My father suggested I do something more practical than astronomy, like math. When I applied to college, there was no local college that taught astronomy, and we didn't have much money. But they [my parents] supported my interest in going to Vassar, where I knew that women could study astronomy. But [I knew] that I would need a scholarship. When the letter came from Vassar, my mother came to school (an unheard of event), so that I could open it. (She must have been convinced I would get in with a scholarship.)"

And, not surprisingly, it turned out to be a good investment for Vassar College. Rubin was certainly one-of-a-kind. Vassar was, at the time, an all-girls' college and she was the only astronomy major. By her senior year, she was the only one in the astronomy class and got one-on-one instruction from her professor. It was good for her to get exclusive attention from the teacher, but if she didn't have her homework done she really had to answer for it. In

1948, at the age of nineteen, Rubin graduated with a bachelors of arts degree in astronomy after only three years, and later married Robert Rubin, a physical chemist attending graduate school at Cornell University.

ROTATING GALAXIES

Rubin followed her husband to Cornell and obtained her master of arts degree in 1951, while he worked on his Ph.D. Her master's thesis involved searching for what was called the residual motion of galaxies. Scientists know that the universe, is expanding. Residual motion is the movement of the galaxies that is still observed after their motion, due to the expansion of the universe was removed. The available data was crude, but to Rubin, the results indicated an additional pattern of galactic motions. Galaxies were rotating as well as moving with the expansion of the universe. The thesis was heavily criticized and rejected for publication by several astronomy journals. She presented this work at the American Astronomical Society (AAS) in 1950 (only a few weeks after she had had her first child, David), but it was not well received there either. Much later, however, she returned to this work with W. Kent Ford Jr., and her basic conclusions were proven correct. It was indeed a hard time for her, but her husband offered a lot of support and they managed to get through it. In retrospect, Cornell offered Rubin a solid graduate education in physics, under some of the best physicists in the world, including Richard Feynman and Hans Bethe.

Robert Rubin was offered several jobs after receiving his doctorate, ultimately deciding to move to Washington, D.C., where both of their families were located. Rubin began graduate studies for her own doctorate at Georgetown University. In Washington, she encountered George Gamow, who was teaching at George Washington University. Gamow was a famous astrophysicist, who was one of the theorists behind the big bang theory. Amid a growing family (her daughter Judy was born in 1952), Rubin lucked out in solving a problem for Professor Gamow that would earn her a Ph.D. As she notes, the problem involved analyzing a lot of data on galaxy locations. The calculations, complex as they were in the 1950s, can be done on a computer today in a few minutes. In 1954, at the age of twenty-six, Rubin received her doctorate from Georgetown.

While teaching at Georgetown, Rubin had had two children, while two more were yet to come. Together, she and her husband managed to make ends meet. She got through graduate school by working into the night, after their children had been put to bed. It's by no means easy living as a scientist (much less training to become one) while supporting a marriage and family. Rubin does credit her husband as being very special and helpful to her, both in her work, being very involved in childcare, and raising their four children. The issue for a better system to support and encourage women to pursue careers in science is one she writes and speaks about frequently.

Once Rubin was awarded a doctorate, she taught courses at Montgomery County Community College (1955) and Georgetown University (1957–1965). Two more sons, Karl, born in 1956, and Allan, born in 1960, joined the family. She managed to arrange a research and teaching schedule that allowed her to be at home when her children returned home from school. In 1965 she confidently walked into the Carnegie Institution's Department of Terrestrial Magnetism and asked for a job. They gave it to her, and she's been working there ever since.

That same year, in 1965, she became the first woman ever allowed to observe at the Palomar Observatory. The astronomers way of life is to apply for time on the few large telescopes scattered around the nation. "Time" allows the scientist to control the direction that the telescope is pointing and to instruct its viewing processes: cameras, spectrographs, charge-coupled devices (a film substitute), or other equipment. Some committee looks at the many requests for viewing time and makes decisions based upon merit of the work. The fact that she obtained time was quite an accomplishment, considering astronomy was primarily a man's field. Rubin was invited to apply for telescope time, despite the fact that the application said, "Due to limited facilities, it is not possible to accept applications from women."[1] The living quarters at the observatory were nicknamed "The Monastery" and women were never allowed near them. This was because George E. Hale, the man who built it, had specifically wanted an observatory where men could go to work, and not be bothered by their wives and families. It was not initially meant to ban women astronomers, but it quickly became that way. When originally built, it only had one bathroom—for men only. Additional facilities have since been added, but the only bathroom on the main floor is labeled "Men" while another, near the large 200-inch telescope console room is unlabeled. Her bright character shone through at Palomar, as well as her sense of humor. On an observing trip in 1990, she drew a picture of a stick woman and stuck it up on the door of the bathroom. It stayed up for the few days she was there, but quickly disappeared, she was told, after she left.

MISSING MATTER

Rubin's work helped change the way that scientists understand the cosmos. When you look up at the night sky, what do you see? If the conditions are good, you probably see a fair number of stars, constellations, planets, meteors, and maybe galaxies if you have very good eyes. But have you ever wondered what you're not seeing? Is the blackness of space just a vacuum, or are there more subtle elements that we can't see? Rubin seems to have made enormous strides in answering that question. She changed the way people perceive the universe because she offered evidence to support the existence of *dark matter*—a nonluminous substance that may account for over 90 percent of the mass in the universe. In plain English, there seems to be a great deal of very black stuff out there that we can't see.

Crucial to an understanding of the puzzle of dark matter is the fact that Isaac Newton's theory of gravitation is the ruling law of the cosmos. Newton discovered that the pull of the Earth on objects near its surface, such as on an apple, is precisely the same as the pull of the Earth, which locks the Moon into its orbit. Precisely the same, that is, after we account for the increased distance of the Moon from the Earth. The gravitational force between two objects decreases as the square of the distance between them. The force is created by the mass of one object and acts on the mass of the second object. The Earth and its fellow planets are pulled toward the Sun which compromises their natural tendency to fly off into space when they orbit the Sun, just as a string pulls on a stone that is being whirled around.

Thus, we can deduce the presence of an invisible massive astronomical object by the gravitational force it exerts on an object that we can see. Dark matter was discovered because it exerted observable forces on nearby visible objects.

For a long time scientists believed that where there was light, there was mass, and vice versa. But early in the twentieth century Jan Oort, a Dutch astronomer, wrote some of the first scientific papers that postulated dark matter, although it was not named that at the time. He asserted that lighht and mass in galaxy NGC 3115 was not distributed the same.

In 1933, astronomer Fritz Zwicky was studying the Coma cluster of galaxies. He observed that these galaxies interacted wtih one another in ways that suggested that there was more mass, exerting gravitational force on these neighboring galaxies, than was visible. It was then called the "missing mass" problem, although this is a misnomer, since there was more mass than "meets the eye."

To understand dark matter and Rubin's work, we need to understand Kepler's third law of planetary motion. Basically, it states that the speed of a body revolving around another body decreases as the distance between them increases. This law can be seen at work in our own solar system. Mercury, the closest planet to the Sun, moves with a velocity that is much faster than Pluto, the farthest planet, does. It was Kepler's laws, determined through careful measurements, that led Newton to his famous inverse square law for gravitational force. Thus, Kepler's laws of planetary motion arise from the gravitational force of the Sun on the planets.

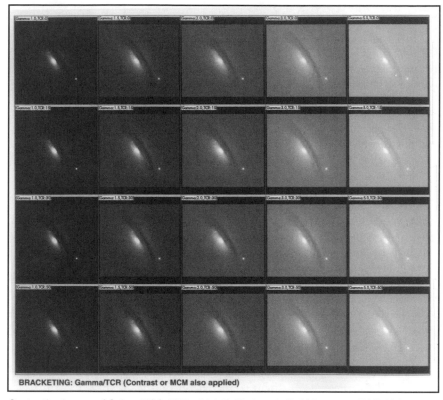

Contrasting images of Galaxy NGC 4526, which Rubin has studied (*Courtesy of V. Rubin*)

Galaxies follow these laws of motion, too. Their billions of suns revolve around the center of the galaxy in the same way the planets revolve around the Sun, drawn to this motion by gravity. The galaxies inside Zwicky's cluster were moving relative to each other, much faster than Kepler's law allows for, given the distances between them. At the speeds Zwicky observed, the galaxies would have flown apart unless there was another, unseen source of gravitational force holding them together. He postulated the existence of a kind of "missing matter" that inhabited clusters of galaxies, adding its gravitational pull to their wildly spinning dance.

Galaxies are vastly larger than our solar system. They contain up to hundreds of billions of suns, each of which *may* have its own planets. The distance between stars is tens of thousands of times larger than the size of a solar system. This should give you a sense of the vastness of space. Yet the law of gravity holds things together. Looking up at the night sky, perhaps with the aid of binoculars or a simple telescope, one can detect a galaxy as a small fuzzy patch, barely larger than the typical star, which is called a point of light. Yet measurements made in the 1900s showed that galaxies tend to cluster, drawn by the tireless force of gravity over distances of countless trillions of miles.

Little progress was made until Rubin hit the scene in the early 1970s, when she conducted her study of the rotation of individual galaxies. As noted earlier, galaxies are somewhat like our own solar system. They, too, have a center of gravity and all the stars in the galaxy rotate around this center, much like the planets rotate around the Sun. Therefore, if you look at a galaxy edge on, while it is rotating, you'll see the stars on one side moving toward you and the stars on the other side moving away. Rubin observed and collected data on the speed of these stars in their galactic orbits (for spiral galaxies like ours), and what she discovered came as a surprise to everyone. According to her data, the stars on the inside of the galaxy, close to the center, were rotating around it *at the same speed* as those on the outer rim, far from the center. Remembering Kepler, the outer stars should be moving much slower than the inner stars. Another force must be at work in order to explain the data that Rubin collected. She investigated further, and it turned out that this behavior could be explained by a rather large amount of invisible mass surrounding the galaxy. Our picture of dark matter is one of a tenuous gas of particles spreading out far beyond the luminous disk of the galaxy: an enormous halo occupying a volume many times greater than the luminous galaxy itself, and in so doing, adding as much as ten times the mass of the galaxy.

This sounds pretty unbelievable. Occam's Razor,[2] a test that is often applied to scientific theories, would seem to cut a big hole in Rubin's theory. Its basic premise is that all other things being equal, the simplest, most straightforward explanation of a phenomenon is probably the right one. And, at first, the theory of dark matter does seem far-fetched. The most difficult part of it is that we can't see it, nor detect it by any conventional means. So how can you prove that this strangely convenient and yet unidentifiable mass is even there? Since Rubin's initial discovery, much of her work has been focused on finding more proof for its existence. Although the first indication of dark matter was in the rotation of stars within a galaxy, the real answer lies in how galaxies interact with each other.

This may sound strange at first because space is an awfully big place. It's time we used the astronomer's measure of distance. Just as a kilometer (km) would be much too big a unit with which to measure the size of a bacterium, so is a kilometer much too small to measure astronomical distances. Light years are used instead. It is defined as the distance light, traveling at a velocity of 300,000 km/sec, travels in a year, which has about thirty million seconds. So one light year is about one trillion km. The Andromeda galaxy, one of our close neighbors, is 2.2 million light years from us and it appears only as a smudge on the night sky. How can two galaxies interact with one another? Space is indeed awfully big, but so are

Rubin observing at Kitt Peak (*Courtesy of V. Rubin*)

galaxies. Consider for a moment our Sun and the nearest star, Proxima Centauri. The distance between them is thirty million times the diameter of the Sun. This distance is far too great for them to have any significant gravitational affect on each other. But a galaxy can be on the order of 100,000 light years across, and it's not at all unusual to find a neighbor not more than one or two times this distance away. So, if one speaks in terms of diameters, galaxies can actually be pretty close, and certainly close enough to attract each other. Dark matter, then, if it does exist, would play a major role in the way they interact. With this in mind, Rubin continued her observations, and came to the conclusion that using visible matter only, the predicted way that two galaxies relate is very different from what you actually see. Thus, there must be unseen matter, dark matter, which influences the interactions of the galaxies that she actually observed.

So many discoveries depend upon the tools of the scientists. In the case of astronomy, the tools are, of course, telescopes, but associated with these are cameras and spectrographs that spread the starlight out into its colors to analyze and identify the atoms and their motion. Other astronomers have looked at galaxy rotations before, but missed this crucial discovery. Why? Rubin was using a state-of-the-art spectrograph in the 1960s to analyze the light from a large telescope. The instrument used electronic enhancement, and was much more sensitive than the instruments previously used for this type of observation.

Of course, with recent advances in technology, the search for dark matter has been much easier. You may imagine astronomers spending all their time looking through telescopes, but now you'll find them much more often looking at computer screens. Computers have vastly improved the field, as they can be used to model galaxies, make predictions for the future, and keep track of the immense catalogue of stellar objects and their places in the sky. Without computers, astronomers would have a much harder time analyzing galaxies.

What composes this mysterious matter? Rubin answers this question with three possibilities: One possibility is that it could be ordinary matter, like the stuff you see and feel every day. Such things as very faint stars, large planets like Jupiter, loose dust, black holes, and cold gas fit into this category. All of these things are too dim for us to see properly, if at all. But can they account for the huge quantity of dark matter that we suspect is out there? The second possibility is that dark matter consists of vast numbers of a new kind of particle, some strange substance that is beyond our realm of understanding and therefore, something we can't detect. (Neutrinos were a popular candidate.) Such a thing would be very hard to prove, however. Since it would be, by nature, ahead of our current ability to detect it, astronomers could not apply the usual methods to it. It may behave in ways that defy everything known about physics, and while constantly moving forth in our ability to comprehend such things, astronomers are not yet able to definitively assert their existence. The third theory, but a rather unaccepted one, is that Kepler's third law is wrong and our idea of gravity is shaky at best.

This is a lot of information to digest all at once. One might wonder why it's important and why Rubin devoted her life to studying it? One of the driving questions in modern astronomy is the destiny of the universe. We know, at least as well as we can, that the universe started with the big bang and since then has been constantly expanding. (The big bang is discussed in chapter 10, the biography of George Smoot.) But will it continue to expand forever? After all, gravity is an attractive force, tending to draw matter together. So, will the expansion of the universe eventually reach a finite point and then start to collapse in on itself?

The key issue in the answer to this question is the density of the universe. Astrophysicists have defined a "critical density" to try to determine the future of the universe. If the actual density of mass in the universe (all the mass in a large sample volume divided by that volume) is greater than the critical density, then the equations predict the attractive force of gravity will slow the expansion, stop it, and reverse it. That's called the *big crunch*. If the density is smaller than critical, the expansion would go on forever. And we need to account for all matter, matter of any kind, in order to start to begin to approximate this actual density. Originally, scientists counted only bright matter. But since then, we have been alerted to the possibility that there is more out there than meets the eye, and this dark matter can have a significant impact. Rubin reports that if someone added up all of the seen bright matter, plus all the suspected dark matter, then it still only account for less than 20 percent of the density needed to halt the eternal expansion of the universe. Our understanding of the fate of our universe is still uncertain.

The story of dark matter is far from finished. It is at the core of the most exciting new developments in astronomy. We should set the stage for this by noting that theoretical astrophysicists have a strong prejudice in favor of the actual density being exactly equal to the critical density; about ten times the density now observed, including dark matter. So until 1998, the theorists called their crisis the missing mass problem. They faced two problems—understanding the nature of the dark matter *and* finding the missing mass needed to achieve theoretical satisfaction. But in 1998 new observations on the rate of expansion of the universe indicated the astonishing result that the expansion is increasing. This changes everything. Now, instead of searching for mass required to achieve a critical density, astrophysicists are searching for a mechanism—a force, that forces the universe to continue to expand.

Rubin considers her contribution to the study of dark matter one of her best achievements in to science. She discussed it in this way, "[My most significant scientific accomplishment was] learning that the stars and gas in galaxies do not orbit with the velocities that we expected, but stars far from the centers of galaxies orbit with velocities much higher than predicted by Newton's laws of motion. This implies that most of the matter in a galaxy (and hence in the universe) is not bright, but dark (not radiating)." She reflected, "It took a while to sink in—initially I was just delighted that we could detect velocities far out in the disk of a spiral galaxy. But after several nights of observing, I knew that something very unexpected was going on. Now, after about twenty-five years, I am disappointed that we still do not know what it [dark matter] is, but that makes it even more mysterious, and perhaps very fundamental." Perhaps Rubin's daughter Judy, also an astronomer, or the next generation of scientists will solve *this* problem. But, without a doubt, the discovery of dark matter has provided us with a clearer understanding of both galaxies and illuminated stars.

AN UNCONVENTIONAL LIFE

The life of an astronomer, and especially that of Rubin, is not what one may expect. As mentioned earlier, an astronomer must apply for time on one of only several large telescopes scattered around the United States. They don't design experiments, but they must carefully plan the observations that they wish to carry out. Rubin described her work like this: "Deciding what to study is perhaps the hardest thing I do. Once that problem is settled, I spend a lot of time asking myself which galaxies will help me find out what I want to know. So I look through atlases and tables of galaxies, searching for the ones that will reveal a few more secrets. Then I make up an observing program, so I will observe each galaxy as it passes overhead (as the Earth turns). Depending on where the Moon is (which I want to avoid), I make up a detailed chart of observations. [This includes] the order of galaxies, how much exposure time on each, and so on, for the whole night. Each day at the observatory I revise what I thought I would do, depending on the weather and success of the previous night. There are always terrible decisions; if the night is poor, do I do the most important galaxy, or do I wait, hoping the next night will be better? I observe spectra, and I take the (now) digital data back to my lab where I measure very accurately the positions of the lines emitted by the hydrogen gas clouds in the galaxy. Then I figure out what it all means.

"In between, I work with my postdoctoral fellows. Sometimes I go observing with them, write papers on what I have observed and discovered, [and I] give formal talks at universities and colleges (about one a month). These take some careful preparation. I answer letters from school children, book writers, and the public.

I attend meetings of astronomers, who also study galaxies. I am a member of several visiting committees, which each college arranges. The committee visits, meets the physics and/or astronomy students, faculty, professors, and reports to the dean about the health of the department, and so on." One should probably also add that her life is very busy, as well as unconventional.

It may seem much was covered here, but Rubin's work encompasses much more than just dark matter. A few years ago, she discovered an unconventional galaxy. "[It] has a single disk, in which half the stars orbit clockwise, half counterclockwise. But in a galaxy disk, stars are very, very, very far apart, so they don't run into each other. Imagine a one-lane road, with one car driving on it about every 1,000 years. There is very little probability that two cars would ever collide." This work is not only extending our knowledge of the movement of stars in galaxies, but also making us think about their movement in different ways. She is also proud of this accomplishment in what she calls her "senior years."

Rubin has authored more than two hundred papers, spanning topics from detailed studies of the Milky Way to the rotation of galaxies, and women in science. She has also received several prestigious awards and honors. In 1981, she was elected to the National Academy of Sciences, received the National Medal of Science in 1993, the Carnegie Mellon University's Dickson Prize for Science in 1994, and the Royal Astronomical Society's Gold Medal in 1996 (the first woman to receive it since Caroline Herschel in 1828). But for Vera Rubin, being a scientist hardly makes her unusual, though she does admit to having an unconventional life. She would never settle for less than every thing that she's capable of, and that dedication has brought her a long way in this world. She compares her child's view of becoming an astronomer with her life in this way, "As a child, being an astronomer meant learning about the stars. So in that respect it is not different. By the time I was in college, I knew I would not live at an observatory, because I knew I wanted a husband and children. I had to learn how to incorporate being an astronomer with being a member of a family. But it has all worked wonderfully."

Still, looking back, she says she feels most proud of her children and her marriage. Indeed, she has an amazing family: Vera, mother, Ph.D. in astronomy; Robert, father, Ph.D. in physics; David, son, Ph.D. in geology; Allan, son, Ph.D. in geology; Karl, son, Ph.D. in mathematics; and Judith, daughter, Ph.D. in cosmic-ray physics. Vera and Judy are one of very few mother-daughter pairs in professional astronomy. Judy, as a child, was interested in science, but it was only when Vera volunteered to teach a college level course in astronomy at her high school that her interests changed. Although they study very different aspects of the galaxies, they occasionally work together. "Judy and I have collaborated, but only a little. She studies molecules in galaxies (with a radio telescope); I study atoms (with an optical telescope). Sometimes I have taken spectra or images for her of a galaxy she is studying, and she has taken radio observations of a galaxy I am studying. We have attended the same meetings, where we have each spoken."

Her advice to students today is probably similar to what she told her children as they grew up: do what you enjoy. It is also how she and her husband modeled their lives, producing four scientists in the family. She said, "*Never give up*! Many people along the way will tell you to find something else to study, and you yourself may wonder if you will succeed. I never dreamed that I would be as successful and make the discoveries that I have. So find something you really want to do, and keep at it. Every one of you can make major advances in science."

You might ask yourself, What else lies beyond our current realm of knowledge? If we push ourselves, expand our horizons as Rubin has done, what will we find waiting? You'll find these answers within your reach; all it takes is a little spirit and a lot of imagination. Scientists are not all men and they're not all supermen or superwomen. They're real people, and all have their stories, hopes, and dreams. They've all made mistakes, met opposition, lived and loved, and most importantly, they have lives outside of what they do. Even Rubin takes time out of a very busy schedule to spend time with her family and do the things she loves. She said, "I garden, play the piano (a little), hike with my husband and family, and travel (often to see [my] grandchildren)."

Anne Katherine Halsall

CHAPTER 9

PAUL SERENO

GRACE J. YANG

P aul Sereno doesn't wear designer suits and power ties to work. And he doesn't wear a trench coat while chasing after criminals through the wet streets of London. Although his job isn't real glamorous, thousands of kids probably would jump at the opportunity to do it—as long as they wouldn't have to do the paperwork that goes with the territory. Sereno is a paleontologist.

Clothed in shorts, T-shirts, and heavy-duty boots, he and his team members search for evidence of dinosaurs and other animals—pieces of bone and teeth that have long since blended with the land. These fossils help Sereno piece together a whole story of the creatures that existed long ago in Earth's history.

Paleontology expeditions require not only brains, but also a lot of endurance. His team arrives at a typical desert location and set up a primitive camp. No one in the camp spends much time thinking about fame and success. It's team work—hot and sweaty; the skin of some team members starts to crack in the scorching desert sun. A couple months later, after miles of hiking and work, Sereno's team members may glue pieces of tire to their thin, worn-out boot soles to give them more traction.

So why does Sereno return to Africa, South America, and other distant places? He loves discovering new dinosaur species and solving mysteries. Sometimes his field feels more like art than science. "The things that I enjoy most about science is that it is almost like creating a painting," Sereno said. "I would do a still life in high school. And in college, I would do abstracts, and I would do paintings. . . . And you get it just right, so the glass looks clear, and you sit back and say that it is a sort of a trick. You play the trick, but it is wonderful. It is beautiful. You've got all the composition working together. Science is pretty much like that. When you do your best science you should look back and say, that is a great trick. By a trick, I do not mean you are fooling somebody. I mean that you put something together that people can only marvel at. That is the best kind of science. I mean that's when I sit back, and I've done maybe the evolution-of-dinosaur paper in *Science*,[1] and I've created a drawing that summarizes all of dinosaur evolution in the skeletal anatomy—in a way that I think that almost nobody else right now will, or at least could conceive of—that's a trick. And it's fun." Sereno, the scientist and artist, performs tricks during his expeditions—pulling dinosaurs out of million-year-old rocks.

AN EARLY INTEREST IN ART

Born in 1958, the second of six children in his family, Sereno grew up in Naperville, Illinois, a suburban neighborhood west of Chicago. He admits that he had "a great sense of mischief" as a child. He disliked school, almost failing several grades before graduating to high school, and showed no signs of his now internationally recognized ability to discover new dinosaur species. He didn't collect rocks and fossils, as one might think, nor did he have a burning desire to become a scientist. His mother, an artist and educator, influenced an interest in art that began while Sereno was in high school. He studied both art and biology at Northern Illinois University (NIU) in DeKalb, and earned a bachelor of science degree in 1979. All of his siblings graduated from NIU, and all six Sereno children have earned advanced degrees in the sciences. Sereno's parents, Rena and Charles, who are very supportive of their children, nurtured young Paul through his rough academic beginning.

A trip with his brother Martin Sereno to the American Museum of History in New York City, during Sereno's junior year at college, ultimately sparked his interest in fossils. During a behind-the-scenes tour of the museum, where students were making sketches, photographs, and reproductions of fossils, Sereno imagined his own world in which he could combine art, science, and adventure. In 1979, he applied and was accepted to the vertebrate paleontology graduate program in geological sciences at Columbia University in New York.

As part of his graduate work, Sereno traveled the world and explored museums looking for dinosaur bones. He realized that the dinosaur family tree was largely unknown and hadn't been studied very thoroughly. He was fortunate enough to be able to explore many museum collections, including some in China, where no American graduate student had been for decades. He identified several new dinosaur species there, and still believes that undiscovered collections like these hold important information about dinosaur evolution.

Sereno earned his doctorate from Columbia University in 1987 and landed a job as an assistant professor at the University of Chicago without ever having organized or led his own expedition. About a year later, he took a team to Argentina and discovered the first complete skull of the dinosaur called *Herrerasaurus*. The researchers also found bones from several other *Herrerasaurus* skeletons, which allowed them to create the first complete description of this dinosaur. Named for Victorino Herrera, who first found this animal's bones, the name means, appropriately, Herrera's reptile.

DINOSAUR DIGS

So what exactly is paleontology? The field encompasses the study of dinosaurs, but it's a bit more complex. Some people confuse this field with archeology. Sereno clarified the difference this way: "As paleontologists, we dig up bones, things that tend to be older than what archeologists study, which is really concentrating on human sites." Paleontologists study fossils of plants and animals (including birds, reptiles, and dinosaurs) several hundred million years old. Archeologists focus on examining the remains of human civilizations, which are only a few thousand years old.

A dinosaur dig is not nearly as glamorous as some people imagine it to be. A dig starts long before anyone picks up a shovel, and ends long after everyone heads home to a comfortable bed, hot shower, and air conditioning. Digs have three stages: the pre-expedition preparation, the actual expedition, and the postexpedition analysis. The first stage involves researching likely sites where fossils can be found, finding or raising the money to take the trip, assembling the dig team, and packing. The second stage includes the back-breaking job of searching for, finding, and removing the fossils from the surrounding rock, and preparing and transporting the materials back to the laboratory. When the fossils arrive in the laboratory, the final stage of analyzing the work and its significance begins. Fossil exhibits at museums are only a small part of the results of a dinosaur dig. Although the research team may be in the field for only a few months, the whole process can continue for many years.

Before anyone goes on a trip to remote parts of the world in search of fossil remains, the expedition must be well planned. Where should one search? What food, supplies, and equipment need to be taken along? Who gets to go? Who packs? Who is going to pay for teams of scientists and students to travel, live, and work far away from home? With literally tons of food, supplies, and equipment to transport, what route should the team take to the dig site? Sereno sometimes spends two or three years answering these questions. He writes grant proposals and solicits funds from philanthropic organizations interested in supporting his work. "But just the amount of leg work involved in organizing an expedition—the amount of paperwork, letters, and answering letters and phone calls, and bills and receipts, and all the stuff that's not the best or most fun part of things. . . . That's the least fun part of my job."

Selection of the dig team is also challenging. "I'm looking for people with special interests, special stamina, and [people who can make] special contributions to the team. Most of these [individuals] are students that I owe training to—graduate students—but I've taken teachers. I've taken engineers . . . The fieldwork is not for everybody, particularly my style of fieldwork—it's gritty. It's wonderfully exciting. It is physically and mentally draining. It's a commitment for three to four months in a foreign land under all sorts of circumstances; the heat reaching 130 degrees, your butt freezing off on other nights. You really have to be—no one gets paid—devoted to this. And so you've got to find the right kind of person. You can find a lot more people who want to go, and who are absolutely sure that they will make great team members, than you can [find] people who will actually make great team members."

Items needed on these types of journeys include dried food,

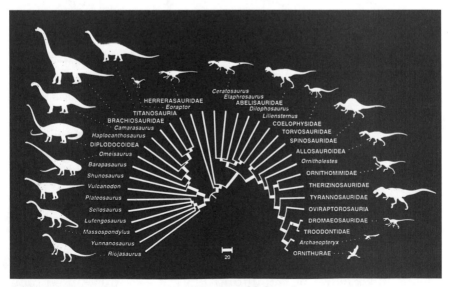

A phylogenetic tree of dinosaur evolution (*Courtesy of P. Sereno*)

plaster, tents, tools, water—anything and everything needed for the dig, as well as for the people to live in whatever climate and country they have traveled. Getting to the site usually is not easy. When traveling to Morocco in 1995, Sereno and his team packed large containers of supplies in Chicago. They were first flown to London. In London, they unloaded everything and repacked it onto trucks, took the ferry to France, and then drove through Spain, crossed the Mediterranean Sea on a boat, and finally reached the dig site in Morocco.

During the past fifteen years, Sereno has led three expeditions to Argentina (1988, 1991, and 1996), three expeditions to Niger (1993, 1997, and 2000), one expedition to India (2001), and one expedition to Morocco (1995).[2] He also has considered making expeditions to Brazil and Australia, having led preliminary trips to these countries to determine whether they have sites that may yield interesting finds. Most recently, in the spring of 2001, he led his first expedition to Inner Mongolia in China, bringing his total digging expeditions to nine. On each trip, he and team members have made significant finds. These include discovering parts of previously identified dinosaurs. Sereno and team members also have discovered more than fifteen new dinosaurs, as well as new species of crocodiles, turtles, and fish.

An expedition may not always be successful in finding previously undiscovered dinosaur species, but Sereno, so far, has never returned empty-handed. This is due primarily to skill and the help of some luck. One example of luck playing a role occurred during the 1995 trip to Morocco. Team member Gabrielle Lyon, who later became Sereno's wife, had to exchange her boots for sandals. Her boots had gotten wet and were unwearable until they dried out. She had to take a different, less steep route down the cliffside she was searching because her sandals were much less stable for walking than boots. On her way, she happened to notice a bone protruding from the ground. She returned with the crew to unearth the bone. What the team soon discovered was a new species, later named *Deltadromeus agilis*, meaning agile delta runner.

Finding a new dinosaur during digs is not easy. The expedition team may excavate more than twenty tons of earth and rocks by hand. There are no bucket-and-crane devices available for digging out the delicate remains or for lifting and moving heavy rocks. Team members commonly lose weight, some as much as twenty pounds. Freeing a fossil from its hundred-million-year-old resting place can require tools ranging from paint brushes to jack-hammers, depending on how the fossils are buried. Other commonly used tools come from dentists' offices—drills and polishers. Paleontologists also use chisels, rock hammers, and awls. Once bones have been found, they are very carefully and painstakingly prepared for return to the laboratory for further cleaning and study.

A process called plaster jacketing is used to protect the bones and artifacts on their long trip back from the site to the laboratory, where they will be studied. Protective layers of wet plaster are carefully wrapped around each piece and allowed to dry and harden, the same way a human's cast protects a broken bone. This insulates the precious remains during the journey back to the lab whether by truck, boat, and/or plane.

After returning from the field, tiring months and even years of unpacking, study, and dinosaur reconstruction begins. Researchers remove the plaster jacketing as well as extraneous materials, which have long encased the bones. Sometimes a single bone must be rebuilt from many smaller pieces. Finally, skeletons are assembled into what researchers hope is a complete and accurate three-dimensional representation of the now-extinct creature. This is when Sereno the artist, not just the scientist, gets a chance to use another set of skills. In a process called fleshing out, paleontologists reconstruct dinosaurs as models of how they might have appeared walking the Earth millions of years ago. Sereno describes it this way: "The reconstruction is something that you have to be very careful with. [At] certain points, there is no artistic license. You're just reflecting something to the opposite side, or just working on intermediates. And others, there's a little bit more license, and you have to go to the nearest species, or set of species, and work your way there, guessing that it probably would be the same. . . . So there is a certain amount of artistry. Actually, the part of artistry that is most important is being accurate and being able to reverse something exactly. If you're an artist, you can do that. A lot of times, people think, 'Oh, you say you're an artist. That means you're just guessing, and you're creating something for which we have no evidence.' In fact, it takes very good artistry to size down, size up, reverse right to left, left to right; to get the animal to the point at which we already know it, but we don't quite have it in our hands yet."

THE ACADEMIC LIFE

Sereno, who now holds the rank of a full professor at the University of Chicago, also has teaching responsibilities, one of which is teaching in the medical school. What's a paleontologist doing teaching medical students? How could dinosaurs, hundreds of millions of years old, offer pertinent information to your future physician? "There's a very general plan, a vertebrate plan, so that every bone in a dinosaur's body, you can find in the human body," Sereno said. "And since we spend most of our time studying bones . . . we're at a pretty darn good position to teach people about bones and muscles. It's not that uncommon that paleontologists, vertebrate paleontologists—paleontologists that study animals with backbones—also are involved in some ways in medical school teaching." It's an option that Sereno chooses in the midst of many other duties and responsibilities. This activity goes to the heart of paleontology, which is the use of plant and animal fossils out of geological history in order to understand, ultimately, the complete history of our planet. Sereno's vertebrate paleontology is also especially relevant to evolutionary theory and the construction of modern living species.

In addition to some of the more dull, paperwork-intensive tasks associated with a dig, Sereno must find the time to document his work by writing scholarly papers. That's why a typical day for him sometimes begins at 5:30 in the morning. Occasionally the day may end at 5:30 A.M., as he works diligently to get paperwork off his desk, so he can turn to the more interesting task of sharing new discoveries with his colleagues. Sereno is careful about discussing his new finds until they have been well studied and documented. Public announcement of the names of new species occurs long after the physical dig is completed. So will Sereno soon announce a new *Paulasaurus* or a *Serenosaurus rex* dinosaur from his latest expedition? Perhaps, but names frequently describe significant characteristics of the animal. Team members will talk and work together to come up with an appropriate name for new species, finally deciding on a name they all agree upon.

PLATE TECTONICS AND EVOLUTION

George Smoot, profiled in chapter 10, studies remnants of the big bang, providing evidence for it as the origin of our universe. The big bang occurred an estimated fifteen billion years ago. The dinosaurs that Sereno discovers and studies were present on the Earth during the Cretaceous period of the Mesozoic era, hundreds of millions of years ago, but very recent compared to the big bang.

Geologists date our Earth back 4.6 billion years and have named several eras. Very little is known about the Precambrian age, an era considered to have ended 570 million years ago. Life on Earth consisted of only simple bacteria and algae—organisms with no hard, bonylike structures—so few artifacts are left to study.

The Paleozoic era, following the Precambrian time, ended 245 million years ago. Geologists believe that during this era, our current seven continents originally existed as one huge land mass—a giant supercontinent—called Pangaea. Primitive plants and fishes were beginning to evolve during this time.

The Mesozoic era, made up of the Triassic (earliest), Jurassic, and Cretaceous (latest) dinosaur periods, followed for almost the next 200 million years, ending about 66.4 million years ago. The beginning of this era is when dinosaurs are first believed to have come into existence. They dominated the Earth because they were the largest animals; the only animals that were more than a meter in length were, in fact, dinosaurs.

During the Jurassic period (approximately 145–205 million years ago), the supercontinent of Pangaea began to split into what geologists call the northern continent of Laurasia (modern-day North America, Europe, and Asia) and southern Gondwanaland (South America, Africa, Australia, and Antarctica). Dinosaurs roamed, and the division of Pangaea began to separate populations of different animals and plants from one another. However, Sereno's research into the dinosaur family tree shows that dinosaurs probably traveled back and forth between the two big land masses; they were not totally isolated from each other.

The Cretaceous period of our Earth's history is the time when the continents, as we now know them, became discrete land masses, further isolating plant and animal species from one another. At the end of the Cretaceous period, and the very beginning of the Cenozoic era, a catastrophic event occurred that caused mass extinction of all dinosaurs and many other species of plants and animals. This event is widely believed to have been a collision between a huge asteroid and the Earth. Only a few reptile species, cousins to the dinosaur, survived to evolve into their present counterparts. Mammals began to emerge at this time on Earth and to dominate the animal kingdom. About four to five million years ago, the first hominids appeared. Hominids are now represented only by modern humans, or *Homo sapiens*, who have been on Earth for only the last one and a half million years.

It was the separation of continents that has helped to provide Sereno with some of his greatest successes. Dinosaurs were present on North America and other continents, but physical separation established the condition for the ancestors of North American and African dinosaurs to eventually evolve into separate and distinct species. About his finds in Africa, Sereno said, "We almost know that if we dig anything up, that it is going to be something new. We are working at a time period in which Africa was isolated, and these species, like today, do not occupy much more than a single continent. We have never found a species [in Africa] that we have found in North America, for example, in the Cretaceous [period]. So the odds are stacked way in your favor that you are going to find something new . . . in the Cretaceous rocks in Africa. That is why it is so exciting to work there."

FASCINATING FINDS

Sereno is credited with discovering more than a dozen new dinosaurs on his various expeditions. These species, along with in-depth study of dinosaurs found by others, have provided the information for Sereno to reclassify some dinosaurs and to refine the dinosaur family tree.

In Argentina in 1991, Sereno and his team found *Eoraptor* near the site where they had found the *Herrerasaurus* bones. *Eoraptor*, meaning dawn raptor, is appropriately named because it is believed to be one of the earliest dinosaur species that existed on Earth, dating back 228 million years.

"If Sereno were a dinosaur, which would he be?" I asked during a recent interview.

"I guess I would want to be *Eoraptor*," he said.

"The oldest?" I asked.

"Yeah. Then you'd give rise to everything else," he said. "Who wants to be out on the little branch [of dinosaur evolution] at the very end of dinosaur life?"

During the 1995 Morrocan expedition, when Lyon discovered *Deltadromeus agilis*, Sereno also found the first complete skull of *Carcharodontosaurus saharicus*, shark-toothed reptile from the Sahara. *Carcharodontosaurus*, estimated to be forty-five feet in length, is larger than the famous forty-foot *Tyrannosaurus rex* that originated in Mongolia. This makes *Carcharodontosaurus saharicus* one of the largest meat-eating dinosaurs ever to have existed on Earth—an incredible and important find for Sereno and his team.

Another very significant discovery for Sereno was *Jobaria tiguidensis*, named after a mythical giant in the lore of the desert nomads of the Sahara. *Jobaria* was found in 135 million-year-old rocks in Niger during the 1997 expedition, and is seventy feet long, making it one of the largest dinosaurs ever discovered. It had a very long neck and ate plants as its food source. Sereno tried to determine how this huge animal, estimated to weigh approximately twenty tons, could stand on its hind legs. Standing on its hind legs might be useful for fighting off predators or obtaining food. He studied the African elephant, today's largest four-footed beast. Paleontologists once thought that a twenty-ton sauropod (lizard-footed dinosaur) like *Jobaria* could never live on land, let alone rear up on its hind legs. The largest sauropod may have weighed more than forty tons. It made more sense that they would live their wholes lives in the water, where they could move effortlessly. How would they support their own enormous weight on land? With detectivelike persistency, Sereno studied the way an elephant distributed its weight, and the thickness of its front and back legs, concluding that it was possible for this mammoth dinosaur to rear on its hind legs.

Sereno and his teams have made many other dinosaur discoveries. In 1993, during the same expedition in Niger that found *Jobaria,* Sereno's team found *Afrovenator abakensis*, the "African hunter from In Abaka." This carnivore was twenty-seven feet in length and 135 million years old. *Suchomimus tenerensis*, the "crocodile mimic" was

Carcharodontosaurus saharicus skull photographed with a human skull (*Courtesy of P. Sereno*)

discovered in Niger in 1997. This animal was thirty-six feet long, had one-foot-long thumb claws, and dined on fish.

PALEONTOLOGY PITFALLS

Several new species of dinosaurs are found each year. While much of the time there is a race between scientists to find and report on new discoveries, paleontologists are also finding themselves in competition with amateur dinosaur hunters. Many fossils, found by such hunters, are sold on the black market, and they end up in private collections, never to be seen again. One of Sereno's goals in Niger is to find fossils before they are stripped from their beds, where they have remained largely undisturbed until the past few years. So who actually owns the fossils that Sereno finds? Sereno feels they belong to the people of the country in which they are found, and he ultimately intends to return the fossils to their museum collections. He is trying, however, to arrange for some permanent loans of bones and to help build facilities to exhibit dinosaur remains in the countries of their origin.

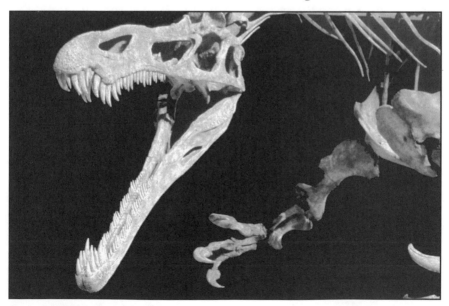

Suchominmus tenerensis (Courtesy of P. Sereno)

In 1998, Sereno and his wife, Gabrielle Lyon, founded Project Exploration. The goal of this nonprofit organization is to educate the public, especially young people, about science. According to their Web site (www.projectexploration.org), Sereno and Lyon hope to reduce the distance between science and the public; involve students and teachers directly with scientists and their research; provide innovative, hands-on experiences to city kids; and inspire segments of student populations that are under-represented in paleontology and the natural science professions. "I think without taking that extra dimension and going to make the stuff that you're discovering meaningful to somebody else, I wouldn't be here in my office," he said. "Because as much as I like the discovery, I can't just sit in the ivory tower and not communicate with what's going on around me. And as a result, I had some real questions about what I was going to be doing, because as fun and exciting as your discoveries are, sometimes you wonder how they relate to the rest of the world."

Project Exploration recruits kids each year to learning about paleontology—the Junior Paleontologist's Program. There is specially designed curricular materials for teachers to use, detailed information on the Project Exploration Web site, and public exhibitions staffed by the Dinosaur Giants Team at Navy Pier in Chicago. The Dinosaur Giants are high school students from Chicago public schools who have undergone seven hours of special training so that they can inform the public about *Jobaria*, fossil hunting, dinosaur history, and other topics relating to paleontology. The students then spend several hours a week interacting with the public. They reflect and evaluate what they have accomplished and often receive community service credit. Some are junior paleontologists that have participated in an actual dig in the western United States.

One time, when an adult asked Sereno a couple questions about dinosaurs, the process of answering the questions allowed him to articulate children's fascination with dinosaurs. "What does finding a new dinosaur do for us?" the adult asked. "What is the use?"

"You know, I have spoken to a half million kids, and no kid has ever asked me that question," Sereno said. "Further, I don't know of any kid that has even contemplated that question. How could that be? I think that the reason why dinosaurs are so interesting to us all, particularly the kids, is because dinosaurs, and their skeletons in particular, force us to imagine, and it is a fundamental human capacity to be born with a great passion for imagination. When you walk in front of the *Jobaria* skeleton, you can only imagine what the animal was like. You really are forced to imagine. You look up, and you see a person's face, and what literally happens is that they get this look of awe on their face. You just wonder what is going through their brain. They are imagining what it would have been like to have been there when this animal was alive. That is an incredible human capacity. . . . Normally people say that kids are interested in it because they [dinosaurs] are extinct, they are reptilian, and they are big. Yes, and that is only a part of the answer, and the more general answer, they like them for all those reasons, but all those reasons feed into the necessity to imagine. . . . But again, I think the reason is because dinosaurs encourage us to imagine, and that is a fundamental human thing. Kids take it for granted, and adults, after a dulling life of twenty, thirty, or forty years, sometimes forget."

Sereno has not lost his childlike awe and imagination. He's also been able to harness an impressive amount of stamina. If there's anything he's known for, it's making discoveries. In his early forties, Sereno has made hundreds of significant finds in countries all over the world, including the identification of more than a dozen new dinosaurs.

He has been honored with numerous awards including: Outstanding Young Alumni Award (1991) from his alma mater, NIU; Teacher of the Year (1992) by the *Chicago Tribune;* 100 Best People in the World (1997) by *Esquire* magazine; Walker Prize (1997) from the Museum of Science, Boston Society of Natural Science; and the University Medal for Excellence (1999) from Columbia University. Many of his awards reflect not only the respect he has earned at a relatively young age from the scientific community, but also his commitment to sharing his knowledge of paleontology with the general public, especially children.

Sereno offered these words of inspiration: "My advice to students is to realize that life is so short that you will never realize all of the talents that you have hidden away, so make sure you let yourself discover a few of them. My advice for teachers or parents is to make sure that each child has his/her day in the sun, one chance to shine, to realize their worth, to be amazed at what they can achieve. It might only take just once. There were a few very important moments like that in my early experience in school, an experience that might otherwise be described as challenged." Paul Sereno, dinosaur detective, is also one very wise man.

Grace J. Yang

CHAPTER 10

GEORGE SMOOT

INDIANA JONES OF SCIENCE

STEPHANIE R. ALLEWALT

Y ou could say he is the Indiana Jones of science. Just like this fictional archaeologist, astrophysicist George Smoot traveled to the badlands and the unexplored jungles, searching for something much older than the oldest dinosaur bones. The key to his search lay six hundred miles above the Earth in a satellite called the Cosmic Background Explorer (COBE). In his 1993 book called *Wrinkles in Time*, written with Keay Davidson, Smoot described what he was seeking. He was searching for "the wrinkles in time, those distant echoes of the early formation of the galaxies."[1] He was trying to determine how the universe was born, and he and his research team found fluctuations in microwave radiation in the cosmos, which supports the big bang theory of the origin of our universe.

L'ATOME PRIMITIF

So what are these wrinkles in time, which outdate even the oldest bones? They are what scientists call cosmic background radiation (CMB). In the late 1920s, the French priest and astronomer Georges-Henri Lemaitre reported a new possibility for the birth of the universe. He named it the "hypothese de l'atome primitif," which translates to "hypothesis of the primordial atom." Today it has been appropriately renamed the big bang theory. Within this hypothesis, Lemaitre stated that the entire universe—the galaxies, planets, and stars—all originated from a single atom of energy. The atom was thought to have basically exploded into the huge universe in which we now live. In Lemaitre's model, the explosion of the "atom" created the space and time that appear in the equations of relativity. Both scientists and nonscientists were doubtful of this theory, but those who thought it possible continued to do research.

Shortly before Lemaitre's idea, Edwin Hubble, an American astronomer, had published the results of his careful study of distant galaxies. Hubble found that the more distant galaxies were moving away from us with a higher velocity than the nearer galaxies. He came to the astonishing conclusion that the universe ,with all its constituent galaxies, stars, and solar systems, was expanding. (The Hubble Space Telescope is named after Edwin Hubble and discussed in chapter 4, which profiles Story Musgrave.)

Hubble's law indicated that all the matter in the universe was expanding from an original point, just as if an explosion had occurred about fifteen billion years ago. But it was not, as pointed out by Lemaitre and others, matter rushing out into space—it was space that was expanding. The Hubble Law seemed to imply that the entire universe started out from some atomic or subatomic size (or from zero) and had been expanding for the past 15 billion years. The Lemaitre big bang theory fit the Hubble measurements very well.

Experimental evidence that the universe started from a very hot, very small state is very strong. But any detailed description of the beginning can only be speculative. One popular version of the big bang idea is that the universe was born in some sort of transition from a state of "false vacuum," which contained a great deal of energy, to a ground state with the release of the energy budget of the universe. The nascent universe was either a point with no dimensions or, more likely, a tiny bubble of volume far smaller than the radius of a proton. The energy density was huge and energy quickly converted to matter and matter back to energy in this boiling, bubbling, foaming soup of primary particles, such as quarks and leptons. The bubble rapidly expanded, creating, as it did, space and time. The early universe had no center and no boundaries, like the surface of an expanding sphere.

Earlier versions of the not-yet named big bang theory led to a huge number of questions, for example: (1) What is the origin of the energy contained in the billions of suns in each of the billions of galaxies? and (2) How do the chemical elements get formed?

George Gamow, a groundbreaking Russian-born astrophysicist, found the big bang hypothesis to be very intriguing. In the late 1940s, he decided to investigate the material Lemaitre called the primordial atom. Gamow proposed a model of the origin of the big bang in agreement with data on the behavior of atomic nuclei being studied in nuclear physics laboratories.

The nucleus of all atoms consists of two types of particles: protons (positively charged) and neutrons (neutral). The number of protons determines the chemical element: one proton is hydrogen, two protons is helium, three protons is lithium, and so on, up to about one hundred protons. One can add a neutron to the proton in hydrogen to make deuterium, a form (or isotope) of hydrogen. Adding two neutrons makes tritium. As the number of protons goes up, one needs more and more neutrons to make stable nuclei.

So now comes Gamow's model. In the beginning, he postulated, the universe began as a very hot gas of neutrons. He called this "ylem," for "primordial matter." The neutrons, when free, soon decay into protons and electrons (neutrinos are also emitted). In this very hot, dense cloud, protons and neutrons could combine to eventually form all the elements.

When the calculations were done carefully, there were many

problems. For two protons to fuse, Coulomb's law requires that they collide with enough energy to overcome the repulsion of like charges. Thus, the very early universe would have to be enormously hot—vastly hotter than the interior of suns. However, as it expanded it cooled or the elements would not be able to have been formed. Working with colleagues Robert Herman and Ralph Alpher, Gamow had some important successes.

The original explosion that created the universe, with all of its mass and energy, was accompanied by an incandescent flash of light. If the universe had indeed started in this way, in a big bang, then after billions of years of expanding and cooling, the universe would still contain evidence of the first flash. This evidence would take the form of a greatly diminished density of radiation, at much longer than average wavelength.

Gamow's group noted that the universe would also cool rapidly as the particles moved outward with the expanding space. They estimated that the initial temperature of billions of degrees would have cooled to about 5° today—this is on the absolute (Kelvin) scale, 5°K above zero or minus 269 degrees on the centigrade (°C) scale. The Gamow group then predicted that the universe would be filled with radiation at wavelengths of about a few centimeters, that is, in the microwave region. This radiation acquired a name: the cosmic microwave background radiation (CMB).

All hot objects radiate. Watch your toaster wire heat up when you depress the lever. Feel the heat before it turns red. Radiation energy is measured by wavelength. The higher the energy, the shorter the wavelength. Visible light covers a narrow band of wavelength from about 4×10^{-7} meters (m) to 8×10^{-7}m. The original flash had wavelengths that were billions of times shorter than visible light (they are called gamma rays). That is long wavelength, heat or infrared radiation. Then as the temperature rises, one sees light, red at first. This is about 10^{-6}m in wavelength. If you could heat the wire way beyond toaster temperatures, the radiation would add the shorter wavelengths, blue and violet, to the red to make it look white-hot.

Thus, all radiation can be connected to a temperature. A heated object radiates a band of wavelengths, but with practice, one can look at the band of wavelengths and estimate the temperature of the body. There are easy to use instruments that will do it for you—point the instrument at an object and read off the temperature, e.g. 275°C (hot). (The toaster, incidentally, goes to about 500°C.) The instrument that measures temperature of radiation is called a radiometer.

The CMB, predicted by the Gamow group as a necessary consequence of the big bang hypothesis, was discovered in 1965 by two scientists at AT&T's Bell Telephone Laboratories in New Jersey. They were assigned the task of finding out why transcontinental radio signals always had a hum that no amount of fiddling could eliminate. There followed an enormous effort to locate sources of noise, specifically connected with a horn radio antenna being operated at the Bell Laboratories in New Jersey. Eventually, all the evidence pointed to the sky; all parts of it were radiating a microwave "noise" at about 5 cm wavelength. The discovery that the hum (CMB) was an essential part of the universe won the Nobel Prize for Arno Penzias and Robert Wilson in 1978. Using a radiometer, they determined the temperature of the CMB to be 2.75 degrees on the absolute scale, in remarkable agreement with Gamow's crude estimate made thirty years earlier.

The big bang hypothesis does not stop there. Scientists realized that all of the matter in the universe, initially smooth, was not distributed evenly throughout the universe. Matter clusters into galaxies, then stars. Here and there, giant clouds of dust and gases swirl. Measuring the temperature of the background radiation should show changes correlating with the eventual clustering of matter, if the big bang hypothesis was correct. However, when they looked at the temperature of the radiation, it appeared to be the same everywhere. How could the temperature of all the radiation be the same if the matter in the universe was not uniform? Something had to be wrong. Either the temperature was not being measured sufficiently precisely, or the entire hypothesis was incorrect.

Smoot believed that the temperature was not being measured with sensitivity to detect tiny fluctuations. So he joined forces with other scientists to build a machine that would measure accurately the temperature of the radiation. He was looking for temperature "wrinkles" in the sea of background radiation. This would provide evidence of seeds that would grow to become the stars and galaxies of our universe.

After a twenty-year quest to achieve his ambitious goal, Smoot succeeded. In 1994, he was named one of eight winners of the 1994 E. O. Lawrence Award by then U.S. Secretary of Energy Hazel O'Leary. He won in the category of physics and was cited "for his leadership in the remarkably accurate measurements of the variations in the cosmic microwave background radiation, thus clarifying our understanding of the early history of the universe, the distribution of dark matter, and the formation of stars and galaxies." Stephen Hawking called it, "the most important discovery of the century, if not of all time."[2]

AN EARLY INTEREST IN SCIENCE

Smoot's interest in science began quite early, thanks in great part to his parents. His father, a hydrologist, and his mother, a science teacher and later a principal, nurtured Smoot's passion for science and math. He describes it this way:, "I was interested in a lot of different things. And a part of it came from my parents. Both my parents had interests in mathematics, science, and engineering, and how the world works and so forth. . . . I have noticed that there is a certain set of people who have to know how things work in either one of two ways. Either they want to take things apart, see what makes them tick, or they want to understand the world, and the universe and how it ticks. . . . There's different levels, depending on what kind of interest you have. And so I think there is a part that's personality type, whether it's inherited or whether it comes from your environment. It's clear to me that some of it must be inherited, or just some form of genetics, because they're people who come from families that have no technical or scientific interest, and they're fascinated by the way the world works. And then there are some people who just want the world to be orderly and sensible. They're looking for meaning and reason and so forth. And so, I just remember as a kid how incredible and wonderful the whole world seemed. One of the things is that I had a lot of access to the outdoors and I could remember there was sort of like these woods between my house and my best friend's house and we would go over, and this is before even first grade, we'd go out into the woods and we would look at the little pool of water and watch the little insects and the fish swim around in it. And all this kind of stuff. And it's all fairly amazing, right? The world is very complicated and very beautiful and there's all these wonderful things going on."

Smoot, as a child, learned that the process of finding out about this world was called science, and he continued to pursue scientific learning throughout his childhood. He enjoyed books by Arthur C. Clarke, a prominent science fiction writer. He also took an interest in football and track during junior high, but chose to concentrate on academics during high school.

Since early childhood, Smoot was fascinated by the night sky, especially the moon. From this, Smoot realized that the world around him was much bigger than he imagined. But what questions occur to Smoot now when he looks up at the night sky? "For me? First how dark it is. It didn't used to be. It used to be, where are the stars? And you think what star is that? And what star is it? And that kind of stuff. Now, if you remember reading about Olbers's Paradox,[3] if there were infinitely many stars, infinitely far, forever, in the night sky, everywhere you look, there should be a star. And so the fact that it's dark means that the universe is changing and evolving, even though on our lifetime scale it's not changing significantly. And so, I get impressed by the darkness and the fact that there are so many things in between. And stars are things of beauty. They're like little jewels put on top of the really beautiful thing, which is the universe, itself."

Smoot pursued his love of science at the Massachusetts Institute of Technology (MIT). Although he enrolled in a premedicine program, he soon realized his heart was with mathematics and physics. Smoot earned a bachelor of science degree in these two subjects in 1966, and a Ph.D. in physics in 1970, all from MIT. The amount of interest in this frontier of science was growing rapidly, so it was to Smoot's advantage to earn an advanced degree. His work focused on the field of high-energy particle physics.

After obtaining his Ph.D., Smoot returned to MIT to work as a research physicist. The field of particle physics was getting very crowded and Smoot simply enjoyed cosmology, the study of the universe, more—so he decided to make a switch. To continue studying cosmology, Smoot left MIT for the University of California at Berkeley. He joined Charles Orth, Luis Alvarez (the 1968 Nobel Prize winner in physics), Andrew Buffington, and other scientists to work on what was called the High-Altitude Particle Physics Experiment (or HAPPE) project. Their goal was to design an experiment that would find evidence to support the big bang theory. One of the puzzles of the time was the lack of experimental data for antimatter. So they designed a machine that they hoped would have the ability to see antimatter.

HAPPE SEARCHES FOR ANTIMATTER

The big bang theory had proposed that matter (planets and stars) had formed from energy. This is the significance of Einstein's famous equation, $E=mc^2$ (Energy = mass times constant squared). If this was correct, then an equal amount of antimatter also had to be created at the same time. Energy, in the form of radiation would be converted to equal amounts of matter and antimatter. A piece of paper made of antimatter looks just like a normal piece of paper, just as a pencil made of antimatter would resemble a normal pencil. But if a piece of paper made of antimatter happened to touch a normal pencil, they both would explode. "For, when matter and antimatter meet," Smoot explains in his book, "each annihilates the other— mass is completely converted to energy in an incredibly violent explosion."[4] Fortunately, the amount of antimatter in our atmosphere is so tiny that explosions like that don't occur very often.

HAPPE's research was structured around this antimatter. The team journeyed to isolated places such as Palestine, Texas, and

Aberdeen, South Dakota, so they could perform balloon launches to study the sky from higher altitudes. There the land was less populated by humans, which allowed their study to be free of pollution and other distractions. The balloons they launched carried spark chambers clamped between the poles of a magnet. They were able to detect possible antimatter entering the Earth's atmosphere from outer space because the negatively charged antimatter would be deflected oppositely to the positively charged protons. Also, antiprotons would be indicated by a burst of energy when they would meet and annihilate a proton. Although the HAPPE team detected several sparks, they were unable to prove that any of them were the result of matter-antimatter interaction. However, the American Institute of Physics recognized the series of flights as one of the world's twelve outstanding physics experiments of 1973. We should note that the failure to observe antimatter turned out to have a surprising cause, which became another strong support for the big bang hypothesis.

DOES THE MILKY WAY GALAXY MOVE?

Although HAPPE's research on antimatter had ended, Smoot found himself preoccupied with curiosity about CMB, the remnant of intense heat from the big bang. When the possibility of using a differential microwave radiometer (DMR), to measure temperature became more realistic, Smoot and Alvarez were enthralled. The differential radiometer would not measure the actual temperature of the radiation, but it had the ability to measure very precisely the difference in temperature between two different places in the radiation (the reason it is called "differential"). One can point it at two sources of radiation and the instrument would compare the temperatures. For example, it wouldn't read the temperature of the top of the mountain as 39°C and the temperature at the bottom as 23°C; it would read the difference in temperature between the top and the bottom of the mountain (16°C). Studying background radiation would not only increase support for the big bang theory, but it also would help determine whether the universe was rotating or simply expanding. Unfortunately, this instrument required a much higher altitude in order to escape microwave interference from water vapor and other atmospheric conditions. The scientists had to place the DMR on a plane. Several planes were considered for this task, but because of the weight and dimensions of the instrument, all were ruled out except one—the U-2 spy plane.

To determine the motion of the Milky Way galaxy, DMR is attached to a plane, which is attached to the Earth, which is attached to the solar system, which is attached to the galaxy. The galaxy is moving (swimming) in the CMB. The radiation ahead of the motion will appear to have a (slightly) shorter wavelength since the waves crowd into the approaching radiometer. This is an example of the Doppler effect. This shows up as a warmer temperature compared to the radiation behind the motion. Some algebra converts the temperature change into a speed.

After several flights, the U-2 returned the DMR with an incredible amount of information, including facts about both the speed of the Milky Way galaxy. If the DMR had examined everything correctly, then they had recorded that the universe was expanding with uniform speed in all directions and that our galaxy was traveling at about six hundred kilometers per second, that is, over a million miles an hour. Both are relative to the *cosmic rest force*. This is defined as the force in which the CMB radiation is isotopic, that is, the same in all directions. Astronomers were shocked at this result. Smoot had set out to measure the motion of the sun relative to the galaxy. What he discovered was an unexpected motion of the galaxy at this huge velocity. This was totally unexpected. Critics claimed that the radiometer's results could have been altered by some atmospheric effect. Those who were doubtful stated that if the team took their DMR to the Southern Hemisphere and the outcome was the same, they would then believe the results.

So a special U-2 team was flown to Peru, along with the special equipment required for the plane itself. The experiments took much longer than originally expected, but at the end of the testing, the DMR showed proof that what they had seen in the Northern

Hemisphere was a reality. Not only was the universe expanding uniformly with high precision in all directions, but our Milky Way galaxy was moving through the CMB "sea" at 600 kilometers per second. This speed was much faster than expected, indicating that we are being pulled through space by the gravity of some large and distant supercluster of galaxies. Galaxies, until this data, were believed to be fairly evenly spread out in the universe. A celestial body so large that it could exert such a force on our galaxy had not been thought to exist. The universe was proving to be very different from what was commonly believed to be the case.

COBE GOES INTO SPACE

While Smoot was engaged in work on launching the DMR via a U-2 spy plane, NASA announced, in 1974, that they were soliciting proposals for astronomy experiments to be carried out aboard satellites. The ability to search for background radiation in space was superior to using balloons and the U-2 spy plane. The books Smoot had read by Arthur C. Clarke proposed the development of a space program, and he had liked the concept. Smoot had hoped to work with NASA since the beginning of his career, so this seemed like the perfect opportunity for him.

Using equipment in space would eliminate the variables of atmospheric noise and bad weather, and would provide Smoot with a longer time for observation and therefore more significant data to analyze. He and Berkeley colleagues began to draft an application composed of two experiments. The first experiment would map the cosmic background radiation to look for evidence of temperature variations or wrinkles. The second one would measure the spectrum of the cosmic background radiation to confirm it was a remnant of the big bang.

Why would NASA encourage and Smoot enthusiastically jump on the bandwagon of spending a major part of his professional life doing more studies of the CMB? This is the reason: Gamow's hot neutron gas had given way in the 1950s and 1960s to a theory of a hot, dense "soup" of primordial particles and radiation. As the universe expanded, the "soup" density decreased, and its temperature began falling. But it was a smooth, homogenized distribution. Somewhere between this early phase and the universe today, matter clumped into galaxies, gas and dust clouds, suns and solar systems. How did this happen?

One theory is that a random clustering of matter could take place by chance. Then this small cluster, by gravitational attraction, would draw more matter toward it. Eventually we would have the makings of a galaxy. Detailed calculations indicated that this theory of clustering of mass would take far too long. It just didn't work. The conclusion was that some kind of "seeds" born in the earliest soup phase were key to the formation of galaxies. Seeds were thought to speed up the gravitational build up of clumps of matter into galaxies. These seeds would show up as places in the radiation where higher than normal density and therefore higher than normal temperatures would appear.

Early studies by Smoot in the U-2 plane and by other astrophysicists in balloons indicated that the temperatures were *very* uniform. No ripples in the constant temperature had been seen and if there were such seed-induced temperature bumps, they were less than one ten thousandths of a degree higher than the normal temperature. Yet they must exist, even if we didn't understand exactly what the seeds were.

So the stakes were high—and Smoot jumped at the opportunity to search for these ripples—or, "wrinkles," in Smoot talk. Little did Smoot suspect that the 1974 call for proposals by NASA would not lead to results until 1990.

The measurement of the spectrum of CMB was another goal of Smoot and his colleagues' proposal to NASA. We noted that all objects emit radiation. They also absorb radiation hitting them. If they are hotter than their surroundings, they tend to emit more than they absorb. Scientists defined a "black body" as an object that absorbs 100 percent of the energy incident upon it. We know that a blue object reflects blue light, but absorbs all other colors. A black car in the sunlight gets very hot to the touch because it absorbs all the sunlight. The full name of the radiation we have been discussing is electromagnetic radiation, which includes microwaves, infrared, visible, ultraviolet, X-rays, gamma rays—listed in order of decreasing wavelength.

At any temperature, a black body would emit different quantities of radiation at each wavelength. This is called the spectrum of radiation. The big bang theory predicted that the CMB should have a blackbody spectrum.

Smoot's proposal was not accepted outright. NASA received over 120 proposals, so they instructed several research groups to work together to evaluate and refine their ideas for observing cosmic temperatures. Smoot worked with Sam Gulkis, John Mather, Mike Hauser, Rainer Weiss, Dave Wilkinson, and all the people in their teams. As Smoot made connections with new people, he hoped to learn an efficient way to convert a balloon-borne instrument to a space-borne one. After much research, Smoot and his collaborators wrote a proposal for a mission named COBE, a nickname for the Cosmic Background Explorer. COBE would carry three instruments: a DMR similar to the ones on the U-2 flights but more sensitive, a far infrared (low frequency) absolute spectrophotometer (FIRAS), and an instrument named the diffuse infrared background experiment (DIRBE). FIRAS would let the scientists know whether the radiation had been created by the big bang or something else, and DIRBE would search for cosmic infrared background, which is the glow from the earliest luminous objects such as primordial stars and galaxies. Smoot would lead the group charged with perfecting DMR for space; Mather was principal investigator of FIRAS and Hauser headed DIRBE. When their design was finished, they had to convince NASA that they knew exactly what to do and how to do it. This took six years to accomplish.

In order to prove that the DMR would work in space, Smoot reluctantly had to return to balloon flight. He performed two experiments in the Northern Hemisphere and two in the Southern Hemisphere. This time the balloon flights were used to find if there was a dipole or a quadrupole effect in the CBR. A dipole is two poles—the warmest and the coolest parts of our sky—which is what they saw in their first U-2 flights. It implied that the Milky Way galaxy was moving toward a supercluster of galaxies. Rumors of other groups detecting a quadrupole anisotropy had been circulating in the scientific community, but weren't proven. The quadrupole shows two warm spots and two cool spots in the CMB and, in fact, would be evidence of the kind of deviation from perfect smoothness expected if the big bang had planted the seeds from which future galaxies, clusters, and voids would form. However, there were more mundane things that could produce quadrupole inhomogeniety. More tests were needed.

The two tests in the Northern Hemisphere resulted in the same findings as the previous tests in that hemisphere: a simple dipole effect. They could not be sure of the results, however, without further testing in the Southern Hemisphere; so they traveled to Brazil. Experiments went well until they were ready to retrieve the balloon from the atmosphere. They pressed the button that should have triggered the drop, but nothing happened. They pressed again and again, and nothing happened. Every attempt to return the balloon to the base failed, leaving them with inconclusive data.

In 1984, two years after the aborted experiments, Smoot received a call from Brazilian authorities informing him that the balloon had been found. A poacher, hunting in a forest preserve, came upon the unbelievable sight of shiny objects clumped together in what he called some sort of strange contraption. He had no idea from where it could have come; for all he knew it could have even been an unidentified flying object (UFO). Because he was removing forbidden plants from the forest preserve, he decided it would be better not to inform anyone about what he had seen. Later in a local bar, however, he told his story of how he saw this conglomeration of metal and scrap, like nothing he had ever seen. Before he could finish his story, there were townspeople searching for Smoot's balloon and its valuable equipment.

When it was found, the townspeople tore it apart, taking various components that they thought would be useful to them. Two of Smoot's colleagues, Phillip Lupin (then a postdoctoral fellow with Smoot) and Thyrso Villela (one of Smoot's graduate students), reached the area and found that their instrument was in pieces scattered all over the town. They drove to homes and apartments and successfully negotiated the recovery of almost everything. The poacher, however, was still holding one of the most important pieces at his home—the gondola containing their data tape. After much debate and a heated argument with the poacher, the team finally obtained the rest of the equipment. Making the trek to recover the balloon worthwhile; they discovered that 98 percent of the data was still useful. The results, however, still failed to confirm a quadrupole effect; their experiment was considered to be successful, anyway.

DISASTER STRIKES THE SPACE PROGRAM

In the NASA application, Smoot and his collaborators had suggested placing COBE on a Delta rocket, but NASA was in the process of shifting experiments to the manned space shuttles. Adjustments began on COBE in January 1986, and Smoot received an estimated launch date—late 1988. On the January 28, 1986, *Challenger* was preparing to launch from the Kennedy Space Center in Florida, carrying seven crew members, one of them a schoolteacher. At around 11:30 A.M., less than sixty seconds after the initial launch, a puffy orange and red ball appeared in the sky. *Challenger* had exploded. (The *Challenger* explosion and the U.S. space program are discussed further in the profile of Sally Ride in chapter 6.) It was a terrible tragedy for the astronauts, their families, and for science. Smoot was in his office when he heard the news. He and his coworkers grieved for the astronauts. Soon they began to realize the effect this would have on their own project. NASA would be experiencing a great delay on future shuttles until an investigation was concluded. Smoot had no clue how long the delay would be, so he and his team members turned to other possibilities. The two types of unmanned rockets that were seriously under consideration, the *Delta* and the *Titan*, both were scheduled for launches not too long after the *Challenger* accident. Unfortunately, the *Titan*—which launched from Vandenberg Air Force Base in California—mysteriously exploded, and the *Delta* rocket lost power in its main engine seventy seconds into flight. NASA was fearful that the *Delta* rocket would fall to Earth somewhere unexpected, so they destroyed it in flight.

At this point, America was becoming extremely weary of the space program, and the team began to consider the French *Ariane* rocket. They had two or three discussions with the French, but when NASA learned that Smoot and his team were considering using foreign rockets, one team member stated, "They ordered us to cease and desist—and threatened us with bodily harm if we didn't." Smoot wrote, "U.S. pride was at stake."[5] Although NASA did not make any promises to Smoot's team, their chances increased for the use of a U.S. rocket.

In late 1986, the COBE project recommended that NASA return to the idea of using the *Delta* rocket to launch COBE. Aside from the previous incident, *Delta* had a good flying record. Smoot's team fought for use of one of the last *Delta* rockets made, and finally, they were successful. The next challenge for the team was to cut COBE's size and weight in half. On October 1, 1986, the team received word from NASA that the launch date was set for early in 1989. With only two years to finish the design modifications for COBE, the team was under quite a bit of pressure and an enormous design task for the engineers of the Goddard Spaceflight Center. Challenging as it was, COBE was completed in time for launch. The entire effort had involved more than 1,500 people and thirty-two companies and organizations. The project consumed many years of effort and cost some $160 million, according to Smoot.

COBE IS LAUNCHED

On November 18, 1989, from Vandenburg Air Force Base in California, the COBE satellite was propelled to space at dawn from a perfect launch. That evening, Smoot traveled to Goddard's instrument operations room. There he waited to see space through COBE's eyes.

Just as the team had hoped, a fuzzy map of radiation was beginning to be assembled. Although the data were not clear, they were extremely excited about the possibilities unfolding before them.

While the data from COBE was being collected and studied for evidence of seeds, Mather and his colleagues had an instant success with the FIRAS detector that was designed to compare the spectrum of microwave background radiation with that of the theoretical blackbody spectrum expected from the big bang. In just nine minutes of data taking, the ultrasensitive FIRAS detector had generated the most accurate CMB spectrum ever seen. It was a blackbody spectrum that agreed exactly with the big bang prediction. When the FIRAS principal investigator, Mather, presented the results at a scientific meeting, the audience burst into a loud standing ovation. This was one of the objectives of the COBE satellite experiment, and it took sixteen years from the NASA announcement in 1974 to the acquisition of this data in 1990.

However, if there are ten good arguments in favor of a theory and one piece of valid evidence that it is wrong, one must conclude that it is wrong. And the early COBE results showed no evidence of the wrinkles in the smooth temperature distribution of CMB. Smoot knew that the sought after effects would be small, perhaps deviations from normal temperatures of only 100,000ths of a degree. This would take lots of data, so he agonized over whether some background effect would simulate the effect of wrinkles induced by the seeds of the big bang. By late 1991, Smoot's data was beginning to show significant deviations from smooth, in terms of quadrupole and even more complex deviations (called octupoles, decapoles, and higher distortions).

The data was getting convincing enough to cause members of the team to urge a public announcement and publication. Smoot was still cautious and urged one more test that could rule out a potential source of distortion that had nothing to do with big bang wrinkles, namely, radio interference from our own galaxy. Whereas much was known about this, Smoot's effect at a part in 100,000, was so small that he felt they had to completely rule out the possibility of interference. How to do this? Galaxy emissions had been studied carefully in the Northern Hemisphere, but not very carefully in the far Southern Hemisphere. This had to be done, but it took the group to Antarctica to make these measurements.

ANTARCTICA—
THE NEXT BEST THING TO OUTER SPACE?

Smoot and his team turned to Antarctica, where the climate—cold and dry, plus lack of pollution—would provide a way to collect data on radio emission from the galaxy with little interference. Smoot, in *Wrinkles in Time*, describes Antarctica as "the next best thing to outer space," but also as "an awful place to do science."[6] The first day in particular was most difficult for the team. Not only was the temperature extremely low, but the altitude was so high that scientists needed to take it easy and drink plenty of water to prevent dizziness and illness. The team started setting up right away, but quickly ran behind schedule. Critical parts to the satellite dish were missing, but fortunately, the parts eventually arrived.

Putting the dish together, making it functional, and collecting data proved quite challenging. Hydraulic fluid froze in the sub-zero temperature. The next plan for changing the tilt of the dish required that modification be made to a hinge. A crew member wanted to haul it inside and make changes, but Smoot knew they were on a tight schedule and thought placing it inside would take too much time. He took a hacksaw and went out into the forty-degree-below-zero climate with strong winds blowing. As Smoot sawed like crazy, he failed to notice how hard he had been breathing. He inhaled so much cold air, Smoot had a medical collapse and had to remain indoors for the next few days to recover from a fever.

Finally, they were able to begin to collect data, only to be confounded by three satellites emitting signals at three of the five frequencies that they were listening to. They were able to collect data for about three weeks, spending about a month in Antarctica. The results were very encouraging. Radio emissions from the galaxy would not be a crucial background.

THE ANNOUNCEMENT

After spending two years organizing everything, analyzing the data and all its possible errors, Smoot was ready to go public. The annual meeting of the American Physical Society was set for April 23, 1992, and Smoot and three DMR team members were scheduled to speak. This was the day they all had dreamed of since the very beginning—the day they could announce to the public that they had discovered wrinkles in time: tiny variations in temperature that indicated the origin of the universe.

Smoot had only twelve minutes to speak about their findings. He went through the process in steps to explain each obstacle they had to go through. On the third step he announced, "We have a quadrupole."[7] This was important because it was the announcement most people had been waiting for; it meant there were fluctuations caused by what they hoped were wrinkles. Smoot continued, astounding the audience by the more complex deviations from smoothness. He revealed that they had detected "a spectrum of wrinkles in all sizes."[8] The discovery stunned the public. Smoot tried to articulate the importance of the discovery by commenting at a press conference, "If you're religious, it's like seeing God."[9]

COBE completed a survey of the sky every six months, traveling 16,800 miles per hour in an orbit 560 miles above Earth. It continued to provide data until 1994 when it was abandoned in favor of other activities. Smoot commutes between his homes in Berkeley, California, and Greenbelt, Maryland, and continues to work with NASA while teaching at Berkeley. Smoot is fascinated with exploration, and continues to do it on a daily basis. His exploration with COBE will have a lasting effect on the world of science.

What would Smoot like children to know about astronomy? "First, the children are the future. I think children already know, somehow, that the future of mankind has to do with space. If you look at it, it's very natural. Think of it as *Star Wars*, it just seemed to be instinctive in children to recognize, at a very early age, that space and the understanding of space, and so forth, is part of their future. They [children] confuse that with the adventure of some of the programs and so forth, but there is an innate fascination with it.

If you look at it, it's very clear there are some topics that are very popular. One of those is dinosaurs (I'm not sure why)—it's clearly genetic and other reasons. But everyone from children through grandparents, all love dinosaurs (see chapter 9 for why Paul Sereno thinks children like dinosaurs). They also all love astronomy and astrophysics and its easy to understand why—it's awe inspiring to realize that there are billions of stars. First, it's so huge. The entire sky is full of stars, unlike the Sun and then when you look at them, some are much bigger then the Sun and some are much smaller. There's this tremendous diversity and range of stars. And the stars themselves are tiny compared to the fact that they're just clustered together in galaxies. And when you look with the big telescope, every time you see a star you can see a galaxy behind it, which is a hundred million more stars out there. And you start looking at it, you start realizing how many wonderful and exciting and unusual things are out there—things left to be discovered and things that will just fill you with wonder.

"How can you look at the night sky and not be amazed? And I think that almost all children know that. And the thing—once they realize that—the thing that I want them to understand is that somehow or another the universe is orderly and relatively simple and it's possible for a human being to understand it, at least so far in any event, and so it's possible for them to learn about the stars and some of them to go on and even contribute and discover new things. There is still a lot of stuff left to be done, to understand, but they're capable of doing it."

Stephanie R. Allewalt

CHAPTER 11

CHARLES TOWNES

LASER LEGEND

DOUGLAS A. HEINTZ

Imagine that you are at the grocery store, and you are purchasing groceries and household items for the week. You need cereal, milk, eggs, bread, paper towels, toilet paper, hamburger meat, buns, ketchup, onion, cheese, broccoli, chicken, pasta, fish, potatoes, rice, peas, corn, green beans, and ice cream. You also need some pens, pencils, and laundry detergent. The list grows longer. You put all of the items into the grocery cart and proceed to the checkout line. A large family, also shopping for the week, is ahead of you, and all the lanes are full. How do you expediently purchase your groceries and get home without your ice cream melting? Are you sure that you are being charged the correct amount of money for everything you've purchased? Today, because of Dr. Charles Hard Townes, you are assisted in a swift departure from the grocery store and assured (barring human error) that the money you paid for your purchases was correct. Townes, with his graduate students, developed the basic ideas behind the laser (light amplification by stimulated emission of radiation), which is used by cashiers in many types of stores across the nation and much of the world. The laser permits bar codes, found on virtually all items for sale in most stores, to be read and rapidly translated by computers into the purchase price. The bar code also offers a lot of other information about store items, and the laser reads this information as well. But bar codes, as practical as they are, make up a small part of the usefulness of the laser.

A VERY USEFUL INVENTION

The laser may well be one of the most useful inventions in history. Its small, focused beam of red light is seen in thousands of products. Lasers are used in compact disc (CD) players and in surveying; their strength is so remarkable that they can illuminate a small circle as far away as the Moon. By timing laser pulses reflected from the Moon, the distance from the Earth to the Moon was determined to within an inch. The laser is so precise that it is used in eye surgery and as a tool to etch reproducible metal plates. The military is currently working with powerful lasers equivalent to the science fiction version of the death ray. One of the most interesting applications of lasers is in scientific research. Lasers make possible for new research, the study of atoms and molecules, of fusion energy, of particle accelerators, and innumerable other studies. Lasers are the basis of an approximately $20-billion-per-year industry, which then pays over $4 billion per year in taxes. So not only is laser technology useful, but it also helps support education, scientific research, and other government expenditures with the taxes generated by laser-related economic activity.

Have you ever wondered how your CD player works, or what makes those mystical bar-code scanners at the supermarket function? The technology that allows these systems to work was being developed nearly sixty years ago. As a young scientist, Townes was interested in studying the basic physics of molecules.

The technique for studying molecules that Townes chose was called spectroscopy. Here is how it works. Molecules are collections of atoms hooked to each other by electrical forces that behave somewhat like springs. The various atoms are always vibrating, and the rate of vibrations (the number of vibrations per second) tells us a lot about the forces that tie the atoms to the molecule. The molecule also rotates, and the rate of rotation gives information about its size.

The physicist has ways of adding energy (by heating or by bombarding it with photons or by pumping in electrical energy). This

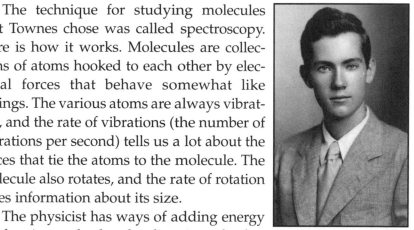

Young Townes (*Courtesy of C. Townes*)

is called "exciting" the molecule. The molecule responds to this by vibrating or rotating more energetically—and these excited motions can be detected. The molecule must de-excite, that is go back to normal, by emitting radiation. The wavelength of the radiation due to rotation is in the microwave region, that is, centimeters (cm) long, while the radiation due to vibration is of shorter wavelength and is infrared radiation. The range of wavelengths emitted is called a "spectrum" and hence the subject is "spectroscopy." By analyzing this microwave radiation, we learn much about the accurate structure of the molecule. Townes was especially interested in molecules that vibrate in the shorter wavelengths that he thought could also be useful in electronic circuits. At AT&T's Bell Laboratories and Columbia University, Townes became a world-class expert on microwave spectroscopy. This would eventually lead him to two very important discoveries: the maser and the laser.

THE EDUCATION OF TOWNES

Townes was born on a South Carolina farm near Greenville on July 28, 1915. His father was a lawyer, and his mother was a homemaker. His interest in nature started early. During a summer vacation, he found a colorful fish that he did not recognize. He preserved it in formaldehyde and sent it to the Smithsonian Institution in Washington, D.C. The staff members there didn't recognize it either and asked him to catch more. Unfortunately, young Townes didn't have the opportunity to look for more, but knowing the Smithsonian considered his work valuable thrilled him. He continued exploring nature throughout his youth. "I've always enjoyed natural history, just looking at things, seeing things, and exploring the woods and seeing what could be found, turning over rocks and looking at insects under them, sometimes snakes and so on. I guess it was my exploratory sense—plus also I like to know about things and to identify them," he said. "If you understand the world, why, it's more friendly."

Townes attended Greenville public schools where he excelled from a young age. Eventually, he became rather bored and needed a bigger challenge, so his parents allowed him to skip the seventh grade. He continued through high school and enrolled in Furman University at age sixteen. Furman, at that time, was all male with only about five hundred students, but Townes was content. He was able to save money by living at home. One problem he was having was deciding what he wanted to do with his life. He was active in the marching band and was a curator at the college's natural history museum. But still, he was uncertain about what to pursue as a career. He enjoyed math and science, especially biology, and he took several classes in modern languages. But then, in his sophomore year, he took his first physics course. He became entranced by the field. "The other sciences were good, too, but physics was still better because it deals with the real world, and it's very precise and quantitative," he said. "You can think through everything yourself, so once you get a solution you can say, 'Yeah, this really has to be right.' And so you really know what is going on, and I found that very satisfying."

At that time, physics wasn't as much a part of popular culture as it is today. It was seen by many as more a part of science fiction than science fact. Perhaps, as a result, only one other person at Furman was majoring in this field. For some of Townes's classes, he read a textbook and then worked on problems until he understood the topic at hand. The physics instructional staff at Furman was small and Townes was often on his own. His dedication to physics, however, paid off. Along with his busy schedule, which included participating in the marching band, competing on the swim team, curating at the university museum, and attempting, but failing, to earn the prestigious Rhodes scholarship, he satisfied the requirements for his physics concentration in only three years. Townes was leery of a fourth year at Furman, but his parents thought he was too young to move away from home. Instead of graduating, he decided to pursue a much different interest in modern languages. Townes mastered French, German, and also studied Latin and Greek during his time at Furman. He graduated in 1935 with a bachelor of arts degree in modern languages and a bachelor of science degree in physics.

Townes went on to earn a master's degree at Duke University. His thesis project involved assembling a Van de Graaff generator,[1] which he finished in only a year. The school was reluctant to let him graduate, even though he had completed his master's work, causing Townes to leave Duke without a diploma in 1936. He wanted to go to one of the very best institutions for physics, eventually choosing the California Institute of Technology (Cal Tech). Duke, meanwhile, mailed him his master's degree, dated 1937.

At that time, Cal Tech was the Mecca of the physics world (and today, still maintains an excellent reputation). It was a melting pot for all types of brilliant scientists. Chemist Linus Pauling and physicist J. Robert Oppenheimer, both top scien-

Townes blowing glass (*Courtesy of C. Townes*)

tists, were on the Cal Tech faculty. Great scientists attended graduate lectures. For a physicist in the 1930s, this was the place to be. When Townes arrived at Cal Tech, he chose to study atomic nuclei using spectroscopy—the study of how light interacts with molecules. In 1939, he earned his Ph.D.

Although his goal was an academic job focusing on basic research, jobs were hard to come by in the late depression era. Strapped for cash, he reluctantly took a post at AT&T's Bell Telephone Laboratories in New York. He earned only $3,016 a year, but considered that to be a hefty premium for a physicist. His work focused mostly on developing a new radar system for military aircraft. The goal was to create a system that made radar more usable for navigation and accurate bombing, first over Europe and then over the Pacific Ocean. To understand and appreciate Townes's achievements with radar systems at Bell Labs, it helps to understand exactly what radar is, what matter is made of, and how light is characterized.

QUANTUM THEORY

The theories through which scientists describe matter were developed mainly in the early part of the twentieth century. Most versions of these theories say that things in the universe (matter) are made of tiny blocks (actually smaller than tiny—absolutely minute) called atoms. The atom has a central, positively charged nucleus and a much larger, negatively charged electron cloud created by the rapid motion of infinitesimally small electrons.

The set of laws science now uses to explain the atom is called quantum theory. Because scientists who created the theory were attempting to understand the behavior of things so incredibly small—100 million atoms fit into a small grain of dandruff—they had no intuition as to how this microworld of atoms would behave. Until about 1900, there were no data on atoms and therefore no need to explain them. New experiments, however, showed bizarre properties of matter at the submicroscopic level of atoms.

Quantum theory, developed between 1910 and 1930, predicted

that any atom or system of atoms (molecules) could exist only in certain discrete and well-defined energy states. This was in sharp contrast to the physics that was known from the time of Newton (1680) when a ball, for example, could be given any speed and it would have a kinetic energy given by $\frac{1}{2} mv^2$ ($E = \frac{1}{2} mv^2$ where E is energy, m is mass, and v is velocity) that could then have *any* value. In the domain of the ultra small, we say energy of an atom or a molecule was "quantized," that is, limited to a number of special values. It is something like the difference between a ramp on which a block can sit at any height above the ground and a staircase, in which only certain heights are allowed, for example ground, step one, step two, and so on. The ramp corresponds to prequantum (called "classical") physics and still works for objects that are vastly larger than atoms. The connection between the quantum world of atoms, molecules and smaller things, and the classical world of beebees and baseballs, appears in this already strained metaphor. The height of the steps would have, in its formula, a term related inversely to the mass of the object. Small, low-mass object, large step—large object, small step. For heavy objects (relative to atoms) the step size is so small (say, one millionth of an inch) that effectively, we have a smooth ramp.

Normally atoms, including their halo of electrons, reside at the bottom of the staircase: "the ground state." Adding energy to the atom or molecule (usually via the constituent electrons) could excite the atom to a higher energy—but only if the added energy exactly corresponds to the difference in energy between the ground state and one of the allowed excited states (one of the steps, say, step 6).

Subsequently, the excited atom will spontaneously de-excite, causing the energy of the atom to tumble down, sometimes a step at a time or by skipping steps, until it rests comfortably in the ground state. In this downward fall, the atom will get rid of its energy by emitting photons of light energy. Again the energy of the photon, given by its wavelength, will exactly correspond to the energy difference of the two states.

However, because many atoms have more than one electron, and all electrons carry negative electric charges, we see complex phenomena that arise from forces between them; attraction of the negative electrons to the positive nucleus and repulsion of electrons from one another. The motion of the electrons, in response to these forces, is constrained by the curious quantum rules of nature which allow electrons to occupy only certain specific regions around the nucleus. The net result is that electrons inhabit shells around the nucleus. Electrons in these shells, depending on their distance from the atomic center, have unique energies. This is a consequence of the fact that the energy of the atom can have only certain discrete values.

To cause an atom to change, the theory says that energy must be added to the atomic electrons. This energy is most conveniently delivered in the form of photons—packets of electromagnetic energy. Photons make up visible light. The energy of a photon depends on its wavelength or color. The longer the wavelength, the less the energy. However, the wavelengths extend from hundreds of meters (radio waves) down to a billionth of a centimeter (X-rays) and to the shortest wavelength detected, gamma rays. Somewhere in the middle is a narrow band of wavelengths that humans can see—visible light from deep purple to deep red. The interesting and important concept to remember here is the idea that because atoms deal with energy in discrete lumps (quanta), electron excitation occurs only when the photon energy is precisely equal to that of the energy required to raise the atoms to the next level of energy.

When, after excitation, an atom returns to its ground state, the amount of energy released (in the form of photons) must be equal to a discrete amount—the difference in energy of the higher quantum states of the atom and the ground state. This difference in energy is equal to the energy of the emitted photon, which also determines the color of the light because of the connection of energy and wavelength. The relationship is: $E = (hc)/\lambda$, where E represents the photon energy, h is Planck's constant, c is the speed of light in a vacuum, and λ is the wavelength. The visible region of light consists of photons of wavelengths of 4×10^{-7} meters (violet) up to 8×10^{-7} meters (red).

Townes's work in the field was in molecular spectroscopy. This means that instead of studying the way single atoms interact with light, Townes studied how groups of atoms linked together, known as molecules, interact. In general, molecules are bigger and heavier than atoms and therefore, on average, the radiation they emit is of longer wavelength. Whereas the atomic radiation is produced by the effective vibration and rotation of atoms in the molecule. Instead of wavelengths of 10^{-7} meters (m), the wavelengths for molecules are 10^{-2} m, that is, microwaves.

ACHIEVEMENTS AT BELL LABS

Townes's last military project at Bell Labs was to develop an accurate navigation and bombing

Townes working in the laboratory, looking for leaks (*Courtesy of C. Townes*)

system for airplanes in the Pacific region. Radar is a system that uses modulated radiowaves (a form of radiation like light, but with a wavelength in the centimeter range) to produce a signal. The radar Bell Labs was developing used radiowaves in the 1.25 cm range.

Townes worked on the problem diligently only to find that the radar being developed would fail miserably because of extreme humidity over the Pacific. Water molecules (H_2O) can readily absorb microwaves in the 1.25 cm range. Therefore, the water vapor would interfere with the transmission of the radio wave. He told the navy about it. They ignored him and installed the system in some of their planes. In a matter of weeks, the systems were junked. "Even good scientists aren't always right," Townes said. "Now, of course, I make mistakes, too. Everybody makes mistakes. Everybody overlooks things, but the point is you mustn't just accept what everybody else says. You have to think it through for yourself if you're going to do something new."

His great success at Bell Labs was his work in the basic research of molecules. Molecules are fairly complicated structures; the "springs" that keep the atoms bound are created by the positions and motions of the electrons. Each of the many atoms vibrates so the number of frequencies is large, but careful spectroscopy could teach physicists much about the shapes of the molecules and any spinning motion they may have. As accuracy improved, even the shapes of the nuclei of the atoms became knowable. Townes's work at Bell Labs was very productive. He was one of the prime movers in this new field of microwave spectroscopy, which would soon spread to physics and chemistry labs around the country. This lead to his next move to Columbia University.

Another big accomplishment for Townes at Bell Labs was his encounter with his future wife, Frances Brown. Townes's work at Bell Labs during World War II allowed him to live in New York City and he chose an apartment near Columbia University and the Julliard School of Music where he studied voice in the evening. There he met his Frances, who had come from New Hampshire and to explore the excitement of New York. Frances had also studied in France and Italy and had a job at Rockefeller-built International House, where foreign students lived. Their meeting was on a ski trip that included a large number of Filipino students who were learning the sport. Frances and Charlie spent much of their time picking the students up from the snow. "It is not just intelligence," he said about his attraction to her. "There are many other things." He found this multitalented woman to have a certain international flare, and they married about a year later in 1941.

THE COLUMBIA EPOCH

Townes stayed at Bell Labs for nine years, leaving in 1948 to accept a professorship at Columbia University in New York City. By that time, Columbia was arguably the most powerful physics department in the nation. While Townes was at Columbia, so were at least seventeen other current and future Nobel laureates. Seven were on the faculty, including the editor of this book—Dr. Leon Lederman.

At Columbia, Townes went back to his roots and resumed his basic research in microwave spectroscopy. He became deeply interested in the properties of ammonia. He found that ammonia reacted well with microwaves and was a pivotal molecule in the development of microwave spectroscopy. He continued his work, partly supported by the joint military services, which were still strongly interested in microwaves for radar, and partly by the Union Carbide and Carbon Corporation. Eventually, he hired his future brother-in-law, Arthur Schawlow, as a postdoctoral fellow in his lab. Schawlow assisted Townes with the development of the laser, and Union Carbide provided monetary support to Townes during most of his time, almost ten years, at Columbia.

At Columbia, military support of basic research in the early postwar years was fairly routine. So it was there in 1950 that Townes was asked to organize a committee to advise the navy on the use of shorter wavelength waves, in the millimeter (mm) region. There was no specific idea, just that the navy, with a great dependence on technology, did not want to overlook anything. This was fine since Townes's molecular research was increasingly using shorter wavelengths. The "millimeter committee," which Townes organized, tried to find some military use, for example for communications between highflying aircraft. But then, how would one produce such waves? The device that could produce these waves would have to have a size of 1 or 2 mm, and yet be precisely machined to tolerate plenty of input power. Not easy!

PARK BENCH EPIPHANY

Now we are tracing the roots of Townes's major discovery. One early morning, on a deserted park bench during April 1951 in Washington, D.C. (Townes was attending a meeting of the American Physical Society), Townes had his great idea. The problem? How to build a device that would generate an intense beam of millimeter wavelength radiation? Townes wrote in *How the Laser Happened*, "What is basically stopping us from doing this? I asked myself. My mind first went back over the practical problems of tiny electron tubes or other resonators . . . my thoughts drifted to a realm that was comfortable and natural for me . . . molecules, especially the molecules to which I had devoted so much of my career and which I know best. . . . The key revelation came in a rush."[2]

We have discussed spontaneous de-excitation of molecules that have been excited to a higher energy state. This produces photons of a precise wavelength. But Einstein had discovered way back in 1917 that the simple nearby presence of a photon of the same wavelength would encourage or stimulate the de-excitation. The vision Townes had is that a dense gas of molecules, all excited to a higher energy state by some external source, would begin to de-excite producing just the photons needed to stimulate further de-excitation. It was like a chain reaction. At each place, more and more photons of precisely the right wavelength would be present to encourage more of the molecules to emit photons. Townes was encouraged by remembering related experiments carried out by colleagues at Columbia and Harvard Universities. Townes actually found an old envelope and scribbled his new idea and calculated how the idea would work. The molecule was ammonia. The park bench calculations proceeded and the idea looked better and better.

When asked to reflect about how he felt on that park bench, Townes said, "It's a great feeling that you've discovered something new, you know, that could be useful and important, and other people will use it and so on. . . . Now, of course, you have to be careful. Sometimes you may think that you've discovered something, and it may be wrong."

The Townes's model went an important step beyond the stimulated emission theory proposed by Einstein. It said that light released from a device would be coherent. Coherence, in this context, means that as the cascade forms, all of the photons line up with each other to effectively make one giant wave. The light emitted from Townes's device would not be that of, say, a typical light bulb because it would not spread out and dissipate with distance. The quantum phenomena involved in the emission would mean that the light would have a very pure frequency and its beam could travel miles and miles without spreading out much.

Townes went back to Columbia and started the long process of building a device. Colleagues in the physics world doubted he would succeed. He did much of his research at Columbia with graduate students. A key person in the development of the first device was graduate student James Gordon. Townes, Gordon, and a young postdoc, Herb Zeiger, worked for three years before glimmers of success appeared. The group's project was plagued by problems with losing radiation and energy from the resonant cavity designed to hold the radiation, but in April 1954, they succeeded in producing the first oscillator and coherent radiation from molecular radiation. At first the group was unsure of what to call the device, but they eventually decided on the acronym maser—microwave amplification by stimulated emission of radiation. Their device used the principles of stimulated emission by targeting a specific molecule that displayed stimulated emission properties; the earliest masers used ammonia. The ammonia was put into a metal tube called a resonant cavity. To obtain molecules excited with energy, Townes's group used molecules streaming through a porous surface, and deflected a beam of those with energy into a hole in the resonant cavity by using an electric voltage.

Even after the group's initial success, many members of the scientific community did not believe the maser did what Townes claimed. The skepticism eventually faded after Townes and his team of researchers successfully demonstrated the phenomenon on multiple occasions. A breakthrough in acceptance came when, at Cambridge University, Townes stumbled upon the work of a group of Soviet scientists from Moscow who had independently designed a somewhat similar device, but had not yet operated it successfully. Ultimately, these two scientists, Nikolai Basov and Alexsandr Prohkorov, shared the Nobel Prize with Townes for their fundamental work on the maser and laser.

In 1955, after completing a three-year term as chairman of Columbia's physics department, Townes took a sabbatical. Supported by a Guggenheim Fellowship and a Fulbright Fellowship, he toured Europe, taught at the University of Paris, and then at the University of Tokyo. During the sabbatical, he made a decision not to concentrate on building a device that worked at high frequencies (i.e., wavelengths shorter than one mm, in the infrared region). His goal changed to something that would eventually lead to his present research. He wanted to build a maser that would amplify microwaves from space.

PUBLISHING AND PATENTS

After some astronomical studies using masers to amplifiy microwaves from space, in 1957 Townes decided to get back to masers toward shorter wavelengths. And in 1958, Townes and Schawlow published a paper on optical masers; the wavelengths were in the infrared and visible region, ranging from wavelengths too long for human eyes to see, to those in the violet. Before the paper was published, Townes had a short meeting with a young scientist named Gordon Gould. Gould was doing research with bright lamps. Such lamps, Townes thought, might be useful in an optical maser. The two talked for a little while with some of the conversation focusing on how patents were documented and obtained. Townes was not expecting any trouble from Gould, but this conversation eventually led to a major conflict.

In the meantime, Townes and Schawlow didn't push hard toward building an optical maser. Theodore Maimann, from Hughes Aircraft, built and then demonstrated the first optical maser that amplified light rather than microwaves. It was dubbed laser in May 1960; the "l" stands for light. The laser started to become part of the standard technological lexicon, and with entrance to this exclusive group came two things—a public fear of death rays and a patent.

Townes tried to be extremely careful with his ideas for the maser and his optical maser. He had the vision to see that this great invention would eventually be a multibillion-dollar-a-year industry. He had the maser and the general principles of amplification by stimulated emission patented by the Research Corporation, a not-for-profit corporation that gives money to support university research. Because Schawlow was working at Bell Labs, Townes felt that the specific optical maser patent would be mainly their concern. So before the paper on optical masers was released, Bell Labs filed for a patent. Eventually, Gould challenged the patent, claiming he was the first to have some of the ideas for making a laser. By then, the term "laser" had been generated by students at Columbia and it rapidly took over from the earlier "optical maser." Through a rather long and tedious process, the challenge by Gould to the Townes-Schawlow patent of 1959, which was owned by Bell Labs, was overturned. They held the patent, as directed by the law. However, in 1976, Gould and Patlex, the company which then supported him, managed to obtain a more junior patent on some types of lasers by claiming some subtle differences from the Bell Labs patent.

RESEARCH VERSUS ADMINISTRATION

With the excitement of the laser and his recent trips abroad, Townes found himself one of the most recognized figures in physics. In 1961 he was appointed provost of the Massachusetts Institute of Technology (MIT), but he found that administrative work did not kindle the spark inside his soul that pure research did. At MIT, Townes also entered the public arena. He was chosen as a scientific advisor to President Johnson, elected president of the American Physical Society, and among others, consulted on the National Aeronautic and Space Administration's (NASA) Apollo project. Townes said he "felt it was sort of a duty, as a citizen, to try and help out and be involved." While provost, Townes was honored with the most prestigious prize in all of science—the Nobel Prize. Along with his scientist colleagues from the Ledebev Institute in Moscow, Townes was honored for "fundamental work in quantum electronics which led to production of oscillators and amplifiers according to the maser-laser principle."

The year before, a Swedish newspaper had called Townes about the possibility of him winning the prize. That happens occasionally, so Townes was not extremely surprised by the award, but he said, "I was obviously pleased. Actually, I was delighted, but it wasn't an enormous surprise. It's a lot like playing a tennis game—you think you have some chance of winning but you don't know." He added, "I didn't do it all. I started it, but a lot of other people contributed. That's typical of science and finding out new things. You start something new, and it grows, and you show something new, and it's right. Then it is always there and always right and everybody can use it, and you just see it grow and get more and more useful." This foundational work was the exact kind of science the Nobel Prize is founded upon—the creation of a better, more interesting world.

Townes continued at MIT until 1967, then decided to completely change the focus of his research. He changed from being a spectroscopist to an astrophysicist. He became a professor at the University of California at Berkeley, a place he describes as a very good place to do astronomy. Some in the scientific community were shocked. Why would someone who was provost at one of the most important universities in the physics world quit and take a job in the most controversial city in America, a town known as a hotbed of political activism—Berkeley, California?

Townes defended his decision by explaining, "Well, they're all very good universities. Berkeley, Cal Tech, MIT, Columbia. All are quite outstanding. They differ in different kinds of ways, but they've all been good. I like the climate out in Berkeley. One reason I'm in Berkeley is because it's a very good place to do astronomy. So, for me right now, Berkeley is the best place. Or, at least, the West Coast is the best place." During his time at MIT he realized how spectroscopy could add new information to our understanding of astronomy. He realized that only three simple molecules of two atoms each had been identified in space using spectroscopy and there might be many more.

The technique is really pretty simple. Scientists take antennae, like the one on a home radio, but much, much bigger, and aim them at points in space. They scan different frequencies, similar to how one might search for a favorite song on the radio. Each of these frequencies is like a radio station, but instead of putting out music, it carries a spectral line, a specific wavelength of light (radiowaves are of long wavelength) that has an energy derived from atomic or molecular de-excitation. By comparing the spectral lines with known energy levels of materials on Earth, scientists can identify interstellar atoms and molecules. The wavelengths may be those of visible light, infrared, or microwaves. When Townes first began his work in astronomy, scientists had detected only a very few microwave frequencies from atoms or molecules in space.

Townes's research group quickly found several very important molecular signals. His first major undertaking had to do with, of course, ammonia. Next, his group found an extremely important molecule, water. Not only is water a prerequisite for life, it turned out to produce a natural maser with a cloud of molecules producing powerful radiation. Townes's discovery in this field led to deeper speculation into the realm of extraterrestrial life. His research continues to focus on astronomy, finding and deciphering molecules in space, detecting a large black hole in the center of our galaxy, flying in airplanes high in the atmosphere to detect infrared radiation at wavelengths that don't penetrate our atmosphere, and measuring in detail how stars behave and emit gas. He is discovering exactly what is out there. At the age of eighty-five, he continues to be an active scientist at Berkeley.

It is interesting that Townes was one of the pioneers in investigating the tiny, which eventually led him to become one of the pioneers in investigating the massive. He doesn't, however, see the laser as his most important discovery. "The laser has an enormous number of uses, but it's more a technology. It's a device. And I've done a lot of science with it, but in terms of new knowledge and understanding of the universe, it's not the most important," he said.

Townes believes that new discoveries in science will always occur and some things are left to chance. Scientists often investigate the same thing, and the successful scientist is simply quicker or more adept than the other one. Einstein postulated a basic mechanism for the laser when Townes was in diapers, and today laser technology is a tool that can be used to investigate the world.

LASERS EVERYWHERE

Currently, the laser is used in almost every industry. It cuts steel used for building skyscrapers. It helps doctors look into living cells, and it may possibly change the future of radiology. It is helping scientists at Lawrence Livermore Laboratory discover the secrets of nuclear fusion, creating a new power source that, if successful, will significantly change the course of human history. The laser helps surveyors and civil engineers build roads. It has opened a new window of hope to many people with vision problems; laser surgery techniques can correct some cases of blindness. Fiber optics allow information to flow at a rate hundreds of times faster than our normal phone lines, allowing Internet connections to grow in speed. And the laser is being used to power a new breed of ultra-high-speed optical computers that may replace resistors in microchips with crystals.

"In terms of its effect on humans generally, yes, I would say that it is my most important work," he said. "It has been generally recognized as a very important part of the science and technology this century, and it's being used very widely in all kinds of different ways, such as the checkout counter at the grocery store, such as long-distance transmissions of information, and computers and all kinds of science. Now we have enormously big lasers putting out more power than all the power we use on Earth, for a short time, of course, because you can't use that much power for a long time. And then very small lasers, very delicate, which can pick up individual cells—laser tweezers they're called, very delicate and very precise. It gives us new standards of distance and time and so on."

AN IMPRESSIVE CAREER

Townes has had a remarkable career in science. He has also had a dynamic, interesting life. From his early days on a South Carolina farm to his acceptance of the Nobel Prize, from White House meetings with four U.S. presidents to his current research about the stars, Townes has remained incredibly active in the scientific community. "It [science] is fun, and I don't particularly intend to stop," he said. "I like to have vacations and travel, and I like to do a lot of things, but science is great fun. So I've never felt that I really have to work. I'm just having a good time . . . I would never stop."

Townes credits a lot of his professional success to a solid family life. He and his wife, Frances, have four married and professional daughters and six grandchildren. He acknowledges that in order to succeed in any of life's ambitions, one has to have more than just brains. "You have to be interested and healthy. . . . My family was willing to move from one institution to another when I felt that it would be worthwhile. I talked with them about it, and they were willing to be flexible," he said.

Townes's work in science has changed the world. He was a creator of microwave spectroscopy, the inventor of the maser, and he was instrumental in developmental work in laser/maser technology and has been recognized for his innovative work in astronomy. He was one of the most important scientists of the twentieth century; perhaps he will be one of the most important scientists in the twenty-first century as well.

Douglas A. Heintz

CHAPTER 12

GEERAT VERMEIJ

SEEING WITH HIS HANDS

ELIZABETH A. GILBERT

S cientists are individuals who are curious about nature. They strive to develop new understandings of our world, based on their own observations as well as what others have discovered. Scientists need to perform experiments, read scientific literature, and communicate their work in written form for their peers to review and build upon. These are all activities that at first, you might think are dependent on sight. How could a blind person ever aspire to become a scientist? Of all the sciences, why would a blind person choose to study biology, the most visual of all the scientific fields? Geerat Vermeij did exactly this. And he chose a field of biology that requires collecting and analyzing specimens from marine habitats from around the world.

Geerat Vermeij has overcome the formidable obstacle of blindness to become a preeminent evolutionary biologist. He studies how living things change and evolve because of environmental pressures. He then uses this information to predict how changes in the environment will affect living organisms. Vermeij (pronounced ver-MAY) specifically focuses his studies on the remains of animals that have shells, such as snails and clams, members of the Phylum Mollusca. This study is called malacology.

Because Vermeij is blind, the process of analyzing the hand-sized shells and fossils of these small creatures suits him very well. Shells are aesthetically pleasing because they have contrasting textures; even the inside of the shell is different from the outside. Vermeij literally feels how the shells change over time and vary in different circumstances. Ironically, his blindness may actually help him to notice by touch what others may have missed by relying on sight.

Vermeij, a professor at the University of California at Davis, has been the editor of *Evolution*, the most respected journal for evolutionary biologists; was an editor of *Paleobiology*; was awarded MacArthur and Guggenheim fellowships; and is a recipient of the Daniel Giraud Elliot Medal given by the National Academy of Sciences. He has also written about a hundred scientific papers and several books, including *A Natural History of Shells*, in 1993, and his autobiography, *Privileged Hands: A Scientific Life*, in 1997.

BLIND AT AGE THREE

In September of 1946, Vermeij was born to a loving family in Sappemeer, a farming community in the Netherlands. He experienced eye pain from birth and was soon diagnosed with an unusual form of childhood glaucoma. Increasing pressure in his eyes was causing him to lose vision, and he spent the majority of his first three years in hospitals. He had frequent eye surgery to help relieve the condition, but the operations were unsuccessful. To eliminate any chance of brain damage, when Vermeij was three years old, his eyes were removed.

Vermeij quickly adjusted to blindness by learning to use his other senses. Echoes and other sounds offered information about his surroundings. Sound, smell, taste, and touch created "a vivid, if nonvisual, picture of the world around me," he wrote in his autobiography *Privileged Hands: A Scientific Life*.[1] "My world was not black and hopeless. It sparkled as it did before, but now with sounds, odors, shapes, and textures."[2]

Vermeij's family was very supportive, yet did not shelter him from the outside world. He was treated as a responsible member of the family and was allowed to do whatever his older brother Arie did. This included fishing, although his mother did warn him about falling into ditches. With the children on the back of the bicycles, his parents would cycle to the countryside or to the shore, where Vermeij was more interested in collecting shells than building sand castles. He has never let his blindness interfere with participation in any activities. He said, "My best advice is not to carry a chip on your shoulder and not to worry about limitations as much as about opportunity."

Vermeij attended the Institute for the Blind at Huizen, a government boarding school. There he learned Braille and the world of reading opened up to him. His family also learned this method of communication so they could translate books into Braille for him to read. Because the Institute was far from home, he could visit his family only every other weekend. The separation from his family left him unhappy and lonely.

THE NEW WORLD

Vermeij's parents had often thought of immigrating to the United States, a land that seemed to hold more promise of opportunity than the Netherlands, which was still suffering from the aftereffects of World War II. The family wanted to live together and not have to segregate Vermeij in a boarding school so that he could obtain a quality education. His father learned that in New Jersey, blind children were educated in local public schools alongside their sighted schoolmates. In 1955, when Vermeij was nine, his family immigrated to the United States.

In New Jersey, Vermeij discovered English, American food, a new school, and different surroundings. The New Jersey countryside offered plenty of opportunity for observations by the budding scientist. The fresh, natural surroundings intrigued him because the new environment contained novel plants and animals that were very different from his native Netherlands. Vermeij frequently roamed the meadows and streams. He began pressing plants, and collecting other natural objects such as feathers and bones.

Vermeij credits his fourth grade teacher, Mrs. Catherine Colberg, with helping him develop his lifelong interest in shells when she allowed him to study some that she had collected in Florida. They were very different from the cold-water shells he had collected in the Netherlands. Cold-water shells are chalky and rough whereas shells from warm water are more smooth and delicate. This difference in the shells made the young boy curious. He said, "For me, curiosity lies at the core of science. Science is a process, true enough, but it is much more; it is a state of mind. It relies first and foremost on observation, looking at the world around us and

Evolutionary biologist Geerat Vermeij (*Courtesy of G. Vermeij*)

seeing puzzles, things that don't make sense but about which we should like to know more. That is where asking questions comes in. Only when we have asked the questions in the right way can hypotheses and tests occur to us, which we can then proceed to investigate with new evidence."

Vermeij frequently traveled to the beach near his home in New Jersey to collect his own shells. He wanted more information about these shells than what was available to him in books. He wrote to the American Museum of Natural History asking if someone would be willing to identify some of the shells that he had collected. The malacologists at the museum agreed to look at Vermeij's shells and even invited him to a private section of the museum. They strongly encouraged his interest in shells and suggested he study biology. At the young age of fourteen, he subscribed to *The Nautilus*, a professional journal of malacology and became a member of the Netherlands Malacological Society.

A SCHOLARLY STUDENT

In high school, Vermeij enrolled in extra courses and participated in a science honors program on weekends with other high school students at Columbia University. He had previously been interested in Darwin's theories. Here, he had the opportunity to listen to lectures from experts in the field and to participate in discussions and debates about these theories with other interested students. Darwinian concepts are based on the belief that organisms best adapted to their environments would survive to reproduce and pass on their genetic material and characteristics. This means that over time, species would change in response to the living conditions surrounding them.

Vermeij was the valedictorian of his high school class. He wanted to pursue a career in biology, but was discouraged by one teacher because much of the field is based on observation. Vermeij remembered the support of the scientists at the American Museum of Natural History and decided that biology was the right choice for him. In April 1964, he accepted a full scholarship to attend Princeton University.

Vermeij missed the comfort and good food of home. However, Princeton was exactly what he had hoped for academically. The faculty delivered stimulating lectures and his fellow undergraduates were enthusiastic about learning. Vermeij's textbooks were not in Braille, so he needed to hire readers. Many students were willing to read out loud to him since they ended up getting paid for reading books that they would have had to read anyway. The Commission for the Blind had to approve of Vermeij's course of study in order for him to obtain funds for readers. They had reservations about the practicality of a career in biology for a blind person. Luckily, his college advisors believed in him and they informed the commission that it was the university's job to counsel their students. The commission never again raised objections about Vermeij's course of study.

Vermeij's heavy course load and adjustment to this stimulating environment left him exhausted. The low grades he earned on his first report card caused him to doubt himself and a career in science. His college advisors reassured him that students often do poorly during their first semester of college. Realizing that he had overextended himself and that he couldn't be complacent about studying as he had been in high school, Vermeij developed good study habits and became a successful student.

Students at Princeton are required to do a senior research thesis that introduces them to the process of scientific research. Vermeij chose an ambitious project: to study the variation in the shell shape of the common blue mussel. He knew that the shell shape ranged from flat to nearly cylindrical. Vermeij planned to measure shells for several weeks during the summer from both coasts of the Unites States. He obtained funds from Princeton to hire a research assistant to help him with his research. This was his first experience with intense fieldwork and from this Vermeij knew that this was the type of career that he wanted to pursue.

Vermeij applied to graduate schools that had close associations with museums, so that he could continue collecting and analyzing specimens. His three top choices were Harvard University, Yale University, and Princeton University. Could a blind person be successful in a competitive and observation-based field? Both Harvard and Princeton claimed to be incapable of meeting the requirements of a blind graduate student who wanted to pursue research in the field. Yale was doubtful as well, but offered him an interview.

When Vermeij arrived for his interview in the biology department, the director of graduate studies was more than a little apprehensive. The director took him down to the university's shell collection, in the basement of the Peabody Museum. Casually he picked up two shells and asked Vermeij to identify them. The director fully expected Vermeij to draw a blank, in which case he would tell him that biology was not an appropriate field of study for a blind person. Fortunately, however, the shells were familiar to Vermeij and he quickly identified them correctly. All of the misgivings of the director instantly evaporated. Thanks to the enthusiastic endorsement of the director, Vermeij was able to enter Yale with a full graduate fellowship that left him free to travel and to carry out an ambitious research project.

In graduate school, Vermeij continued to study how environmental conditions affect shell shape. He was especially interested in molluscs that lived in the region of the tide zone called the upper shore. This is the region where land and sea meet. It is a hostile region where molluscs must tolerate long periods when the tide fails to reach them, as well as low food supplies, intense sunshine, and rainstorms. Vermeij noted that shells from the highest regions of the shore, where the habitat was harshest, were shaped differently from those found in lower zones, where the tide was always present. He also found that different molluscs coped with the harsh region in different ways. Some molluscs have tall spires, reducing the surface area that is directly exposed to the Sun. They also have ribs on their shells that reflect heat. In contrast, other molluscs have compactly built shells that rely on water evaporation for cooling. The interiors of those shells act as water reservoirs. Shells at lower shore regions do not have the problems of heat and water loss and, therefore, do not have the same structure as shells from the high shore levels. He was granted his doctorate for this work.

After completing his dissertation, Vermeij found himself facing yet another challenge. He wanted an exciting academic position that would allow him to teach, perform research, and achieve the financial independence that he lacked while attending school. He also wanted to stay near Yale University where Edith Zipser was pursuing her Ph.D. in molecular biology. Vermeij had met Zipser when he first arrived at Yale in 1968 and they dated briefly. Two years later, they renewed their acquaintance when she volunteered to be a reader for him. Zipser was an excellent reader, but they also discovered that they had a lot in common, such as a love for science, classical music, and nature. Soon they found themselves in love. Vermeij proposed marriage in 1971 before leaving New Haven for a position at the University of Maryland at College Park. Zipser finally accepted a second proposal in the summer of 1972. (Here's Zisper's version: She wanted to give the relatively inexperienced Vermeij time to be sure he knew what he was doing by marrying her!) They married in the fall of 1972, but Zipser did not move to Maryland until she successfully defended her doctoral dissertation in the spring of 1973.

Vermeij knew that the next few years of work at the University of Maryland would be very strenuous and important in establishing himself as a tenured professor. In academic life, tenure is a guarantee of permanent employment given to a professor after a probationary period. He wrote grants and used the money to travel and to pursue research comparing shells from the West African coast, the Caribbean, the Indo-Pacific coasts, and Alaska. To help him with his travels, he hired assistants to accompany him in the field. Later, Zipser left molecular biology for evolutionary research and became his colleague, accompanying him in the field. (Their daughter, Hermine, born in 1982, has also taken an active role as a field companion.) At home, he achieved independence by traveling about with a white cane and learning how to cook simple meals. In 1974, after being out of school for only three years, he was granted tenure because of the quality of his published research, which was considered a major milestone.

PREDATOR–PREY INTERACTIONS

Vermeij's research on shell variation in different habitats led to a publication in *Evolution* in 1974 in which he hypothesized that regional variations in shells were the result of predation by mollusc-eating crabs and other predators. He speculated that the molluscs would have thicker shells in regions where there are mollusc-eating crabs with strong claws compared to the molluscs found in regions where the mollusc-eating crabs have less robust claws. Since little was known about mollusc predators, he traveled to Guam and studied shells to test this hypothesis. Guam contains a good representation of the molluscs that are found throughout the Indian and Western Pacific Oceans. When Vermeij was a boy, his brother gave him a shell as a gift. Vermeij was grateful for the gift but disappointed because it contained a scar that he thought had been incurred by human handling. His new research forced Vermeij to change his previous ideas. He realized that many shells had these irregularities, and human mishandling did not cause the marks. Rather, they were reminders of times when the shell had been attacked. Organisms inhabiting those shells that were strong enough to survive such assault could live on and mend themselves. Evolution would occur leaving only the molluscs with stronger shells to live and reproduce in the Western Pacific and Indian Oceans. But in other locales, shells had developed differently.

Further research indicated that different types of predators lived among the varying shell forms. Molluscs with resilient shells lived in areas that were also occupied by crabs that had very strong claws. The predators would need such physically powerful claws and teeth to crush the shells and eat the soft creature inside. This evidence supported the concept that predators, not just geographical environment, can affect evolution of species. Crabs with powerful claws were found in the Pacific tropics, where shells of molluscs are thick. Crabs with less robust claws are found in other tropical areas where the shells of molluscs are thin.

This predator-prey interaction is an example of *coevolution*, a process in which two interacting organisms evolve in response to each other. Coevolution is really little more than natural selection, but the selection in this case is one in which both organisms affect each other. Charles Darwin was aware of this phenomenon when he wrote in his 1859 book, *On the Origin of Species*: "Thus I can understand how a flower and a bee might slowly become, either simultaneously or one after the other, modified and adapted in the most perfect manner to each other."[3] In fact, in 1862 Charles Darwin predicted the existence of an insect pollinator, the hawkmoth, based on the structure of a flower, the star orchid. The star orchid of Madagascar has a flower spur that is 20 to 35 centimeters (8 to 14 inches) long. This means that an insect with a very long proboscis (tongue) must be responsible for pollinating this flower. But in 1862, no insect with such a long proboscis was known. Darwin was ridiculed for this prediction. In 1903, he was vindicated when a hawkmoth with a proboscis of 22.5 centimeters (9 inches), was found. The hawkmoth and the star orchid had coevolved; the star orchid depends exclusively on the hawkmoth for pollination, and the hawkmoth depends on the star orchid for nectar. The hawkmoth was named *Xanthopan morganii praedicta*; the term "praedicta" in the moth's name acknowledges the prediction Charles Darwin made.

The term coevolution was coined by Paul Ehrlich and Peter Raven in 1964 in a famous article, "Butterflies and Plants: A Study in Coevolution," published in the journal *Evolution* (coincidentally, the journal that Vermeij eventually came to edit). They studied butterflies that fed on only certain families of plants. They believed that diversification (the creation of multiple forms) in either the butterfly or the plant could occur only when one gained an advantage over the other. For example, the plant could develop a chemical that would make any butterfly that tried to eat it sick. To counter this, the insects might evolve new ways of neutralizing the plant's toxins. Only the butterflies that were immune to the toxin would survive and reproduce. The better-adapted generation of butterfly would then still be able to eat the plant, so the plant would have to change again to fend off hungry butterflies.

Vermeij added to the theory of coevolution by suggesting that there is escalation (an increase) in a predator/prey race. As prey defenses get continually better, so do predator weapons, so that after a period of evolutionary time, the two would still be roughly balanced. This means that if a current predator could be exposed to prey from the past, the current predator would easily overcome earlier prey. Likewise, present-day prey would be protected from predators from the past.

Vermeij reconsidered his observations of tropical shells that he had made in Mrs. Colberg's fourth grade classroom. Shells are mainly composed of calcium carbonate, a mineral that is abundant in oceans. Vermeij speculated that the difference between shells from warm and cold water might have developed because the process of making a shell from calcium carbonate is less carefully controlled in molluscs that live in cold water compared with those that live in the tropics. Because calcium carbonate forms more readily in warm water than in cold, warm water molluscs require less energy to build a shell than cold-water molluscs. Besides the energy costs, predator-prey coevolution might also play a role in the shell differences. There are many more demands placed on tropical molluscs than on temperate ones. These include demands by predators such as organisms that bore into shells that are not found in cooler water. Overall, for a mollusc to survive in the tropics, the shell must be stronger than the shell of a temperate mollusc.

Adaptations are beneficial features of organisms that improve performance in the environment, allowing them to survive and reproduce. There are two schools of thought about how organisms adapt to their environment. One view is that most of the big adaptive breakthroughs come through coincidences within organisms. This means that most changes in organisms would occur randomly and without cause and would not have necessarily negative or positive effects. The other school of thought states that since selection favors characteristics that give a competitive edge, all organisms are adapted. This viewpoint, which Vermeij holds, suggests that adaptation is the dominant theme in evolution. He believes that adaptation cannot be escaped and that populations will change over time due to pressures from their environment.

In 1987, Vermeij accepted a position at the University of California at Davis (UC-Davis) where he remains today. At UC-Davis, he began to notice how occurrences of coevolution in nature parallel trends in civilization. He compares the case of predatory crabs and their mollusc prey to the phenomenon of an arms race between countries. The argument he poses is that just as there is no organism on Earth that doesn't have competitors, there is no human on Earth that doesn't have competitors. Competition for mates or food is a given whenever there are resources that can be used by more than one organism. Many plant and animal adaptations, as well as adaptations of humans and of human societies can be interpreted as responses to competitive environments. The arms race is one manifestation of that.

Vermeij also argues that evolutionary and economic principles are in many ways identical. His ultimate aim is to see what the economic history of life can tell us about how to construct human economies that are not dependent on perpetual growth. "Evolution is descent with modification; it is a powerful world view that affects every branch of science. Economics is an important part of evolution because both it and evolution are about success in a changing environment. Molluscs led me to economics and evolution through the arms race and through the realization that the availability of resources dictates how far arms races can go."

To this day, his ideas on predator involvement in change and how systems are related continue to shape science and how the world is understood. He has received the Daniel Giraud Elliot Medal from the National Academy of Sciences and the MacArthur Award. He continues his fieldwork along the coasts of California, French Polynesia, and New Zealand. Vermeij has faced many obstacles and taken many risks. His blindness has caused trepidation among colleagues, and he has had to earn respect through hard work and patience. He has always believed that he should be treated completely equally, with no special advantages over others. He holds himself to very high standard and continues to work hard as he adds new ideas and observations to the field of evolutionary biology.

Elizabeth A. Gilbert

CHAPTER 13

EDWARD O. WILSON

DILIGENT NATURALIST

NIA H. DUKOV

T hrough the bottomless darkness of night in the Amazon forest, groping along the edge of the world, a solitary figure traces a path of light, searching for hidden life. And suddenly—the cold eyes of a friend or enemy, or maybe just what our insistent observer has been seeking emerges from the dark. He will not flee, but instead, will face it. Our intrepid observer is Dr. Edward O. Wilson, noted naturalist and Pulitzer Prize winning author. He has devoted much of his life to studying ants and confesses in his autobiography, *Naturalist*, written in 1994, "In my heart, I will be an explorer naturalist until I die."[1]

Wilson strives to discover the secrets of nature, sometimes from the reference point of even the smallest creatures. Influential ecologist, controversial biological theorist, and a world-renowned authority on a single kind of organism, ants, Wilson is probably most famous for his contributions to the field of sociobiology, the study of the biological basis of the behavior of different organisms.

Wilson is one of the preeminent scientists of the twentieth century. Accomplished as both a scientist and a writer, he has won two Pulitzer Prizes in addition to his numerous science awards, which include the National Medal of Science. He has also authored over three hundred and seventy scientific publications. As in the encounter in the Amazon forest, Wilson is always eager to probe into the challenging unknown.

INTO THE WOODS AND FIELDS

Edward Osborne Wilson was born on June 10, 1929, in Birmingham, Alabama. His life-long passionate interest in nature developed early in childhood. His family moved frequently and his ever-changing social relationships as the new kid on the block made Wilson turn to the outdoors. Driven to study nature, Wilson might have chosen any particular organism to explore. However, at the age of seven he lost the vision in his right eye in a fishing accident. As a teenager, he lost hearing to high-pitched sounds, such as bird calls, possibly due to an inherited disorder. This made it difficult for Wilson to observe animals that require a keen sense of sight and sound to observe, such as birds and frogs. "I have always loved nature. The ants where I was growing up in the American South were extremely abundant and diverse. I couldn't see as well as other people as I lost my vision because of an accident in one eye. The other eye was very sharp, but seeing through one eye makes it difficult to see birds, because you do not have in-depth vision. So as a result I turned to insects to learn to be a naturalist, because they were so abundant and interesting," said Wilson. "But others have had similar experiences and handicaps and have hit upon other kinds of organisms and even different subjects like geology. It doesn't matter as long as you find something you love to study." (This sentiment is echoed by Geerat Vermeij, profiled in chapter 12, who is a blind malacologist.)

When Wilson was nine years old, his family moved to Washington, D.C., which was within walking distance of the National Zoological Park and a short streetcar ride to the National Museum of Natural History. Also close by was Rock Creek Park, which didn't have the exotic large animals of the National Museum or zoo, but was a place full of live insects that could be observed and collected. Butterflies first captured Wilson's interest, but that passion was soon redirected toward ants when he found a huge colony of yellow ants that smelled like lemons under the bark of a rotting tree. These childhood experiences are what made Wilson resolve to venture into entomology (the study of insects).

Wilson's family moved back to Alabama when he was twelve. Though he often found school to be dull and pointless, he maintained passing grades. During his senior year in high school, his father's health began to fail, and Wilson realized that his father might not be able to support him in college. Wilson tried to enter the U.S. Army in order to benefit from the G.I. Bill, which helped finance a college education, but was not accepted because of the blindness in his eye.

The University of Alabama was open to all graduates of Alabama high schools with minimal expense, so Wilson pursued his studies there, earning both his bachelor's and master's degrees in biology. As an undergraduate, he was recognized as an expert in ants and was asked at the young age of nineteen to conduct a study on the imported fire ant for the Alabama Department of Conservation. Wilson later began his doctoral studies at the University of Tennessee, but transferred after a year to Harvard University because it had the largest collection of ants in the world and a greater academic setting. During his years of graduate study, Wilson was able to fulfill a boyhood dream of traveling to the tropics, where he did research on ants for his doctorate. After receiving his Ph.D., Wilson remained at Harvard, eventually becoming a professor and a curator of the ant collection. Although he has recently retired from teaching at Harvard, he remains a research professor and honorary curator in entomology at the Museum of Comparative Zoology.

ANT ODYSSEY

As a graduate student at Harvard, Wilson became intrigued by the work of Konrad Lorenz and Nikolaas Tinbergen, who studied animal behavior under natural conditions, a field known as ethology. Ethologists believe that behavior is mainly instinctive, or innate, that is, inherited from genes the same way physical traits, such as coat color, are inherited. This means that behavior is under the influence of natural selection (pressures from the environment that cause some characteristics or traits to be retained and others to be lost by differences in ability to survive and reproduce) in the same way as physical traits such as size and strength.

Lorenz and Tinbergen studied the nesting behavior of geese. (They shared a Nobel Prize for this work with Karl von Frisch, who studied behavior in bees.) Geese make nests by digging out shallow holes in the ground. If a goose sees an egg that has been accidentally pushed out of the nest, it will first extend its neck toward the egg, then get up and roll the egg back into the nest with its bill. Even if the egg is removed while the goose is retrieving it, the goose will complete this behavior.

According to ethologists, the egg retrieval behavior is triggered by detection of a stimulus that, in this case, is the egg out of the nest. The stimulus can be thought of as a cue from the environment that triggers a certain behavior. The cue is detected by a component of the goose's nervous system, called the innate releasing mechanism. The innate releasing mechanism provides the neural instructions for the motor program to carry out the behavioral act, in this case, rolling the egg back into the nest. Even geese who have never performed this egg, rolling do it completely the first time.

Intrigued by the idea that animals respond to stimuli with built-in motor programs, Wilson turned to ants to learn the triggers of their innate behaviors. Ants are social insects that live in large colonies. In a successful colony, the queen, soldiers, and workers must communicate with each other about the location of food, the presence of enemies, or to simply find one another in their nest. He knew that ants couldn't be communicating with each other through

Wilson at 13 years of age, collecting insects near his home in Mobile, Alabama
(*Courtesy of E. O. Wilson*)

motor programs that are triggered by sight and sound, like birds, because ants live in dark tunnels and there is little evidence that they can hear. Wilson reasoned that ants must use chemicals that can be tasted or smelled to trigger their behavior.

Wilson began to decipher ant social behavior by searching for the chemical stimuli of ant communication. He conducted an impressive experiment, in which he worked with his favorite ant species, the imported fire ant. He observed, for example, that each time an ant found food, it would crouch to the ground on its way back to the nest, depositing drops of a chemical substance. He crushed various internal organs of individual ants and used them to mark a trail along a surface. Only when he experimented with crushed Dufour's gland, a tiny finger-shaped organ at the base of the sting, did other ants pour from the nest and follow the trail.

Wilson concluded that ant communication is governed by chemical signals called *pheromones*, chemical messengers produced by an organism that influences the behavior of others of its species. Chemicals may carry messages over long distances, unlike sight or sound. Pheromones may not even be detected by other species, including predators, who might be attracted by the sight or sound cues of their prey.

Pheromones can act in one of two ways. Releaser pheromones cause an immediate behavior in the animal detecting them. Wilson's fire ants were responding to a releaser pheromone laid down in the trail. In nature, this pheromone is produced by successful foragers which send the message of the location of food to other ants in the colony. Primer pheromones cause a physiological change (a change in a biological function) in the animal detecting them. This type of pheromone may either enter the nose or be eaten by the receiver. Most primer pheromones affect the reproductive state of the receiver and are important in the maintenance of complex insect societies such as those of ants. For example, the ant queen produces a primer pheromone called queen substance that is eaten by her colony mates. The queen substance prevents other females in the colony from becoming sexually mature, and thus ensures that the current queen remains "in charge."

Following his discovery of the pheromone trail, Wilson continued to search for pheromones that triggered other behaviors. He soon discovered pheromones, for example, that attracted ants to each other and sent an alarm to the colony in response to an invader. However, finding pheromones that triggered behaviors other than alarm and attraction was very difficult without advanced training in histology (the study of tissues) and chemistry. Wilson stopped doing this line of research knowing that his work with ant pheromones was going to be continued by other scientists who called his research groundbreaking in the study of chemical communication.

It was also during his graduate school years that Wilson met his future wife, Renee Kelley, from Boston. Although not a scientist, Wilson describes her in *Naturalist*, as "a scholar by temperament . . . [a person] able to understand my dreams of pursuits in faraway places."[2] Soon after they were engaged, Wilson left for a ten-month field trip to New Guinea. In the 1950s, jet and telephone service to remote areas was not common, so Wilson and his fiancée had to make do with daily letters. Six weeks after he returned from this trip, they were married. The following winter, at the age of twenty-six, Wilson was offered an assistant professorship at Harvard.

ISLAND BIOGEOGRAPHY

During the same period, Wilson developed his theory of *island biogeography*. Biogeography is the study of the past and present distribution of plants around the world that bring together concepts from biology, geology, paleontology, and chemistry. Biogeographical regions are isolated from other regions by impassable land barriers, or in the case of islands, by water. Regions isolated from others have distinctive plants and animals, because these isolated organisms have undergone evolution by natural selection. There may be similar environmental conditions in two different regions, but even then, both regions may not contain the same plants and animals. Instead, the organisms may resemble each other because they have adapted to the similar type of environment. For example, coyotes in western North America and jackals in Africa resemble each other physically and behaviorally. Both have also adapted to grasslands and are carnivorous predators, as well as carrion eaters.

Wilson developed the theory of island biogeography with Robert H. McArthur in the early 1960s. The researchers predicted three relationships: (1) The number of species on an island increases with the increasing size of the island. (2) The number of species on an island decreases with increasing distance to the nearest source of new species, usually a continent. This means that the farther an island is from a continent, the fewer species it is likely to have. (3) A constant turnover of species occurs as new species arrive and compete with the ones already on the island. However, the total number of species remains approximately the same. These three relationships mean that the number of species inhabiting an island represents an equilibrium between colonization, increasing species, and extinction, decreasing species.

Wilson needed to test the accuracy of his theory on islands where recolonization could be studied. Wilson and his graduate student Daniel Simberloff found the ideal island laboratories in the Florida Keys. The Keys were relatively close enough to Harvard that Wilson would not need to be away for months at a time, and they weren't so remote that he couldn't bring along his wife, Renee, and new daughter, Catherine. All arthropods (animals with jointed appendages and a rigid external exoskeleton, such as insects, spiders, and crabs) on several mangrove islands were removed by fumigating these small islands with pesticides, but vegetation was left intact. The recolonization process was then monitored for three years. They found that all islands, except the most distant one from the mainland, had recovered initial species numbers within one year. They also found that species turnover rate was high, even after species had reached equilibrium. The most isolated island had the fewest species and the lowest rate of recolonization. Wilson's predictions held true; this research confirmed some of the key results of his 1967 book with MacArthur, *The Theory of Island Biogeography*.

The results of the island biogeography studies applies not only to islands, but can also be adapted to any series of isolated habitats such as forest fragments, which are small sections of forest isolated from one another. Thus, Wilson's island biogeography work is a cornerstone of biological conservation and ecology, informing the planning of natural parks and reserves. For example, a group of interconnected reserves would help protect and save more species than scattered reserves. The major threat to the survival of a species is the reduction of its habitat, because a small area cannot support very many organisms. "We have lost a great many species. Humans have already cut and destroyed half of the forests of the world. A lot of species have gone extinct. One percent [of species], for example, in the United States have gone extinct. That is a small figure, but that's a lot of species. In other countries, and in some places like Hawaii, that figure is closer to one-fourth of all the species. In some parts of the world with the largest number of species, like the Atlantic forest of Brazil and the Madagascar island, the number of species that has been lost is probably in the thousands and can become catastrophic if the forests continue to be cut," states Wilson. He believes that everyone should be concerned by this erosion of biological diversity.

SOCIOBIOLOGY

During the 1970s, Wilson conceived one of his grandest ideas, the theory of *sociobiology*. Sociobiology is the systematic study of the genetic and evolutionary basis of social behavior in all organisms, including humans. A basic tenet of sociobiology is that cooperative behaviors among members of a society exists only because such behavior increases the frequency that an animal's genes are passed on to the next generation relative to other animals in that population, a term called fitness. In other words, by cooperating with other members of its group, an animal will be able to have more offspring, and thus contribute more genes to future generations. Wilson already knew from his work with ant communication that behaviors that maintain the social order in colonies are inherited, which means that social behaviors in ants are adaptations to the environment, just as physical features in animals are adaptations to the environment. Wilson extended these ideas of adaptive behaviors to all animals.

An important event leading to the formulation of sociobiology occurred when Wilson read an article by William D. Hamilton, a British entomologist, in 1964. The article addressed the controversial problem of altruism among insects. Altruism means that an animal is acting for the good of others rather than from self-interest. For instance, in ant societies, only the queen lays eggs and most of the colony is made up of workers that do not have any offspring themselves. The problem here is how such a society can increase the fitness of the workers. The self-sacrifice of the workers poses an apparent problem for natural selection. Natural selection is the weeding out of failures and the reward of success by increased reproduction. Since workers don't reproduce, it appears that the workers are reducing their own fitness in favor of helping the queen increase her fitness. Why aren't the workers being weeded out?

The answer lies in the unusual sex-determining mechanism in social insects of the Order Hymenoptera (ants, bees, and wasps). Unfertilized eggs, which are haploid (contain half of the genetic complement) develop into males, whereas fertilized eggs, which are diploid (contain the full genetic complement) develop into females. (Queens are diploid and develop when fed special nutrients from the workers.) This unusual way of determining sex means that worker ants share, on average, three-quarters of their genes with their sisters, unlike organisms such as humans who only share one-half of their genes, on average, with their siblings. Because worker ants share three-quarters of their genes with siblings, but only one-half with their parents, the fitness (passing genes to future generations) of the worker ant is increased when it raises siblings rather than offspring. This means that when a worker ant helps the queen in what appears to be an altruistic act, in actuality, the worker ant's own fitness is increased. Thus, altruism in ants has a biological basis in that the frequency of the workers' genes in the next generation is increased when they care for the colony rather than reproduce.

Hamilton's ideas, and Wilson's own work in biogeography, seemed to be a source of inspiration to further fuel Wilson in developing his new theory. "They [sociobiology and biogeography] are very close because of my studies of the distribution of ants . . . where different species are found in particular. When I studied ants in the South Pacific, I developed the first ideas about island biogeography. That was theoretical, but I helped to explain the distribution of ants that were discovered in the field. From the study of the social systems of ants, I developed an interest in the general principles of sociobiology, so it followed very naturally," said Wilson.

The synthesis of these ideas by Wilson led to the landmark work, *Sociobiology: The New Synthesis*, published in 1975. In this book, he declared that an organism's primary function is to pass on its genes to the next generation. Drawing on his previous work, Wilson traced the evolution of cooperative behavior and animal communication. Such behaviors are inherited in the same way that physical traits are inherited, and evolve in response to natural selection. This means that since cooperative behavior helps to insure the successful transmission of genes, each organism develops behaviors that assure the greatest reproductive success of the group.

In the last chapter of his book *Man—From Sociobiology to Biology*, Wilson turned to the evolution of human behavior. He interpreted human behavior in terms of its ability to pass on genes to the next generation. For example, Wilson concluded that aggression, religiosity, and conformity in humans help (or have helped in humanity's past) propagate genes and, therefore, have a genetic basis. In a sociobiological interpretation, parental love is clearly selfish in that it promotes the likelihood that an individual's genes will be present in the next generation. The sociobiological interpretation of polygamy (having more than one wife) in some societies shows it to be an adaptation to the environment. It is reproductively advantageous to the male to have more than one wife, so that he can have more opportunities to pass his genes to the next generation. In areas where sources of protein are scarce and early weaning poses a threat to the health of the child, it is also advantageous for the woman to be married to a man with several wives. By this arrangement, she has fewer children and they are thereby assured a more nutritious diet.

Sociobiology: The New Synthesis provided a new way to analyze human behavior. It has given rise to closely related fields such as evolutionary psychology. Even though it is widely accepted today, it sparked great controversy when the work was published. Wilson was not expecting the disturbance created by the suggestion that genes govern human behavior. "Perhaps I should have stopped at chimpanzees when I wrote the book," he commented wryly in *Naturalist*.[3] In a bitter struggle, Wilson was falsely accused by a group of scientists for allegedly providing a scientific justification for exploitation and oppression of certain groups in society. The worst incident of protest came in 1978, when Wilson was presenting a paper at a meeting of the American Association for the Advancement of Science in Washington, D.C. Just as Wilson began to speak, demonstrators poured a pitcher of water over him, chanting, "Wilson, you're all wet!"[4]

Withstanding these assaults with dignity and maintained by a belief in the correctness and value of his theory, Wilson participated in the debates, both in the academic and lay press, that followed the publication of his book. In 1978, he published *On Human Nature* to explain his theories to the general public. The book was awarded the Pulitzer Prize in 1979. Wilson gave examples of inborn fear of the dark, of heights, and of certain facial expressions that people of all cultures can understand as some examples of behavioral patterns that have evolved for survival.

After the publication of *Genes, Mind, and Culture: The Coevolutionary Process*, in 1981 and finally *Promethean Fire: Reflections on the Origin of the Mind* in 1983, Wilson withdrew from the debate about sociobiology. In his opinion, he had provided enough evidence for the defense of his theory. "I always felt that I was fundamentally correct. I knew a lot about the subject and it seemed so logical and so consistent with the evidence that I never had much doubt that it was basically correct. Of course, nobody likes criticism unless it is constructive, such as: 'Here let me see how I can help you.' or 'Here is more information to consider.' or 'Maybe that is not quite right and what do you think of the following?' That is constructive criticism. But twenty-five years ago it was often destructive, by people saying 'Oh no, that is no good.' 'No, it is false and is going to cause people to have the wrong political beliefs.' That has largely vanished. There is little criticism of that kind now."

In 1990, Wilson won the Crafoord Prize of the Royal Swedish Academy of Sciences, ecology's equivalent to the Nobel Prize. In 1991, Wilson won his second Pulitzer award with Bert Hölldobler for *The Ants*, a treatise that represents a lifetime's work on these organisms.

A NEW SYNTHESIS

Unlike a few scientists who became increasingly specialized in one very small area of research early in his career, Wilson's expertise has constantly been expanding throughout his career. In his most recent book, *Consilience: The Unity of Knowledge*, published in 1998, Wilson argues that science and the humanities must be reunited and the ideals of the thinkers of the Enlightment must be revisited. The natural sciences should inform the study of philosophy, history, psychology, and economics, among others, because human affairs make sense only when explained by the biological sciences. *Consilience* means the uniting of knowledge from the different disciplines into a common harmonious system of explanation. Consilience in science—the fact that information from one branch of study agrees with another—is evidence for the success of science. For example, medicine is grounded in molecular biology, which in turn agrees with genetics. The laws of genetics are consistent with the laws of physics. Wilson affirms that the social sciences should be a part of this continuum. "Very little social change in the future is not going to be biological. In this century, it is going to be social and cultural. We are what we are. We have a human nature that is a million years old and we are not going to change that much for better or for worse, because we cannot change our heredity that quickly—and maybe we don't want to. But we obviously will be able to make huge changes by more knowledge and a cultural revolution."

CHAMPION OF BIODIVERSITY

Driven by his deep understanding and love for nature, one of Wilson's ongoing projects and greatest legacies has been global conservation. By the late 1970s, he was actively involved in the conservation movement. A pioneer in the field of ecology, he is a very persuasive champion of the cause. With unmatched dedication, Wilson has spoken out for the preservation of *biodiversity*. The word "biodiversity" is a contraction of the term "biological diversity." Diversity means variety; biological diversity thus refers to variety within the living world. Biodiversity refers to the variability within and among groups of organisms with respect to genetic composition and/or the numbers and types of species or species assemblages in a given area. In its broadest use, biodiversity is a synonym for "life on Earth."

Wilson has pointed out many times that the existence of our very own species is dependent upon the survival of biological diversity on the planet. "I think right now, the most important thing is setting aside more natural reserves around the world. Equally important is education and raising political awareness around the world; making economic arrangements so that the developing countries can find it profitable to set aside large forest reserves and coral reef reserves. It is also evident that the world is waking up to the problem. For example, ten years ago in Brazil hardly anyone had heard about the problem. Now, a large majority of the citizens of Brazil believe that the Amazon forest should not be destroyed any further."

Wilson also believes that creating a world biological survey, completed in 2000, would have greater benefit for humanity than even the mapping of the human genome, "It [a biological survey] is terribly important because we know that the world is extremely rich in biodiversity. We are discovering new species every day. We know about as few as ten percent of the species in the world. We know they are disappearing fast due to habitat destruction, that we could lose half of the species by the end of the present century, unless we change our practices in cutting forests, polluting, and introducing alien species. It is important to understand how to save the world's biodiversity and make full use of it, because if it disappears it is gone forever. That makes it urgent. In order to do that we need to know what biodiversity is. So I have called for a global biodiversity map that will engage the efforts of ecologists and museum biologists in the same way that working out the human genetic map engaged the geneticists and molecular biologists. We must make this a major scientific effort because it is urgent and so many benefits could come from it."

In his book, *Biophilia*, published in 1984, Wilson argued that humanity's innate attraction to the environment has an evolutionary and psychological basis. The concern for the environment that humans exhibit is genetically based because it is a quality that assures the survival of our species.

Scientists still do not know very much about biodiversity on a global scale. The total number of species on Earth is estimated to be between 10 and 100 million, but only about 1.4 million have been identified. Yet, even as our knowledge is expanding, the rate of extinction of species is increasing. In many cases, the damage is greater than imagined, because what is lost is the particular genetic heritage of an organism. This information is extremely valuable, because each species has evolved a unique defense mechanism to survive in its environment. A few advantages of preserving and studying these genetic assets include developing new pharmaceutical and medical products from plants, finding pest-resistant crops, and manufacturing new industrial products. This means that preserving the fragile ecosystems that support threatened species is the ultimate act of self-preservation.

Wilson's current project continues with his goal of the preservation of our natural resources. "What I am working on right now is a book on the subject of conservation. I call it *The Future of Life*. It is about the state of the world's biodiversity and why it is important to save it, and what the methods are that are being used around the world to do just that—what the best hope is for the future."

"The rule that my career has demonstrated is that you can be a successful scientist if you find a subject to love, like a group of organisms, like ants, birds, trees, or bacteria. Then as you study them, you ask the question of what they can tell us about the natural order. . . . Each group of organisms has something special to offer." He affirms, "I celebrate ants."

It is difficult to summarize Wilson's research, life, and contributions to humanity in a few sentences. One reason for this is because his work continues to be a work-in-progress, even after his retirement from teaching. Another reason is that he has, at the time of this writing, authored, coauthored or edited twenty-four books, written over 370 scientific articles, mentored twenty-seven students to completion of their doctorates, and lead the development of the fields of biogeography, sociobiology, and chemical communication. He has been awarded two Pulitzer Prizes along with more than seventy other awards and honors. *Time* magazine named him one of the twenty-five most influential *Americans* in 1995 and both *Time* and *Audubon* magazines labeled him one of the century's one hundred leading environmentalists in 2000. One can only wait to see wait to see what revolution and controversy his next book will bring, but also what long-lasting positive effects it will have on humanity.

Nia H. Dukov

CHAPTER 14

EDWARD WITTEN

MARIA E. WILSON

T wo of the most powerful forces in the universe are in conflict. One is very, very large and affects every large body in the universe. The other is very, very small, yet is everywhere and influences everything deep within the universe. For years no one has been able to reconcile these two superpowers. They are both part of the universe, but they just cannot seem to get along. One cannot exist without the other; and yet, they seem intent on alienating each other. The universe and the world of science cannot be whole until they find a way to compromise. Who can help reconcile the two? We need someone who is brilliant in math *and* in science; someone who has contributed to the world of science several times before; someone whose charming, dark curly hair, captivating speaking skills, and amazing intelligence could not be withheld from the science world. This individual is Edward Witten.

Edward Witten is a professor of physics at the Institute for Advanced Study in Princeton, New Jersey. *Time* magazine recently called him the most brilliant physicist in the world, perhaps the most brilliant physicist who ever lived. This kind of praise, bordering on hype, need not be taken literally, but it does reflect the tremendous respect, approaching awe, which Witten is accorded among his scientific colleagues who are liberally quoted in *Time*. Interviews and articles about Witten appear frequently in the popular press. This attention is earned by Witten's willingness to try to explain the very exotic theories of physics with which he is involved. In the past few years, articles in *Encyclopedia Britannica*, *The Guardian*, *Baltimore Sun*, and *Scientific American*, as well as this author's interview with him, profile one of America's leading physicists—insofar as it is possible to have a picture of a very prominent scientist whose creativity is still evolving.

With this kind of worldwide recognition, one would think the personality of the man would be terribly distorted. Not so. Witten "dismisses with a shrug all suggestions and comparisons to Einstein and Newton." He seems unaffected by the attention he gets from the press. Witten is an impeccable role model in his ability to maintain his modesty, despite a great deal of media attention.

SUPERSTRING MAN

Edward Witten was born August 26, 1951, in Baltimore, Maryland, into a family which valued education. Witten's father was (and is) a theoretical physicist, and later became a professor at the University of Cincinnati. One of the things he worked on was classical general relativity—a topic that would later play a large role in his son's career. When Witten was very young, he loved astronomy and space, which is not surprising since he was raised in an environment where they were often discussed. He grew up during the beginning of the space race, an exciting time for scientists. The world's enthusiasm and the father's influence molded him into a very committed young researcher. When he was growing up, he wanted to be an astronomer. Using a small telescope, he enjoyed exploring the universe, including the rings of Saturn that he saw for the first time while on vacation in New Hampshire. He said, "Looking back at it now, it seems to me that it should have been quite easy to find Saturn from my own backyard in Baltimore—I am puzzled that it seemed necessary to bring the telescope to New Hampshire to see Saturn."

Witten was identified as gifted early in his schooling. He managed to skip a couple of school grades during a period of time when educators frowned on acceleration as a way of coping with giftedness. The ability to excel in school must have been connected with the influence of his physicist father, who engaged the preschool aged youngster in discussions about science.

An aunt tells the story of teaching ten-year-old Witten how to play bridge before he accompanied his family on an ocean voyage. A week later, the aunt heard that "Eddie had won the bridge tournament on the way over."[1]

When he was older, after about the age of eleven, when that childish excitement began to disappear, Witten thought he would be a mathematician. To this day, he is not sure why he became a physicist instead of a mathematician. Perhaps it is his destiny to serve as a bridge between math and physics, as his work creates new links between two vital areas of science. Though his father served only one side, Edward strives to bring balance to them.

Witten attended Park School as a ninth grader where recognition of his "problem" was immediate. The school engaged a professor from John Hopkins University to teach him math. A classmate at the Park School remembers his first impression of Witten in ninth grade: "He was two years younger than anyone else and at least 2000 years smarter than anybody else—and that makes for an awkward time."[2]

One of his high school friends was quoted as saying, "I suppose it is common that kids in any high school sit around and talk about who is the smartest kid in the class. But when Ed wasn't there, we used to sit around and talk about how he was the smartest person in the world!"[3]

In high school, Witten also displayed a great deal of interest in history and politics. He succeeded in getting several letters published in the *Baltimore Sun* against the war in Vietnam. In many issues related to politics and world affairs, Witten exhibited qualities of compassion, outrage at injustice, and a willingness to espouse unpopular opinions on important topics.

Witten did his undergraduate work at Brandeis University, graduating in 1971 with a bachelor's degree in history. He also studied economics and linguistics. He was interested in politics and wrote briefly for the *Nation* and the *New Republic*. He even volunteered to work in the campaign of George McGovern for U.S. president in 1972.

But the pull of physics won out and he obtained a Ph.D. in physics from Princeton University. By the age of twenty-eight, he was a full professor—a monumental achievement. In due course, recognition of Witten as a leading physicist was confirmed by his acceptance of many very prestigious awards, such as the Einstein Medal, the Dirac Medal, the Field Medal (the highest prize given in mathematics), and a MacArthur "genius" award.

Witten is now deeply embroiled in what may well be the most mathematically sophisticated and abstract effort in the history of physics: the theory of superstrings. But he is very proud of his early work in theoretical particle physics, which was directly connected to then current experiments. As an example, he was invited to give the opening lecture at the twentieth International Conference on Neutrino Physics in June 2000. This field is dominated by experimental results and Witten's talk skillfully wove in the most exciting elements of current understanding. This may be a reaction to some critics who are not yet convinced that string theory will produce well-defined predictions.

The young genius more than fulfilled his promise to become a leading scientist. The work he has been most associated with is both very complex and may be supremely important to the future of physics—indeed to the future of our understanding of the universe. String theory, sometimes called superstrings, attacks the biggest puzzle in physics: the unification of relativity with the quantum theories of the forces of electromagnetism and nuclear physics. Witten, the "pied piper of superstrings," waxes eloquently at the "magical" properties of the theory which probes the deepest symmetries of the world. He feels this theory will bring about a revolution. This revolution, in Witten's view and in that of his colleagues, will be more profound than any that has shaken up physics in history.

The two forces of the universe he is trying to reconcile are not demon forces; they are parts of the mechanics of the universe—theories about how it works. They are perhaps the two most important pillars of physics, foundations upon which modern physics has grown and developed. These two 'superpowers' are the two revolutionary theories of the twentieth century: the laws of quantum mechanics and Einstein's general relativity.

In order to set the stage for the reader to gain some appreciation of string theory, it is imperative to review the main ideas in physics leading to the entry of Witten. This will take us to Isaac Newton, through Faraday and Maxwell, through Bohr and Schrodinger and Heisenberg, to Einstein. Dare we put Witten on this list? The string theory Witten has investigated decades of his life to has no lesser ambition than to combine and, in some sense, replace all of the physics from the past four hundred years.

THE WORLD OF ISAAC NEWTON

To understand the revolution that Witten is leading, it is only proper to review the state of the knowledge of physics that developed toward the end of the twentieth century. For a fuller picture, however, we have to start even earlier, with the work of seventeenth-century English physicist and mathematician Isaac Newton. Newton invented a theory of gravity to explain why apples, for example, fall down from trees—always down, even though the trees may be on opposite sides of the Earth. Newton was also familiar with data from astronomers who had tracked the motion of planets and were tending to conclude that this was planetary motion around the Sun. He also understood that the Moon orbited around the Earth. Moreover, Newton discovered the basic laws of motion—his key law was that objects would move only in straight lines at constant speed unless there was a force acting upon that object. He then, if the force were known, devised a way of determining the motion of any object.

Newton put all these ideas together. Apples fall down because a force, gravity, pulls them toward the center of the Earth. Planets move around the Sun because the Sun exerts a force, again gravity, drawing the planets toward the Sun just as a string draws a stone toward your hand as you whirl the stone around over your head. If the string breaks or gravity stops, the planets would fly off in straight lines, tangent to the orbit. And the Moon is drawn toward the Earth by a similar force of gravity. Newton wrote down exact equations that precisely explained the motions of apples, moons, and planets, and would anticipate those of baseballs and artillery shells. Today, Newton's laws are used to design bridges, buildings, and airplanes. Newton's laws are used by astronomers to study the motion of stars over vast distances and by the National Aeronautics and Space Administration (NASA) to steer the voyage of artificial satellites and *Voyager* space vehicles around the solar system. However, Newton's great theory of gravity turned out to be slightly inaccurate when its predictions were compared to the exact measurements of the motion of the planet Mercury, the planet closest to the Sun and, therefore, under the strongest gravitational influence. It is impossible to exaggerate the influence of Newton's mechanics on the course of world events; from the general principles that the world was an orderly machine subject to laws of motion, to the specific countless inventions and discoveries, to the development of subjects such as mechanical and civil engineering. When, in the nineteenth century, Newton's laws were supplemented by the laws of Michael Faraday and James Clark Maxwell, of electricity, magnetism, optics, and the laws of heat and thermodynamics, physicists had some justification in believing that everything worth understanding was already understood. Classical physics, the physics of Newton and Maxwell, should be a consequence of the much more encompassing postulates of the string theory that Witten and his colleagues are developing.

QUANTUM MECHANICS

But the last decade of the 1900s brought a host of new discoveries: radioactivity, X-rays, and the electron, and in the first decade of the twentieth century, the structure of the atom.

In the early years of the 1900s, physicists were beginning to study the properties of atoms. It was known for a long time that all normal stuff around—paper, pens, air, water, sand, and clouds—were made of atoms. Chemists had identified about a hundred different atoms that were defined as the smallest units out of which the chemical elements were made. Thus hydrogen, the lightest element, was composed of hydrogen atoms, the simplest atom, made out of one electron in an orbit around a tiny nucleus, consisting of a single proton. The force holding the parts together was not gravitation, but a much stronger force, electricity. Each of the chemical elements had a different structure, the major difference being the number of electrons and the mass of the nucleus.

In contrast to the theories of Newton and Einstein, quantum mechanics was the creation of many minds, but we may list Neils Bohr, Erwin Schrodinger, and Werner Heisenberg as among its prime movers.

Data from the detailed behavior of atoms indicated very weird behavior. Remember that atoms are unimaginably small; one hundred million hydrogen atoms in a straight line would equal one centimeter. Again, Newton's theory of force and motion didn't work inside the atom and a new theory had to be constructed.

By the mid-1920s, a new theory was indeed invented. It was very strange and posed a challenge to even the greatest minds. Nevertheless, it worked and was known as quantum mechanics. In this strange theory, electrons could exist only in certain arrangements around the atom. Light, which had been understood as being composed of electrical and magnetic (electromagnetic) waves, was instead found to consist of streams of small bundles of energy called photons. In quantum mechanics, everything comes in "lumps" and "jumps." A photon, hitting an electron in an atom, can cause it to jump to a new orbit or, better, a new state in the atom. Only certain special states are possible. Later the electron can jump back to its original state, generating a new photon.

The contrast of quantum theory and Newton's "classical" theory is somewhat like the difference between a cup of water and a cup of fine sand. If you don't look too closely, they both pour and appear similar. But if you look very closely, the sand comes in units—one grain, two grains, and so on—whereas the water is smooth and continuous. Quantum mechanics enabled scientists to invent the transistor, the laser (Charles Townes, its inventor, is profiled in chapter 11), the tunnel diode, and the scanning tunneling microscope—just to give a few examples. It enabled scientists to understand how atoms work, how atoms can combine to make simple molecules (like H_2O), that is, to more completely understand chemistry and how to make very complex molecules like DNA.

Again the revolution of quantum mechanics was a major change in humankind's understanding of the microworld. Its economic impact was also monumental—it gave us quantum chemistry, molecular biology, lasers, transistors, microelectronics, computers, and the Internet. But the concepts underlying quantum theory were also very profound: discreteness, quantum uncertainties, continuous waves replaced by lumpy particles, all outside of our human experiences and our intuitions.

Quantum mechanics also allowed us to break atoms apart, into their pieces: electrons, protons and neutrons—and what is inside *these* objects (quarks, for example). In Witten's ambitions, string theory will provide a newer and deeper foundation for quantum mechanics. So the next stage in taking things apart is called particle physics, which provides the stage upon which Witten's string theory can play.

PARTICLE PHYSICS

All the phenomena of the physical world and the biological world can be reduced to the properties of a relatively small number of fundamental and irreducible particles, interacting with each other through a small number of forces. This strong statement is far from being accepted by all scientists, but it has enough validity to make the search for such particles and forces a major objective of physicists. Over the past fifty years, particle physicists, using an ever more powerful array of machines and instruments, have established a standard model, a table of the primordial particles and forces which we can summarize as follows:

I	II	III	
u	c	t	Quarks
d	s	b	
e	μ	τ	Leptons
ν_e	ν_μ	ν_τ	

Strong force carried by gluons
Electromagnetic force carried by photons
Weak force carried by $W^+ W^- Z^0$
Gravitational force carried by gravitons?

Quarks should have names; they are called up, down, charm, strange, top, and bottom by the same logic that gives people names like Tom, Dick and Mary. Quarks experience each of the four forces listed in the above table, whereas leptons seems to be unaffected by the strong force.

The objective of the standard model is to present a table of the primordial particles and forces that form the basis of all of matter and energy. A metaphor helps; Dr. Lederman stole this one from the Roman poet Lucretius. It seeks the smallest unit that will create a library. (The library stands for "universe.") You start with books—millions of books: poetry, history, religion, humor, travel; fat books, skinny books; a countless variety. But each book has chapters, the chapters have paragraphs, and these have sentences. The sum total of sentences is like the number of grains of sand on a huge beach. But, ah! Sentences are made of words and there are a finite number of words—all listed in some convenient order in a thick book found at the library entrance and labeled "dictionary." Now we are excited. All the trillions of sentences in the millions of books can be constructed with this dictionary set of words, provided that we use rules for combining words. We call this (for simplicity) grammar. So the laws of grammar and the dictionary full of words can construct all the books. But wait, we can further reduce things. All we need is twenty-six letters and a new law called spelling. This will make all the words in the dictionary that will—but any six-year old will dismiss your reduction with contempt. "All you need, old fellow, is a zero and a one." Kids now grow up with digital toys in their cribs. So we are down to zeros and ones and a new rule, a computer algorithm which then constructs the letter which, with spelling. . . . Now if it doesn't make any sense to take the "zero" apart or the "one" apart, we have arrived at the bottom line. The universe/library can be reduced to zeros and ones (the fundamental particles) and a set of rules (laws of nature). The standard model is just this reduction: everything we know about our universe can be constructed by these primordial particles and the laws of nature (forces) which control how they combine to make the nuclei, the atoms, the molecules, the DNA. Of course, we are not there yet.

This summary, with all the mathematical equations which describe the forces in detail are consistent with a vast number of experiments. For example, the strong, weak, and electromagnetic forces are more fully described as quantum field theories. Gravity, the theory of relativity, is different and sort of hangs uncomfortably below the standard model.

Quantum field theories obeying a deep symmetry known as gauge symmetry implies the existence of a new class of particles—the quanta of the fields, which carry the forces between participating particles. For example, the force between a positively charged nucleus and a negatively charged electron (Coulomb's Force) is transmitted from nucleus to electron and back by a force transmitted by *photons*. When all the math is done, out pops Coulomb's inverse square law. In this way, we have come to understand, with great precision, the strong forces holding nuclei together, the weak forces responsible for radioactivity, and the electromagnetic forces which account for the behavior of atoms and molecules.

There has been some progress in the hope for a simpler model, one in which we have fewer than six quarks and leptons inter-acting under the guidance of four forces. The quest for a simpler picture ("As simple as possible," opined Einstein, "but no sim-pler") looks for unification of the forces and some model in which the variety of quarks, leptons, and their antiparticles are aspects of some much simpler system. Looking ahead, could "strings" be the answer? It should finally be noted that if we add up all the num-bers that are associated with the standard model table (the masses of all the particles, the strengths of all the forces, the range or reach of the forces, and so forth), we need about twenty numbers that are known by direct measurement with varying degrees of precision. The test of any good theory is to have these numbers emerge as a consequence of the theory, rather than have them inserted into the theory. One of the properties these fundamental particles don't have is a radius. It has become standard to refer to quarks and lep-tons as points with no internal structure. Thus, as we will see, the string theory, led by Witten and his colleagues, is a departure in that tiny, vibrating strings replace the "point" particles.

EINSTEIN'S THEORY OF GENERAL RELATIVITY

Slight inaccuracy of Newton's theory was no surprise to Albert Einstein. In 1916, Einstein invented a new theory of gravity. The new theory had the same successes as Newton's theory when it was applied to apples, moons, and planets, except that it predicted precisely the behavior of the planet Mercury. Einstein's theory was able to correct the small discrepancy in Newton's treatment. And whereas Newton postulated the inverse square law of the gravity force, this came out of relativity. It made many new predictions. One was that light, passing near a large mass, would be attracted to the mass (for example, the Sun) and would thereby bend from its usual straight-line motion.

Einstein's view of gravity was as a distortion in a new geom-etry of space and time. So masses distort space and this curved space influences the motion of bodies just as if there was a force acting upon them. This geometry could explain that the force of gravity was revolutionary. When it was discovered by careful measurements that light indeed bends toward heavy masses, Einstein's theory became widely accepted.

In the past thirty or so years, the theory of relativity has been tested in many different ways with increasing precision. One dramatic test is that the theory of relativity predicts that when the gravitational forces are very strong and produce changing motion of very heavy objects, then gravity "waves" could be generated that would travel away from the sources of the gravitation. Astronomers are aware of stars orbiting one another—binary systems. When both stars are neutron stars, then they demonstrate a loss of energy, presumably because they are radiating gravitational energy. This is an effect predicted by relativity and not by Newton's laws.

Another of the great successes of Einstein's theory is its prediction that stars that have a large enough mass will, when they exhaust their nuclear fuel, eventually collapse to form a black hole.

A black hole is a bizarre object. Its gravity is so strong that nothing, not even light, can escape from it; thus the description "black." Today we are aware that the universe is full of these objects and we know that the theory of relativity is an essential part of the way scientists can understand their behavior.

Einstein's relativity was based upon a very simple concept: the laws of nature should not depend on the state of motion of Earthbound scientists who are trying to figure them out. One additional idea was needed: the gravitational force that pulls down on a person (say, standing on a scale) is in every way the same as the effect if the room containing the scientist and scale is accelerating upward in free space. That is, the gravitational force on an object is in every way equivalent to an acceleration of the object in free space.

We must stress that Einstein's theory of relativity is a classical theory in that the geometrical picture of space and time is smooth and has no hint of the quantum lumpiness characteristic of atoms. Many attempts were made to join relativity and gravity to the other forces and to their quantum nature. In anticipation, the quantum of the gravitational field was given the name *graviton*. It was even deduced that, if indeed such an object existed, it would have a spin of 2 units (quarks and leptons have spins of $1/2$ unit). Again, this partially successful grand scheme must somehow emerge from the superstring efforts.

CONFLICTING THEORIES

There are phenomena in the universe nonetheless, that demand both quantum theory and relativity be used simultaneously. One is black holes. Black holes are places in the universe from which nothing, not even light, can escape, as was stated earlier. Black holes, though not entirely understood, raise some interesting questions. And to answer these questions, black holes require that both quantum mechanics and general relativity be used. As mentioned earlier, quantum mechanics is applied to the very, very small and very low-mass objects. General relativity is used to explain the very, very large and heavy objects, such as stars and galaxies. The matter in black holes is both very small and very massive. Some black holes weigh a million times the mass of our Sun. (Although some black holes are very small.) Thus, both theories are needed here, even though with our current understanding, they are in conflict with one another.

EARLY UNIVERSE

Another important domain where Einstein's gravitation and quantum mechanics must work together is in the early universe. Cosmologists are historians charged with the responsibility of tracing the origin of the universe, its evolution to where it is now, and where it will be one hundred billion years from now. Their progress over the past century has been remarkable. We know a lot more about the origin and evolution of the universe now than a century ago. And overwhelming evidence points to a time, about fifteen billion years ago, when the universe was born in a cata-clysmic explosion (see the profile of George Smoot in chapter 10).

The size of the entire newborn universe was much smaller than the nucleus of an atom; therefore, the physics that is relevant has to come under the domain of quantum mechanics. In detail, the relevant physics is the quantum mechanics of elementary particles. This is because the incredible heat energy typical of the universe at this initial period decomposed matter into its most basic fundamental particles. But the incredible masses squeezed into a microscopic dot demands an explanation through general relativity. In order to fully understand what happened in the first few trillionths of a second, it requires the unification of quantum mechanics and general relativity.

Key to the hope for unification is in the details of the building blocks of atoms, the fundamental particles. Particle accelerators (atom smashers) give us clues to these fundamental particles and thus quantum mechanics.

THEORETICAL PHYSICISTS

So what do theoretical physicists actually do? Are they just physicists, who sit around and contemplate their toes all day and don't actually accomplish anything? Some people believe that. Theoretical physicists, however, claim that they are in fact full-fledged physicists. They deal in ideas or concepts that can explain large numbers of facts or data. The contrast is that experimental physicists work in laboratories, using instruments to collect data on whatever topic interests them. They may, for example, be interested in the behavior of matter at extremely low temperatures, near absolute zero. They may be fascinated by the structure of atoms and thereby design delicate instruments that will torture atoms into providing facts and processes about how atoms are structured. They may be astronomers, studying the distribution of stars within a galaxy or clustering of galaxies in the vastness of space. Out of all of this experimentation and lots more work pours a plethora of precise measurements and observations.

Then enters the theoretical physicist who seeks to find some hopefully simple explanation in terms of a new concept (or theory) that would explain the data. When Newton invented his theory of gravity, he successfully explained the orbit of planets and moons as observed and measured by astronomers. He explained in precise detail how things (like apples) fall near the surface of the earth. Newton's gravity explained tides, and such known facts as the Earth not being an actual sphere, but bulging slightly at the equator. Theories, invented by theoretical physicists, usually explain not only known facts, but are capable of predicting new phenomena. Einstein, theoretical physicist par excellence, explained why Mercury's motion, suffering the strongest gravitational force of the nearby sun, was not in agreement with Newton's gravity. But he also predicted that starlight, passing very close to our Sun on its way to a telescope, would be deflected toward the Sun. Relativity was first published in 1915 when a solar eclipse permitted close observation of the light near a star that could not be seen in the full glare of sunlight. Astronomers rushed to South American and Africa to observe the starlight and verify the predictions of Einstein.

It takes an enormously creative person, such as Witten, to be a theoretical physicist. Theoretical physicists have to ask questions like the one asked by Albert Einstein: "If I were riding on a beam of light, and I was holding a mirror, would I see my reflection in it?" Imagination and intelligence work together to fuel the mind of a great theoretical physicist. After an ingenious theory is concocted, hard work must be done to explore its possibilities, and, ideally, prove it.

Although the class of theoretical physicists is a very select group among physicists, even within this class there are large variations in ability. Brian Greene recounts these stories about Witten: "The breadth and depth of Witten's productivity is legendary. His wife, Chiara Nappi, who is also a physicist at the institute, paints a picture of Witten sitting at their kitchen table, mentally probing the edge of string theory knowledge, and only now and then returning to pick up pen and paper to verify an elusive detail or two."[4] Another story is told by a postdoctoral fellow who, one summer, had an office next to Witten's. He describes the unsettling juxtaposition of laboriously struggling with complex string theory calculations at his desk while hearing the incessant rhythmic patter of Witten's keyboard, as paper after groundbreaking paper poured forth directly from mind to computer file.[5]

SUPERSTRING THEORY

The efforts to find a unification of the forces, to combine gravity and quantum mechanics, and to account for the fundamental particles, has kept many theoretical physicists busy over the past four or five decades. Most of these hopeful efforts ran into mathematical and physical problems, leading to no result. Then the work of a young Italian theorist, Gabriella Veneziano, came to the attention of the theorists.

Veneziano was trying to find a model to explain data obtained by experimentalists on so-called resonances—that is, seemingly excited states of combinations of quarks (hadrons). Veneziano found that the masses of these excited states were correlated with the spins. His model was "mere mathematics," but reminded others of the properties of ordinary strings. A popular Physics I experiment shows a long rope, stretched across the lecture table, which is caused to vibrate by being connected at one end to a mechanical arm driven by a motor whose speed, can be changed.

At certain frequencies, the long rope's vibrations became coherent, the rapid up and down motions of the string forming a wave shape. As the frequency of the driving vibration is increased, other resonances appear. This property of strings, to vibrate preferentially at certain frequencies, is the basis of many musical instruments: piano strings hit by key hammers, violin strings caused to vibrate by the frictional force of the bow, and so on. But could the quarks really be strings? This gave rise to a string model for particles, admittedly a crude approximation. Then, in the 1970s, physicists discovered that string theory seemed to describe, not the spin $1/2$ quarks, but a zero mass particle with spin of 2, that is, a graviton. Could string theory describe the quanta of gravitation, that is, a quantum theory of gravitation? Interest in this theory exploded. All fundamental particles are, in this picture, not point particles—but tiny vibrating strings and the frequencies of the vibrations determine the various masses.

WITTEN AND SUPERSTRING THEORY

Witten, appointed professor at the Institute for Advanced Study in Princeton, New Jersey, made many contributions to theoretical particle physics and to quantum field theory. He and his colleagues developed new insights into an old problem of why one never sees an isolated quark—only clumps of quarks that make protons and other hadrons. He became intrigued by higher dimensional theories and it was perhaps this that led him into string theory. Witten's attitude toward research is especially interesting to potential scientists. He states, "Doing research means (apart from being interrupted a lot) spending most of one's time floundering around, not sure of what one does want to do. The hardest part is to find a problem that is hard enough to be worth doing, but easy enough that one can actually do. It is something that we all (that is, all theoretical physicists I know) have trouble with."

The "string" idea replaces the point particle as the basic structure out of which matter is made. Instead of point particles of different masses (i.e., quarks and leptons), you have tiny vibrating strings and the various frequencies at which the strings vibrate represent the particles of different masses. The strings are very short—a billion of a trillion times smaller than the proton. That's a problem in experimental verification. We will not ever (probably) check this directly, but we will surely look at the consequences of this string structure.

Witten is a leader in many senses of the word in the latest effort at what the media now calls a "theory of everything" or TOE. The idea is a unifying, overarching theory, which would, in principle, explain all phenomena from human psychology to the origin of earthquakes, from quasars to quarks and DNA to dinosaurs.

Witten and many of his colleagues don't like the appellation TOE, because they would be overjoyed with a theory out of which would emerge the standard model, unified with a quantum theory of gravity, even if it left other questions unanswered. The joining of this TOE to other branches of physics, chemistry, biology, and more complex fields would still be left to do. In this way, the string theorists look at their theory as the beginning of a new phase of explaining the world.

Witten was attracted to string theory by the possibility of reconciling gravity with quantum mechanics. Witten said this was a central problem in physics for longer than he'd been in the field. The inconsistency of gravity and quantum theory "emerged more and more as *the* central problem in theoretical physics. Perhaps the most inaccessibly difficult problem."[6]

Witten's personal attitude toward his as of yet incomplete contribution to science is given in response to an interview question. "I will say that I really believe that string theory is leading us to a fundamental new level of physics, comparable in scope to any of the advances that have been made in physics in the past—it would involve a revolution in our concepts of the basic laws of physics—similar in scope to any that occurred in the past."[7]

As we listen to Witten, realize that we are eavesdropping on one of the leading physicists of our time, discussing what he believes is a revolutionary theory at the very core of our understanding of the world in which we live. It may still be a chimera, and it may still be that Witten and the large group of string theorists are following a blind alley. History does tell us such stories. However it is also very possible that the innovations in modern research, and the great advances in communications has enabled us to get a glimpse of a profound event in the history of science, as if Isaac Newton or Albert Einstein were exposing their innermost hopes as they were working on their own revolutionary theories that changed the world.

Brian Greene goes on to write, "Edward Witten's razor-sharp intellect is clothed in a soft-spoken demeanor that often has a wry, almost ironic, edge. He is widely regarded as Einstein's successor in the role of the world's greatest living physicist. Some would go even further and describe him as the greatest physicist of all time. He has an insatiable appetite for cutting-edge physics problems and he wields tremendous influence in setting the direction of research in string theory."[8]

Witten's major contribution to string theory (as of the year 2000) was made public in a famous talk he gave at a conference on strings called STRINGS 95. The talk pointed out a dramatic discovery that would unify many different approaches to the ultimate string theory—the TOE. As Brian Greene writes in his book, "Witten's discovery stunned the audience and has since rocked the string theory community."[9]

Largely because of Witten, 1995 is considered a start of the second superstring revolution. The period from the mid-1980s to 1995 was one of enormous effort on the part of upward of one hundred physicists and mathematicians, at which time they undertook the highly ambitious program of unifying and understanding all of nature's fundamental material objects and forces.

The mathematical concepts were mostly brand new. In the history of physics, Newton had to invent calculus in order to solve problems in gravitation. Calculus is now one of the most useful branches of mathematics. On the other hand, quantum mechanics required a branch of mathematics that had already been developed by mathematicians for their own enlightenment. They were delighted and astonished when physicists swarmed all over the mathematics of matrices and finite dimensional vector spaces. In string theory, it was mostly new stuff.

Witten said, in 1985, "String theory at its finest is, or should be, a new branch of geometry. Einstein's great achievement in general relativity was to base the theory of gravity on geometry. If string theory is to be a worthy successor, it must likewise have a geometrical foundation of which, at present, we only have glimmerings.

"We are probably living in what might prove to be the early stages of a long process, like the process that led to quantum electrodynamics—which took fifty years to emerge."[10]

By the mid-1980s, string theorists had constructed five different superstring theories. In each of these, the extended nature of strings enables the theories to embrace compatibility between gravity and quantum mechanics. Each of these theories has a mind-numbing property that its description of space includes not only the three space dimensions we are accustomed to and which satisfied Newton and Einstein, but six other space dimensions, each perpendicular to all the others. Imagine only four space dimensions if you can; you probably cannot. You may come close by imagining "Flatlanders," creatures who live in two dimensions, say, knowing only about east-west and north-south. Ask *them* to imagine a third dimension. From our superior view it is simply up-down, but to the Flatlanders it would be unimaginable.

Mathematically, we can describe any number of orthogonal (mutually perpendicular) systems, but our experience prevents us from visualizing more than the three of our experience. String theory, it turned out, needed a total of nine space dimensions and one time dimension in order to achieve the unification of forces. Without these extra dimensions, the mathematics would predict total nonsense: quantum mechanical probabilities that were greater than unity (i.e., greater than 100 percent) or even negative probabilities.

So where are these new dimensions? Curled up into tight little shapes with spatial extents that are characteristic of string lengths, that is, 10^{-33}m, ten million billion times smaller than the smallest distance we have ever been able to measure!

Each of the five string theories had its supporters and each had some glimmers of success. But you can't have five theories of everything. Witten's 1995 breakthrough talk resolved the crisis. Here, at the expense of adding one more space dimension, Witten was able to convince a discouraged community that these five approaches were a kind of Roshomon[11]—that all five were different pieces of a master superstring theory he called M-theory. Whereas mother-of-all-theories is as good an interpretation as any, one reason for M is that not only do one-dimensional strings vibrate to make particles, but two-dimensional membranes can also play a role. Whatever there is after Witten in 1995, a strong feeling that all five string theories are describing different pieces of a new, unified string theory.

Witten has accomplished so much in the fields of mathematics and physics, and earned so much academic prestige, that he would have every right to consider himself a "superhero." But that is not the case. Witten even admitted, "Perhaps I was just a little bit 'geeky' at that age [junior high]." He added, "I try not to take what other people say about me too seriously." He works very hard, and his time is in great demand from his colleagues, but he also enjoys other activities. He is a tennis player and enjoys chess, as well as observational astronomy. He has always spent a great deal of time with his children (the oldest of whom is now twenty), sometimes taking them stargazing. He has shown them some of the things that excited him as a child, such as the Andromeda galaxy and the Orion Nebula, conveying to them the same wonder he felt when he first saw the rings of Saturn through that small telescope. He is a teacher as well as an explorer, taking great joy in sharing his passion.

Is the theory of everything the end of science? Brian Green, in *The Elegant Universe*, writes, "The universe is such a wonderfully rich and complex place that the discovery of the final theory . . . would not spell the end of science. Quite the contrary: The discovery of the TOE—the ultimate explanation of the universe at its most microscopic level, a theory that does not rely on any deeper explanation—would provide the firmest foundation on which to build our understanding of the world. Its discovery would mark a beginning, not an end. The ultimate theory would provide an unshakable pillar of coherence forever assuring us that the universe is a comprehensible place."[12]

Witten said, "I don't like talking about [the] 'theory of everything' as it is too grandiose sounding. Besides, string theory can be a major advance if it just turns out to be a theory of a lot without being a theory of everything."

Either way, it will connect two pillars of science by placing a larger pillar underneath them. The handsome, dark-featured man, aided by many colleagues, may lift up these pillars with superhuman strength and place on them the strongest foundation of existence. He may take the baton and direct the cosmic orchestra for his theme song during the credits. Because, once accomplished, our understanding of the universe will have been truly united.

In an interview with the *Baltimore Sun*, Witten was quoted in a perceptive revelation of what it means to be a scientist. He said, "Whether you think of them yourself or learn about them from the work of others, good ideas—really good ideas—in math and physics, are just much more beautiful than what you meet in other walks of life. And part of the beauty of math and physics is that they're universal. If there are other civilizations in other galaxies, they've discovered the same math we've discovered—because it's true. They might organize it differently, but they've discovered the same truth."[13]

And finally, we read Witten's opinion of his field. "I can only speak for myself. I think that it is a tremendous stroke of good luck to be working in physics during the epoch in which string theory is developing. I personally believe that in future centuries people will look back and say that this was one of the great times to do physics.

"I think that we are in a similar period with string theory. I think that even most people who are enthusiastic about string theory tend to underestimate how radical it will prove to be in its impact on how we understand physical law. We are uncovering part of the structure, but we haven't got to the nub of things yet. Again, as with quantum mechanics, I think that without coming to the nub of what string theory really is, it's hard to foresee what theoretical physics is going to be like after that. I think that theoretical physics will be on a plane that we can hardly imagine today. What the problems will be in that epoch I wouldn't care to speculate about."[14]

Maria E. Wilson

CHAPTER 15

DAWN WRIGHT

MAPPING THE ABYSS

MIKE STUKEL

There are regions of our planet where light cannot penetrate, regions teeming with bizarre life forms never seen by the human eye. These strange places can range in temperature from just above the freezing point of water to a scalding 660 degrees Fahrenheit. They are filled with poisonous chemicals. Yet somehow in this dark hostile land of extremes, life can survive. In the absence of light and photosynthesis, unique organisms have adapted to use new forms of energy unlike anything we have ever experienced before, thriving on the very chemicals that would spell death for most species.

This may seem like a scene from a science fiction novel or from explorations of a foreign planet, but strangely, this ecosystem is closer to Earth than we are. These fantastic places and creatures are located around hydrothermal vents in some of the deepest regions of the Earth's oceans. Here, mineral-rich, magma-heated water rises from holes in the ocean floor, carrying with it nutrients capable of supporting a food chain based solely on chemosynthesis, the production of energy from chemical compounds.

Before 1977, when the first such vent was discovered in the Galapagos, an ecosystem devoid of all solar energy would have been inconceivable for biologists. Yet, hidden in the depths of the ocean, it exists. Oceans cover more than seventy percent of the Earth's surface, yet we know less about the depths of these oceans than we do about the surface of Mars. Most people don't know what strange and fascinating secrets the ocean holds, but it is the task of oceanographers and geophysicists, like Dr. Dawn Wright, to find out.

When Wright was in high school and college, she was a great athlete. She was a national qualifier in collegiate bicycling, a United States Cycling Federation licensed racer, and an Olympic hopeful in the long jump. The passion and energy she once brought to sports is now focused on unraveling the mysteries of the deep.

ATTRACTED TO THE SEA

Throughout most of her childhood, Wright lived in Hawaii where she developed a deep love of the ocean. This natural attraction to the sea influenced many of her activities—from the books she read, to the televisions programs she watched, and the pastimes she enjoyed. She cherished her relaxed life on the island of Maui in Hawaii surrounded by the beauty and grandeur of the endless blue water.

She recently reflected upon her childhood: "I grew up on Maui, Hawaii as a very happy, only child and loved the 'island life' (being barefoot all the time, swimming, snorkeling, and having friends from many different Asian cultures). This also prompted my interest in the oceans and I first considered growing up to be an underwater photographer. This quickly changed to wanting to be an oceanographer as my interest in science grew.

"Our grade school teachers always encouraged us to read for

pleasure and I read every 'classic' sea novel that I could get my hands on: *Mutiny on the Bounty*, *Treasure Island*, and *20,000 Leagues Under the Sea* were my favorites.[1] I was also very active in team sports (basketball, track and field, and volleyball) and this carried over to when my family was transferred to California so that my mom could teach an exchange year at a community college (during my 8th grade year).

"For my freshman year of high school we moved back to Hawaii but then, due to the illness of my grandmother, moved to Maryland to be close to her and the rest of my extended family. So [I] finished high school in Columbia, Maryland, and continued to have a great interest in oceanography and science in general.

"In addition to being involved in sports, I also enjoyed participating in the state science fair as a senior in high school (won 2nd prize). My project was about bioluminescent (glow-in-the-dark) marine bacteria."[2]

Wright was always more interested in geology than the other sciences, and as a result, geological oceanography was her field of choice, instead of the more glamorous and popular marine biology. She obtained a bachelor of science degree (cum laude) in geology from Wheaton College in Wheaton, Illinois, a master of science degree in oceanography from Texas A&M University in College Station, and ultimately a Ph.D. from the University of California at Santa Barbara in geography and marine geology. She loves studying the formation and structure of rocks, and this interest led her to study the morphology of the seafloor, the field in which she works today. Scientists in this field study the structure and composition of the ocean floor.

OCEANOGRAPHY, AN INTERDISCIPLINARY FIELD

Oceanography is an interdisciplinary field that incorporates not only biology, chemistry, and physics, but also geology and meteorology. Oceanographers also rely on engineering to a great extent because exploring and researching the depths of the ocean requires state-of-the-art submarines and other sophisticated equipment. Many oceanographers use incredibly high-tech instruments, such as satellites, to measure small fluctuations in the height of the oceans, which reflect—on a much smaller scale—the shape of the ocean floor beneath. At times, however, discoveries are made through simple curiosity and exploration, such as the discovery of the coelacanth—a fish thought to be extinct for sixty-five million years—by a group of fishermen trawling off the southeastern coast of Africa in 1938. This same curiosity and interest in the world around us drove men and women to begin studying these great bodies of water thousands of years ago.

Since the dawn of civilization, our great societies have grown near enormous bodies of water. Our ancestors relied on rivers and seas for their livelihood. The Euphrates-Tigris River valley contained the world's first cities, which thrived using these two massive rivers not only for drinking water, but also for crop irrigation and transportation. Later, the Egyptians created their immense pyramids and monuments with the assistance of the world's longest river—the Nile—and the Greeks and Romans became the rulers of the known world, a world centered on the Mediterranean Sea.

Society's reliance on water has fueled the field of oceanography. The importance of transatlantic commerce led Benjamin Franklin to systematically measure water temperatures in the Atlantic and plot the route of the Gulf Stream, a current of water that flows east across the ocean. In 1855, U.S. Navy Lieutenant Matthew Fontaine Maury published the first modern textbook on oceanography after years spent collecting data from navy ships.

Out of its roots in shipping, navigation, and the navy, oceanography has grown into a popular field of study. (World War II, with much of the fighting take place at sea, helped prompt the practical need for an understanding of the ocean.) Jacques Cousteau helped raise public awareness of the mysterious ocean depths. Marine science continues to expand our understanding of the world in many distinct areas. Using submarines deep within the ocean as well as satellites far above it, oceanographers are constantly increasing our knowledge of the underwater world.

There are four main categories of marine science: physical oceanography, marine biology, chemical oceanography, and marine geology/geophysics. These four groups encompass most of the pure scientific research taking place in the ocean, whether it is work with climatology, marine life, or the ocean floor. Along with oceanographic engineering, or applied oceanographic science, they represent the vast amount of knowledge that is currently being generated by marine scientists.

MARINE BIOLOGY

Marine biology is probably the most popular of the four main oceanographic sciences, due largely to the work of Jacques Cousteau. Wright was influenced by his achievements to pursue a career in oceanography. Cousteau was coinventor of the aqualung, a device that allows divers to stay underwater for more than an hour without any connection to the surface, as well as the creator of several underwater photography techniques. With his newly developed instruments and his ship, the *Calypso*, Cousteau introduced people to the underwater world through several documentaries, hundreds of books, and a long-running television series. He showed his audience the marvels contained within coral reefs, the majesty of large marine mammals, and the carnal energy of the shark.

As far back as the time of the ancient Greeks, the creatures living under the ocean's surface have captivated the imagination, as they have for Wright. Whether it was the great whale of *Moby Dick*,[1] or the intelligent dolphin, Flipper, stories and images of these creatures have intrigued readers and moviegoers. What image does she recall about the ocean from her childhood? "The giant squid in Disney's *20,000 Leagues Under the Sea!*" The magnificent, yet frightening images transfixed a generation. That the water can support such awe-inspiring creatures unlike any others on the Earth and the desire to understand them—this drives marine biologists every day.

Many marine biologists study coral reefs, which are some of

the most diverse and valuable ecosystems on the planet. Wright feels strongly that we should be protecting these coral reefs. "Reef systems are storehouses of immense biological wealth and provide economic and ecosystem services to millions of people as shoreline protection, areas of natural beauty and recreation, and sources of food, pharmaceuticals, jobs, and revenues. Unfortunately, coral reefs are also recognized as being among the most threatened marine ecosystems on the planet, having been seriously degraded by human overexploitation of resources, destructive fishing practices, coastal development, and runoff from improper land-use practices." Scientists working with these fragile coral systems are involved in a race against time to educate those who use the reefs and to protect these beautiful parts of the oceans.

Marine biology is specifically the study of all the biota of the ocean, from the tiniest plankton to the largest whales. It is a field in which new discoveries are constantly being made, such as the recovery of the prehistoric coelacanth and the detection of life around hydrothermal vents. Research in marine biology is also being applied to world problems, such as global warming, one of the major environmental problems confronting the world today.

Global warming is caused by the carbon dioxide that is released into the atmosphere through the burning of fossil fuels (coal, oil, natural gas, and wood). When it is in the atmosphere, this carbon dioxide traps some of the Sun's energy that would be radiated out by the Earth, much as the glass in a greenhouse traps heat. Photosynthetic organisms, such as plants, are able to take some of this carbon dioxide out of the atmosphere, but not as quickly as we are putting them in. Many scientists, environmentalists, legislators, and concerned citizens are trying to find solutions to this problem. A fascinating twist to such a large-scale problem is that a tiny, unicellular, photosynthetic creature, phytoplankton, may be the answer. Phytopankton produce more than ninety percent of the world's oxygen. Many scientists are working to understand these tiny organisms, with the hope of increasing their productivity, and thereby removing carbon dioxide from the atmosphere. If they succeed, this would mean that Wright and her colleagues are at the forefront of science that could have a major impact on the Earth for generations to come.

MARINE PHYSICS

Another field of oceanography that relates to global warming is marine physics. Many climatologists are attempting to create computer models that will predict the effects of increased carbon dioxide in the air. In order to make accurate predictions, however, the scientists must first understand the interactions between the ocean and the atmosphere. They need to learn how much heat can be held by the ocean and how the increased heat will affect the polar ice caps. They also must consider the effect of increased water vapor in the atmosphere as the surface of the ocean slowly evaporates.

Physical oceanographers also study the thermocline. The thermocline is a layer of water in the oceans in which the temperature changes rapidly with depth. It usually begins about three hundred feet below the surface, but it can vary greatly in different parts of the ocean and at different times. The temperature differential above and below the thermocline is able to reflect and refract the sound signals used by Sound and Navigation Ranging (SONAR) arrays inside seagoing vessels. SONAR is a method of sending out sound pulses and then measuring the time that it takes for them to bounce off an object and return to the receiver, in order to determine the distance to objects underwater. Forms of this echolocation are used not only by boats and manmade objects, but also by sea creatures such as dolphins. As just one example of the interdisciplinary nature of oceanography, dolphins have been studied to provide information to physicists and engineers about the workings of their sophisticated echolocation ability. They, in essence, learn from dolphins. SONAR has been used by hundreds of submarines, such as those depicted in the movie *Hunt for Red October*,[3] to avoid detection. As a result, it is the subject of much naval research.

One of the most interesting and important uses of chemistry in the ocean is the study of the sea's salinity, or salt concentration. For billions of years, salt has been washed off the land, down through our rivers and lakes, and finally out into the oceans where it has pooled in high concentrations. Living organisms in the oceans have evolved to live with the particular salinity level of their surroundings. For that reason, many fish and other marine organisms are incapable of moving from fresh to salt water, or vice versa. Many engineers working at the ocean's coasts are attempting to discover affordable methods of removing the salt from seawater, to make it suitable for human consumption and irrigation.

The fourth major subsection of marine science is the field in which Wright conducts most of her work. Wright and other marine geophysicists study the formation of the oceans, the composition of the ocean floor, and the processes that cause change in the structure of the seabed. They also investigate underwater volcanoes as well as the polar ice caps, and they attempt to create more accurate and informative maps of the ocean.

SEAFLOOR-SPREADING

Wright concentrates her time and energy on topics related to seafloor-spreading centers such as the East Pacific Rise, a submarine chain of volcanic ridges that parallels the western edge of South America and includes the Galapagos Islands. Seafloor-spreading centers are areas in the ocean where new portions of the Earth's crust are being formed and pushed up from beneath the seafloor. At these areas, it is common to find volcanoes, hydrothermal vents, and other dynamic geologic activity.

These seafloor-spreading areas confirm one of the most dramatic theories in geology: the theory of plate tectonics. Proposed in the 1960s, plate tectonics was a ground-breaking new theory in the field of geology. It was a coherent explanation for such distinct phenomena as earthquakes, volcanoes, and the absence of evidence of seafloors older than the Mesozoic era. By providing explanations for such varied geological phenomena, the theory of plate tectonics became one of the pillars of modern-day geology. It can now help us to predict catastrophes such as earthquakes so we can warn people living near them.

The theory of plate tectonics grew out of an earlier theory proposed by Alfred Wegener in 1912. Wegener realized that the continents seemed to fit together like a jigsaw puzzle and proposed that at one time they had been a part of one supercontinent. (This played a role in dinosaur evolution and is discussed in the profile of Paul Sereno in chapter 9.) In the 1960s, geologists proposed that the Earth's crust was really not one whole piece, but instead included several different crustal plates that floated on the Earth's asthenosphere, the fluid inner portion of the Earth. The asthenosphere is composed of much of the Earth's mantle, the layer below the crust. The incredibly high pressures put upon the asthenosphere by the crust above it cause the rock in this layer to be compressed at high temperatures into a molten fluid material. The lithosphere, or the layer containing the earth's crust, floats upon this molten layer. The gigantic crustal plates flow slowly, averaging a rate of about two inches a year. The regions where two plates join together are known as plate boundaries. There are two major categories of plate boundaries, divergent plate boundaries and convergent plate boundaries. Divergent plate boundaries form when two plates move away from each other, and convergent boundaries form when they move against each other.

The seafloor-spreading areas that Wright studies form at divergent boundaries under the ocean. At these areas, oceanic crust flows away from another nearby plate. This creates a gap in the floor of the ocean. But into this gap, molten material flows up from the asthenosphere and rapidly cools to become a new portion of the oceanic plate. At these spreading areas, the crustal plates are usually very thin. Of course, thin is relative to other plates because oceanic crust is, on average, five to ten kilometers thick. Because the crust here is much thinner than that in other areas, molten rock is able to force its way up through cracks and create volcanoes, hydrothermal vents, and mid-ocean ridges.

BENEATH THE SEA, TO THE OCEAN FLOOR

During her studies, Wright has traversed to the floor of the ocean in the Alvin Submersible three times. This venerable sub was the same vessel used on many other famous excursions, including Dr. Robert Ballard's discovery of the *Titanic* in 1985. The vehicle can withstand the pressure of water more than twelve thousand feet deep. In this three-passenger sub, under the direction of a pilot, scientists can descend to the depths of the ocean.

"While the pilot steers Alvin through the black depths, in and around lava pillars and sulfide spires created by deep-sea hot spring hydrothermal activity, we [Wright and her partners on the voyage] look out the two portholes on the sides of the vehicle and describe into a tape recorder what we see within the perimeter illuminated by the sub's lights," said Wright. "We often instruct the pilot [about where to maneuver] and sample biota or rocks using the robotic arms that extend from Alvin's bow. We know that few others have ever visited the site that we are diving on, and, due to the dynamic nature of the ocean floor, many surprises may await us."

Wright describes what it feels like to be under the surface of the water, completely hidden from the outside world. She recalls experiencing a feeling of peace not found on land—almost as if she'd been transported to a foreign world, lacking everything familiar to her. Beneath the waves, the rigors and worries of daily life are replaced by a feeling of tranquility enhanced by the beautiful natural setting. The calm movements of marine life and the soothing motions of the waves replace the chaotic sights and sounds of human existence above the sea. Wright has felt the temptation to simply step out of the submarine and walk around on the ocean floor, although of course had she tried, the immense pressure would have crushed her body.

Also known as decompression sickness or Caisson's Disease, the bends occur when scuba divers ascend to the surface too quickly. The problem occurs because the compressed air that divers breathe has a great deal of nitrogen in it, which expands under the lessened pressure near the surface, causing extreme pain. Decompression sickness can be prevented by ascending slowly. Air embolisms are bubbles formed in the blood stream when divers surface and the nitrogen expands. These can be prevented just as easily as the bends—by rising slowly to the ocean's surface, with a five-minute pause at a depth of ten feet.

A VOLCANIC ERUPTION

On one of her dives in the Alvin submersible, Wright and her colleagues came closer than anyone else had to witnessing an underwater volcanic eruption. One of her Ph.D. advisors, Dr. Rachel Haymon, and Dr. Karen Von Damm went down to the seafloor on April 14, 1991. When they reached the seabed, they noticed the remains of tubeworms and mussels from an ocean-floor animal community. The creatures had been scorched by fresh lava that was still partially covering their bodies. The scientists noticed that the remains were still free of the marks of scavengers and were covered in ash, which normally dissolves rapidly under water. This evidence convinced them that the volcanic eruption had taken place very recently.

Using the submarine's robotic arm, they collected samples of the dead organisms and brought them to the surface. Shortly after the dive, the samples were analyzed in a lab using state-of-the-art equipment. The rocks and ash samples were estimated to be less than two weeks old. This confirmed that they had come closer than anyone to witnessing an underwater eruption; in fact, it is unlikely that a submersible could withstand direct exposure to a volcanic eruption. This and subsequent dives to the region, referred to as "tubeworm barbecue" by Haymon and her colleagues because the tubeworm samples recovered smelled like grilled hamburgers, provided new insights into the effects that volcanic eruptions have on deep-sea hydrothermal communities. Wright made her dive to the tubeworm barbecue on April 21, 1991, helping to elucidate life in this hot climate. Wright explained, "By and large, the organisms that live at these hotsprings can live there and only there, as they depend on the sulfides at the springs for their food supply. The fluids emitted at the springs may increase to temperatures in excess of 800°F and thus boil the animals alive. On the other hand, if the hydrothermal activity dies completely the animals will starve. It is still a mystery as to exactly how these organisms manage to migrate for several miles to new undersea hotspring sites in order to survive."

ADVENTURES AT SEA

Wright has experienced many other adventures on the open ocean during her explorations as an oceanographer. She was on board a vessel that rendezvoused with some of Dr. Bob Ballard's crew on their way to photographing the wreck of the *Titanic*. She also saw the crew of the *Sea Tomato*, a small rowboat that an adventurous group used to row across the Drake Passage, a passage that connects the Atlantic with the Pacific near Antarctica and has some of the roughest seas in the world. On the same trip, Wright was able to enjoy the experience of watching penguins, whales, and seals in their habitat near Antarctica.

Wright described an old naval ceremony that takes place when oceanographic research boats cross the equator. Those on board who have already crossed the equator are called "shellbacks," and those who haven't are referred to as "pollywogs." In order to earn the right to be honored as shellbacks and be accepted into King Neptune's realm, the pollywogs are required to undergo one of several initiation experiences. Some have to crawl through garbage or be dipped in bins of disgusting material. Others are hosed down or forced to drink and eat horrible-tasting foods. Another punishment Wright described was known as kissing the baby, which meant kissing the belly of the fattest man on the boat while it was smothered with gross things, like unusual combinations of food—ketchup and chocolate mixed with fish for example, or worse! Wright now carries a card certifying her status as a shellback so that she will never have to bear such treatment again.

Wright is confident of her abilities, particularly as a woman on a sea vessel. She had this to say: "Overall, I don't really think that my life has been any more difficult, which is a great testament to the women and people of color who have gone before me. Right now, I'm just trying to move ahead to achieve and do the best that I can just as anybody else would in my profession.

"Things can get interesting when [one is] at sea on an oceanographic research vessel though, particularly with the rough, physical work. For instance, if you are trying to deploy equipment over the side, it takes quite a bit of upper body strength. There have been times when a man would come by and take something out of my hand or wouldn't have confidence that I could do the job that I had been assigned to do. There can be two reasons for this. One, the person might just be concerned for my safety. The other side of the coin is that the person just doesn't think that I can do the job or that women do not belong at sea. This has happened to me at sea a couple of times. I think for at least most of the women I have worked with who have faced the same sorts of situations, we just keep doing our jobs the best that we can. Ninety-nine percent of the time, at least in my experience, women have been able to pull their weight and do extremely well at sea."

TEACHING AND RESEARCH

Wright is an associate professor at Oregon State University where she was recently granted tenure. She really loves her work, even though while seeking tenure she often had to work seventy-hour weeks. She teaches classes on oceanography, geography, and geographic information systems (GIS). She also advises graduate students and does her own research. Her life is very busy, but she still has time to ride her mountain bike, weather permitting, and she can bring her dog Lydia (rescued from the Lincoln County Animal Shelter) with her to work.

What does Wright find most rewarding about her work? Does she prefer research to teaching? She said, "Hearing from students who really enjoyed one of my courses and felt as though they really learned something or were inspired; or hearing from colleagues who thought a presentation or paper or book that I completed was excellent. I prefer research [though], especially going to sea on big research ships and working with the equipment at sea (devices for mapping the ocean floor)."

Despite her busy schedule, she manages to reserve time for her spiritual well being. She said, "My spiritual life (being a Christian and deepening my relationship with God) is most important, as well as keeping healthy and active in sports. I love cycling (both road and mountain bike), watching cartoons with my dog, and going to movies with friends (particularly foreign or independent films). I also never turn down an opportunity to ride a roller coaster."

One of her typical problems in the office involves running a computer program time after time until it finally works. "Science takes perseverance," she says. She makes extensive use of GIS (geographic information systems) to help her find patterns in the ocean floor and has become an expert in their many applications.

Geographic information systems are used to manipulate and map different types of geographic information. A GIS stores and compiles information into a series of maps. These systems can take events and objects and make it easy for scientists to look at them together to find patterns. For instance, if you thought that there was a correlation between elevation and the density of trees in an area, you could take a tree density map and an elevation map and input them both into the GIS. Then the GIS could compile these two maps into one map that showed elevation and forest cover together, so that you could easily see any relationship that might exist. Many GISs can also answer simple or even analytical questions that are posed to them, such as how many trees are in an area of land or what type of soil seems to best suit maple trees?

Wright uses GIS to make maps of the East Pacific Rise, one of the fastest seafloor-spreading areas in the world. She described it this way: "This is a place where the ocean floor is literally being split apart and created anew by a process called 'seafloor-spreading.' This site is where the rate of seafloor-spreading is known to be among the fastest on the entire planet. I am trying to figure out how the cracks in the ocean floor that are created by this process of seafloor-spreading are related to the ages and shapes of lava flows and the occurrence of 'hydrothermal vents' or hot springs on the ocean floor in that area. With the GIS, I can overlay maps of different themes on top of each other and figure out if any patterns in the maps match either other (e.g., the co-occurrence of cracks with the locations of hot springs). If patterns match, this might be related to a physical process in the earth that can be explained."

Wright uses the GIS to overlay maps of the cracks in the ocean floor with maps of the locations of lava flows and hydrothermal vents. She then looks for patterns and correlations in the maps, to see if there is a relationship between the cracks caused by the seafloor-spreading and the other geologic features of the seafloor. She added, "My work in seafloor mapping contributes to how much we know of what is on the surface of our own planet. We still know more about the surface of the Moon, Venus, and Mars than we know of our own planet (this is because we have better sensors for seeing through the atmosphere than through water)."

Wright sees a bright future for her career and for the fields of geography and oceanography in general. She hopes someday to become the director of a major research center that focuses on environmental and geospatial studies in the ocean and on the coasts. She would like to design and implement a combined effort to conduct research and educate the general public about the value and appeal of the oceans, coasts, reefs, and shelf environments. She envisions a center that would encourage cooperation between oceanographers around the world while conducting research of its own. The center would correlate the data generated by marine scientists and geographers in different locations and create an on-line database that would make information readily available to all.

If brought to fruition, Wright's visionary center could tremendously accelerate the pace of our exploration of the oceans, and allow us to come to a much greater understanding of the processes that shape life in the heart of our planet. Her individual contribution may lead to a better understanding of the formation of hydrothermal vents and underwater volcanoes as well as the theory of plate tectonics.

Wright urges those who aspire to be future scientists and oceanographers to persevere in their work. "Once you decide on what you would like to do, pursue it with great passion! This will tide you over during discouraging, difficult, and tedious times. Find a hero or heroine to inspire you, and follow their work and accomplishments. Don't shy away from math and computer programming. Watch the Discovery Channel for science specials—they are great. For would-be oceanographers, get some hands-on experience at sea, such as a short internship or semester at sea, if at all possible. And if you really want to lead a fulfilling life as a scientist, you should definitely think about going to graduate school."

Wright is a talented young scientist who received a Faculty Early Career Development Award from the National Science Foundation in 1995 and, in 1999, received an Outstanding Professor Award from Oregon State University Honors College and was named Woman of the Year by *Clarity* magazine. Also, in 1999, she was invited to present at the TED conference (Technology, Entertainment, and Design), an interesting eclectic mix of innovative thinkers for the new millennium. She's made an awesome start to what is sure to be a long and successful career.

Mike Stukel

EPILOGUE

LEON M. LEDERMAN

W e have seen how observatories on mountaintops and satellites have given us a coherent account of the creation and evolution of the universe. Somehow in this vast and seemingly chaotic condensation, our planet was made to remarkable specifications.

We have examined this planet from the chemistry at the top of the atmosphere to the phenomena at the dark bottom of our deepest oceans. We have delved into the structure and behavior of the prehuman creatures that roamed the Earth millions of years ago. We have looked at the infrastructure of our sciences and the benefits to medicine and measurement of our ever-deepening understanding and control of molecules. The application of the ubiquitous laser for a million uses is one direction this knowledge has taken us. The grasp of the structure of living organisms as an example of the explosive growth of molecular biology is another. The structure and function of one branch of living objects, molluscs, is still a third example. We have examined the frontier of how our minds work and how humans organize their societies. We have ventured to glimpse efforts to understand the basic laws of physics at their most primordial level and followed astronaut/scientists to the most romantic personal explorations of the space around our planet.

Our students, who have selected their scientists, have given us a wondrous spectrum of disciplines. But their task was also to give us a sense of how scientists evolve from students, pretty much like the authors, to world famous scientists. Our introduction was designed to describe the enterprise of science that, as these portraits show, span so huge a variety of personalities, of qualities and styles of thinking. To really do justice to our selected scientists, each would require a book of his or her own. The difficulty of summary is, as usual, best illustrated by an unexpected passage in Richard Feynman's *Lectures on Physics*. In the course of commenting on the difficulty of imagining electromagnetic fields, Feynman generalizes to comment on scientific imagination:

> [Physicists] can't allow ourselves to seriously imagine things which are obviously in contradiction to the known laws of nature. And so, our kind of imagination (LML: perhaps in contrast to poetic or artistic imagination) is quite a difficult game. One has to have the imagination to think of something that has never been seen before, never been heard of before. At the same time, the thoughts are restricted in a straitjacket, so to speak, limited by the conditions that came from our knowledge of the way nature really is. The problem of creating something which is new, but is consistent with everything which has been seen before, is one of extreme difficulty.[1]

This Feynman statement clearly applies to all the scientists we have described in this book. Small wonder that all scientific breakthroughs are initially met with skepticism usually based upon the constraints of prior knowledge. This is perhaps why so many of those portrayed were so young when they made their discoveries. As opposed to musicians and artists whose creative works improve with experience, scientists very often do their best work when they are at the beginning of their careers.

The handicap of too much intellectual baggage was most eloquently expressed by Wolfgang Pauli, the great Swiss-Austrian physicist who at age forty complained: "Ach, I know too much!"

The scientists depicted here have been somewhat too modest to praise the life of science. Like so many other activities, it has its periods of frustration, hard labor, failure, and discouragement. But these are punctuated by periods of intense involvement, satisfaction, joy, and exultation. The real purpose of this book is to invite its young readers to consider a career in science. Scientists love the work they do. And often to their surprise, they even make a living! And what is unique is that scientists are adding to an intellectual edifice, a monument, about three thousand years in the making. Here we add a few bricks, there a lintel, perhaps a small tower. This monument, contributed to by scientists from all regions of the world and over many epochs, is humanity's expression of its desire to understand the world and humankind's place in it. But it is also the source of hope that the structure will be essential for human welfare and fulfillment. Scientists love to communicate. We belong to an international community. In the cafeteria of a great U.S. laboratory, we can see a Pakistani physicist in heated discussions with colleagues from South Africa, Japan, and New Jersey. In a European laboratory there is a sign: Official Language: Broken English. Although there is no secret handshake, no standard T-shirt, there is a bond of understanding between all scientists. I am sure that all the scientists portrayed within these leaves join me in a warm welcome to the next generation of scientists.

NOTES

PREFACE

   1. Paul DeKruif, *Microbe Hunters* (1928; reprint, New York: Harcourt Brace and Co., 1996).
   2. Paul DeKruif, *Hunger Fighters: Dramatic Stories of Great Scientists* (1942; reprint, New York: Harcourt Brace and Co., 1985).
   3. Bernard Jaffe, *Crucibles: The Story of Chemistry from Ancient Alchemy to Nuclear Fission* (1930; reprint, Dover, 1977).

INTRODUCTION

   1. Richard Feynman, *What is Science?* unpublished essay given at the California Institute of Technology. N.D.
   2. S. Chandrasekhar, *Truth and Beauty* (Chicago: Chicago University Press. 1987), p. 59.
   3. Ibid., p. 62.
   4. Ibid., p. 64.
   5. Edward O. Wilson, *Consilience: The Unity of Knowledge* (New York: Knopf, 1998), p. 277.

I. CLIFFORD GEERTZ: ANTHROPOLOGICAL AMBASSADOR

1. Clifford Geertz, *The Interpretation of Cultures*, 2000 edition (New York: Basic Books, 1973), p. 412.
2. Clifford Geertz, *Available Light* (Princeton, N.J.: Princeton University Press, 2000), p. 83.
3. Ibid., pp. 18–19.
4. Ibid., p. 19.
5. Clifford Geertz, *After the Fact: Two Countries, Four Decades, One Anthropologist* (Cambridge, Mass.: Harvard University Press, 1995), p. 98.

2. MARY-CLAIRE KING: PIONEERING GENETICIST

1. The journals *Science* and *Nature* both devoted their February 16, 2001 issues to publication of results and information about the Human Genome Project. Many popular books have also been written, including *Genome: The Autobiography of a Species in 23 Chapters*, by Mattew Ridley (New York: HarperCollins, 2000) and *Cracking the Genome: Inside the Race to Unlock DNA*, by Kevin Davies (New York: Free Press, 2000). The National Institutes of Health (National Human Genome Research Institute) heads the United States public sector project (www.nhgri.nih.gov). Celera Genomics, Inc. (www.celera.com) is a private company that also plays a very key role in the project.
2. There are two types of cells: eukaryotic, which contain a nucleus, and prokaryotic, which do not. Plants, animals, and fungi are made of eukaryotic cells. Bacterial cells are prokaryotic.
3. A nucleotide is a single molecule composed of a five-carbon sugar (pentose), a nitrogenous base (a one- or two-ring structure composed of carbon and nitrogen), and a phosphate group. The composition of the base portion determines whether the molecule is adenine, cytosine, guanine, or thymine. These single molecules are linked together to form a piece of DNA.

3. MARVIN MINSKY: MIND MAKER

1. Harry Harrison and Marvin Minsky, *The Turing Option* (New York: Warner Books, 1993).
2. Constructivism is a teaching methodology based on student

understanding constructed from experiences and true understanding of a topic. This is in contrast to teacher-directed education and students simply memorizing lots of facts.

4. STORY MUSGRAVE: SPACE DOCTOR

1. *Newsweek,* 9 July 1990.
Robert W. Smith, *The Space Telescope: A Study of NASA, Science, Technology, and Politics* (New York: Cambridge University Press, 1993), p. 416.
2. Gary Larson, *Far Side,* Universal Press Syndicate, 1990. Smith, *The Space Telescope,* p. 415
3. Smith, *The Space Telescope,* p. 399.
4. The Hubble telescopes "fixes" on known stars as a way of orientation. This is similar to the way that sailors use stars at night as a reference point for where they are located.

5. STEVEN PINKER: LANGUAGE'S BAD BOY

1. Noam Chomsky was one of the first to study language and the brain in a scientific manner. He advanced a new theory of the way that language is acquired. He is a professor at MIT and has been there since 1955. Influential in Pinker's early career selection, the two are now colleagues.
2. As stated in the text, this is an extreme example of genes determining characteristics. It is incorrect, but overstated to make the argument in favor of heredity.

6. SALLY RIDE:
FIRST AMERICAN WOMAN IN SPACE

1. This is modified from the introduction to *Star Trek,* the television series createded by Gene Roddenberry. It ultimately spawned three additional television series, nine movies, hundreds of books, and countless numbers of "Trekkies" (individuals who are devoted fans).
2. President Ronald Reagan's speech from the White House Oval Office, after the *Challenger* explosion, 28 January 1986.

7. F. SHERWOOD ROWLAND: CONTROVERSIAL CHEMIST

1. Mario J. Molina and F. Sherwood Rowland, Stratospheric Sink for Chlorofluoromethanes: Chlorine Atom-Catalyzed Destruction of Ozone," *Nature* 249 (1974): 810–12.

8. VERA RUBIN: INTERGALACTIC PROSPECTOR

1. Vera Rubin, *Bright Galaxies, Dark Matters* (Woodbury, N.Y.: American Institute of Physics Press, 1997), p. 156.
2. Occam's Razor is derived from William of Occam (1284–1347), a noted English scholar who played a role in the development of scientific thought. Using available data, the simplest explanation for a phenomenon should be considered the best one.

9. PAUL SERENO: DINOSAUR DETECTIVE

1. Paul C. Sereno, "The Evolution of Dinosaurs," *Science* 284, vol. 5423 (June 25, 1999): 2137.
2. Sereno's Web site at the University of Chicago contains many details of his expeditions (www.dinosaur.uchicago.edu).

10. GEORGE SMOOT: INDIANA JONES OF SCIENCE

1. George Smoot, *Wrinkles in Time* (New York: Avon Books, Inc. 1993), p. 18.
2. Ibid., p. 283.
3. Olbers's Paradox refers to a nineteenth-century physician and astronomer Heinrich W. M. Olbers. If there are an infinite number of stars evenly distributed in the universe, then the night sky should be not be dark, unless something is absorbing their light. He was the first to propose the presence of interstellar matter. This is not the reason, however, for the dark night sky. The poet Edgar Allen Poe proposed that light from the most distant stars just hadn't reached us yet. This is regarded as correct. The dilemma of why the night sky is dark is known as Olbers's Paradox. See Smoot, *Wrinkles in Time*, p. 28.
4. Smoot, *Wrinkles in Time*, p. 92.

5. Ibid., p. 221.

6. Ibid., p. 252. Smoot borrowed the quote "This is an awful place" from Antarctica explorer Robert Scott, and added "to do science."

7. Ibid., p. 282.

8. Ibid.

9. Ibid., p. 289.

II. CHARLES TOWNES: LASER LEGEND

1. The Van de Graaf generator is a device that makes and stores a static electric charge. One may have seen this device in a physics class; the large silver ball that a student places his hand upon to make her hair stand on end.

2. Charles H. Townes, *How the Laser Happened* (New York: Oxford University Press, 1999), pp. 55–56.

12. GEERAT VERMEIJ: SEEING WITH HIS HANDS

1. Geerat Vermeij, *Privleged Hands: A Scientific Life* (New York: W.H. Freeman and Co., 1997), p. 15.

2. Ibid., p. 14.

3. Charles Darwin, *Origin of Species: By Means of Natural Selection or the Preservation of Favoured Races in the Struggle for Life* (1859; reprint, Amherst, N.Y.: Prometheus Books, 1991).

13. E.O. WILSON: DILIGENT NATURALIST

1. Edward O. Wilson, *Naturalist* (Washington, D.C.: Island Press, 1994), p. 363.

2. Ibid., p. 164.

3. Ibid., p. 328.

4. Ibid., p. 307.

14. EDWARD WITTEN: THE THEORY OF EVERYTHING

1. Alice Steinbach, *Baltimore Sun*, 12 February 1995.

2. Ibid.

3. Ibid.

4. K. C. Cole, *New York Times*, 18 October 1987, p. 20

5. Brian Greene, *The Elegant Universe* (New York: Vintage Books, 2000), p. 274.

6. P. C. W. Davies and J. Brown, eds. *Superstrings: A Theory of Everything?* (Cambridge, England: Cambridge University Press, 1988), p. 94.

7. Ibid., p. 96.

8. Greene, *The Elegant Universe*, p. 274.

9. Ibid., p. 309.

10. Davies and Brown, *Superstrings*, p. 95.

11. Roshomon is illustrated by the five blind men, in the oriental myth, who explore an elephant. Each one tells a radically different story of what an elephant is, depending on what part they are feeling.

12. Greene, *The Elegant Universe*, p. 17.

13. Alice Steinbach, *Baltimore Sun*, 12 February 1995.

14. Davies and Brown, *Superstrings*, p. 106.

15. DAWN WRIGHT: MAPPING THE ABYSS

1. The classic books that are Dawn's favorites continue to be published and are found in most book stores.

2. Bioluminescent bacteria live symbiotically with some fish in the ocean. It is believed that these bacteria assist the fish in some way with communication.

3. The movie *Hunt for Red October* is based on the Tom Clancy novel of the same name.

EPILOGUE

1. Richard Feynman, *Lectures on Physics* (Menlo Park, Calif.: Addison Wesley. 1964), p. 77.

BIBLIOGRAPHY

1. CLIFFORD GEERTZ: ANTRHOPOLOGICAL AMBASSADOR

Geertz, Clifford. *After the Fact: Two Countries, Four Decades, One Anthropologist.* Cambridge, Mass.: Harvard University Press, 1995.
———. *Available Light.* Princeton, N.J.: Princeton University Press, 2000.
———. *The Interpretation of Cultures.* New York: Basic Books, 1973.
———. *Islam Observed: Religious Development in Morocco and Indonesia.* Chicago: The University of Chicago Press, 1968.
———. *Works and Lives: The Anthropologist as Author.* Stanford, Calif.: Stanford University Press, 1988.

2. MARY-CLAIRE KING: PIONEERING GENETICIST

Davies, Kevin, and Michael White. *Breakthrough: The Race to Find the Breast Cancer Gene.* New York: John Wiley and Sons, Inc., 1995.
Varmus, Harold and Robert A. Weinberg. *Genes and the Biology of Cancer.* New York: Scientific American Library, 1993.

3. MARVIN MINKSY: MIND MAKER

Artificial Intelligence. Alexandria, Va.: Time-Life Books, 1986.

Kurzweil, Raymond. *The Age of Intelligent Machines.* Cambridge, Mass.: MIT Press, 1990.

Levy, Steven. *Artificial Life: The Quest for a New Creation.* New York: Pantheon Books, 1992.

Minsky, Marvin. *The Society of Mind.* New York: Simon and Schuster, 1985.

Minsky, Marvin, and Seymour Papert. *Preceptrons: Introduction to Computational Geometry.* Cambridge, Mass.: MIT Press, 1968.

4. STORY MUSGRAVE: SPACE DOCTOR

Smith, Robert W. *The Space Telescope: A Study of NASA, Science, Technology, and Politics.* New York: Cambridge University Press, 1993.

5. STEVEN PINKER: LANGUAGE'S BAD BOY

Pinker, Steven. *How the Mind Works.* New York: W.W. Norton and Co., 1997.

———. *Language, Learnability, and Language Development.* Cambridge, Mass.: Cambridge University Press, 1984.

———. *Learnability and Cognition.* Cambridge, Mass.: MIT Press, 1989.

———. *The Language Instinct: How the Mind Creates Language.* New York: William Morrow and Company, 1994.

———. *Words and Rules: The Ingredients of Language.* New York: Perseus Books, 1999.

6. SALLY RIDE: FIRST AMERICAN WOMAN IN SPACE

Ride, Sally, and Susan Okie. *To Space and Back.* New York: William Morrow and Company, 1986.

Ride, Sally, and Tam O'Shaughnessy. *The Mystery of Mars.* New York: Crown Publishers, Inc., 1999.

———. *The Third Planet: Exploring the Earth from Space.* New York: Crown Publishers, 1994.

———. *Voyager: An Adventure to the Edge of the Solar System.* New York: Crown Publishers, 1992.

7. SHERWOOD ROWLAND: CONTROVERSIAL CHEMIST

Gribbon, John R. *Hothouse Earth: The Greenhouse Effect and Gaia.* New York: Grove Weidenfeld, 1990.

Rayner, Steve, and Elizabeth L. Malone. *Human Choice and Climate Change.* Columbus, Ohio: Battelle Press, 1998.

Rowland, F. Sherwood. *Stratospheric Ozone Depletion* (in Annual Reviews of Physical Chemistry). Palo Alto, Calif.: Annual Review, Inc., 1991.

Soroos, Marvin S. *The Endangered Atmosphere: Preserving a Global Commons.* Columbia: University of South Carolina Press, 1997.

8. VERA RUBIN: INTERGALACTIC PROSPECTOR

Krauss, Lawrence. *Quintessence: The Mystery of Missing Mass in the Universe.* New York: Basic Books, 2000.

Rubin, Vera. *Bright Galaxies, Dark Matters.* Woodbury, N.Y.: American Institute of Physics Press, 1997.

Wasserman, Elga. *The Door in the Dream: Conversations with Eminent Women in Science.* Washington, D.C.: Joseph Henry Press, 2000.

9. PAUL SERENO: DINOSAUR DETECTIVE

Carpenter, Kenneth, and Philip J. Currie. *Dinosaur Systematics: Approaches and Perspectives.* New York: Cambridge University Press, 1990.

Farlow, James O., and M. K. Brett-Surman, eds. *The Complete Dinosaur.* Indianapolis, Ind.: Indiana University Press, 1997.

Sereno, Paul C. "The Evolution of Dinosaurs." *Science* 284, no. 5423 (June 25, 1999): 2137.

Tarbuck, Edward J., and Frederick K. Lutgens. *Earth: An Introduction to Physical Geology.* Upper Saddle River, N.J.: Prentice Hall, 1999.

10. GEORGE SMOOT: INDIANA JONES OF SCIENCE

Hawking, Stephen. *A Brief History of Time.* New York: Bantam Books, 1996.

Smoot, George, and Keay Davidson. *Wrinkles in Time.* New York: Avon Books, Inc., 1993.

II. CHARLES TOWNES: LASER LEGEND

Chiao, Raymond Y. *Amazing Light: A Volume Dedicated to Charles Hard Townes on his 80th Birthday.* New York: Springer-Verlag, 1996.
Townes, Charles H. *How the Laser Happened.* New York: Oxford University Press, 1999.

12. GEERAT VERMEIJ: SEEING WITH HIS HANDS

Vermeij, Geerat J. *A Natural History of Shells.* Princeton, N.J.: Princeton University Press, 1993.
―――. *Biogeography and Adaptation to Marine Life.* Cambridge, Mass.: University Press, 1980.
―――. *Privileged Hands: A Scientific Life.* New York: W.H. Freeman and Company, 1997.

13. E. O. WILSON: DILIGENT NATURALIST

Hölldobler, Bert, and Edward O. Wilson. *The Ants.* Cambridge, Mass.: The Belknap Press, 1990.
―――. *Journey to the Ants: A Story of Scientific Exploration.* Cambridge, Mass.: The Belknap Press, 1994.
Lumsden, Charles, and Wilson, Edward O. *Genes, Mind, and Culture: The Coevolutionary Process.* Cambridge, Mass.: Harvard University Press, 1981.
―――. *Promethean Fire: Reflections on the Origin of the Mind.* Cambridge, Mass.: Harvard University Press, 1983.
Wilson, Edward O. *Biophilia.* Cambridge, Mass.: Harvard University Press. 1984.
―――. *Consilience: The Unity of Knowledge.* New York: Knopf, 1998.
―――. *The Diversity of Life.* New York: W.W. Norton and Company, 1993.
―――. *In Search of Nature.* Washington, D.C.: Island Press, 1996.
―――. *Naturalist.* Washington, D.C.: Island Press, 1994.
―――. *On Human Nature.* Cambridge, Mass.: Harvard University Press, 1978.
―――. *Sociobiology: The New Synethesis.* Cambridge, Mass.: Harvard University Press, 1975.
―――. *The Theory of Island Biogeography.* New Jersey: Princeton University Press, 1969.

14. EDWARD WITTEN: THE THEORY OF EVERYTHING

Davies, P. C. W and J. Brown, eds. *Superstrings: A Theory of Everything?* Cambridge, England: Cambridge University Press, 1988.

Greene, Brian R. *The Elegant Universe.* New York: Vintage Books, 1999.

Lederman, Leon M., and David N. Schramm. *From Quarks to Cosmos.* New York: Scientific American Library, 1995.

Lederman, Leon M., with Dick Teresi. *The God Particle.* New York: Bantam Doubleday Dell Publishing Group, 1993.

15. DAWN WRIGHT: MAPPING THE ABYSS

Ballard, Robert D., with Malcolm McConnell. *Explorations: A Life of Underwater Adventure.* Winnipeg, Canada: Hyperion Press, 1998.

Cousteau, Jacques. *The Ocean World of Jacques Cousteau.* Winnipeg, Canada: Danbury Press, 1975.

Earle, Sylvia A. *Dive: My Adventures in the Deep Frontier.* Washington, DC: National Geographic Society, 1999.

Pinet, Paul. *An Invitation to Oceanography.* Sudbury, Mass.: Jones and Bartlett Publishers. 1996.

Van Dover, Cindy Lee. *Deep-Ocean Journeys: Discovering New Life at the Bottom of the Sea.* New York: Perseus Press. 1997.

———. *The Ecology of Deep-Sea Hydrothermal Vents.* Princeton, N.J.: Princeton University Press, 2000.